THE CHRISTIAN CHURCHES OF THE EAST

THE CHRISTIAN CHURCHES OF THE EAST

VOLUME 1: CHURCHES IN COMMUNION WITH ROME

By DONALD ATTWATER

The Church of Jesus Christ is neither Latin nor Greek nor Slav but Catholic; accordingly she makes no difference between her children, and Greeks, Latins, Slavs and members of all other nations are equal in the eyes of the Apostolic See.— POPE BENEDICT XV

THE BRUCE PUBLISHING COMPANY
MILWAUKEE, WISCONSIN

THE BRUCE PUBLISHING COMPANY
400 North Broadway
Milwaukee 1, Wis.

Revised edition 1961

© DONALD ATTWATER 1961

PRINTED IN GREAT BRITAIN
BY WOOD WESTWORTH AND CO. LTD.

INTRODUCTION TO VOLUME I

THIS book was first published in 1935, in the United States of America, under the title of *The Catholic Eastern Churches*. It has now for the second time been revised and brought up to date. With its fellow on the Eastern churches not in communion with Rome, it is intended as a modest and elementary contribution for English-speaking people to the wider spreading of knowledge about the Christian East; familiarity with whose history, religious life and present state has been so often urged on Catholics (and by implication on other Christians) of the West by recent popes from Leo XIII onwards.

Though the expression "Eastern church" is often met, bearing various meanings, there is not in fact, and never has been, a single unified Eastern church corresponding to the Western church over which the Bishop of Rome presides as patriarch as well as supreme pontiff. The "Eastern church" now consists of four unrelated divisions, of which the first two (*Nestorians* and *Monophysites*) are esteemed heretical and consist of six separate churches; the third also is separated from Rome (the *Orthodox*) and consists of some fifteen self-governing churches, most of which are national and all in communion with one another; and the fourth division consists of several fully organized churches and a number of groups, one in Catholic faith and the communion of the Holy See, known as the *Catholics of Eastern rite*. It is with the last-named division that this book is concerned. Charity begins at home; and until we of the West learn more about the Orientals of our own communion and (I regret to have to add) realize that they are every bit as fully and unequivocally Catholic as ourselves, and act accordingly, it is in vain that we consider all the millions of non-Catholic Orientals, work towards whose reconciliation with the Holy See was such an outstanding activity of Pope Pius XI's pontificate and clearly holds so important a place in the mind of John XXIII.

Successfully to present Catholicism to others needs that we should first ourselves try to realize Catholicism at its best and most authentic. A study, however slight, of the Catholic East contributes to this by emphasizing the variousness and all-embracingness of the Church, and helps powerfully to break down that exclusive occidentalism and Europeanism of which we Western Catholics are so often, and not always unjustly, accused: a narrow particularism that is not compatible with Catholicity and is a formidable barrier for non-Catholics of other ancient civilizations, the more so since they themselves are frequently corrupted with particularism, especially in its nationalist form.

I also hope that in a modest way this book may serve another purpose. "So far from being an obstacle," wrote that distinguished scholar and monk, Dom Fernand Cabrol, "the exact knowledge of facts is, on the contrary, of the greatest assistance to true piety." I include in these pages a considerable number of facts (which I have done my best to make exact) about the various aspects of the Catholic Eastern churches, and especially about their public worship. There is no need to apologize for and explain the amount of space given to this last to those who appreciate the fundamental identity of true Christian life with the life of common worship, and who know how strongly the recent Roman pontiffs have encouraged a "liturgical movement" in the Western church. The religious life of Eastern Christians is notably centred in the Mass as a communal sacrificial meal and in the daily observances of the Church's year; we may therefore profit by a consideration of their example, and "be moved to a yet warmer love for the true Bride of Christ" by looking upon her "entrancing beauty in the diversity of her various rites" (Pope Pius XI).

This book aims simply at being an elementary introduction to a little-known subject for the general reader. Years ago the writer had some personal experience of Christian life in the Near East, and he has maintained his contacts; but for the historical parts and accounts of more remote churches he has had to rely on the work and information of others, and has done no original research of his own. Some of the numerous books consulted are noted in the bibliographies that follow each section, and further information can be found in the general reference books mentioned at the end. These bibliographies, being meant mostly for the general reader, do not, except here and there, include technical works or those in more esoteric languages than English and French.

It may well appear absurd that no more than a dozen or so pages is given to the relations between East and West during the first fourteen hundred years of the Church's history. But on that subject many volumes have been written, and this writer's concern is with more recent times and contemporary conditions. Nevertheless the earlier centuries must on no account be ignored by anyone who wants to get a good general grasp of the present-day situation; of no subject is it more true that "The roots of the present are in the past". As Professor A. D. Ritchie has observed, "You cannot expect to understand what a living thing is except by seeing how it has come to be what it is, and considering all the relevant data. That is just the trouble: there are too many data. Writing history consists principally in leaving things out, and the shorter the history the more you leave out."

The perhaps rather daunting schematic arrangement of Chapters IV to VIII was necessary for the clear and orderly treatment of a very complex subject; for the same reason I gave up any attempt to treat the various groups in chronological order or according to ethnic or geographical affinities: to have done so would have resulted in complete confusion. I have instead primarily taken them in alphabetical order of liturgical families, and secondarily in the chronological order of the renewed adherence of the different bodies to the Holy See. But on account of their importance the churches of the Byzantine rite are dealt with first, and for convenience their liturgical rite is considered before the people instead of afterwards as elsewhere; and it was found convenient for historical reasons to treat the ("pure") Syrians before the Maronites, and the Melkites before other Byzantines.

I have not attempted to be consistent in the transliteration or translation of foreign names—it seems impossible in all but erudite works. With little knowledge of tongues at my disposal, I have endeavoured to make respectable words out of them, without doing outrageous violence to any forms that are well known in English. Another tiresome problem was statistics of numbers of people. The figures given in printed and other sources, even when in some degree official, sometimes show remarkable discrepancies, for which various reasons can be adduced. Where Catholics are concerned, I have in general followed the diocesan statistics given in the *Annuario Pontificio* for 1960.

As regards customs, ritual, etc., I have concerned myself only with typical Catholic usages, which do not necessarily hold good for non-Catholics of the same rite, though to a very large extent they are identical. Only occasionally do I note divergences under this head, though they are often implied by the context (e.g., when a Catholic body uses a Roman office translated into its own liturgical tongue).

The categories and names used for the different bodies of Catholic Easterners are those in official use in Rome. They have the advantage of being clear and in accordance with past history and present fact; they have the disadvantage of often being different from what the people concerned call themselves or are called locally, especially in North America. The commonest colloquial name is "Greek Catholic", for any Catholic of the Byzantine rite; apart from the scientific inadmissibility of such a usage, it is unsuitable in a book like this because of the difficulty of distinguishing between Rumanian and Melkite and Greek and other "Greek Catholics". I suppose that within limits people are entitled to call themselves what they like; but a writer on the subject can hardly be expected to grapple with such atrocities as "Ruthenian-Greek-Roman Catholic"—which I once saw in an American paper.

Catholic Orientals are sometimes called "Uniates". This word is derived from Latin *unio*, "union", through the Polish *unia* (Russian *unya*, Greek *ounia*), whereas the word for "union" is ordinarily *jednosc*, *soedinenie* and *enosis* in those languages respectively. It was coined as a term of contempt by the opponents of the Union of Brest (p. 73), and for that reason alone its use by Catholics is to be deplored. It is often used in a hostile sense by non-Catholics and it is repudiated by those of whom it is used;[1] moreover, it is never found in official ecclesiastical acts at Rome or in such publications as the *Annuario Pontificio*. "Catholic of such and such a rite" is more trouble to say and write, but it is strictly accurate and void of offence or regrettable association.[2]

A word, too, about "rite". This term primarily means the words to be said and actions to be done in carrying out a given act of religion; e.g., the rite of Baptism. By extension it means a complete system of ritual and prayer to be used in the worship of God and the ministration of the sacraments; so we have the Antiochene rite, the whole complex of prayers and offices originating at or associated with the city and patriarchate of Antioch. In time this gets modified, on the one hand into what we call the "Syrian rite" and on the other into the "Maronite rite". (The English technical word "use" [*"ad* usum *ecclesiae Sarum"*] is obviously fitted for the sub-rites, e.g., the Maronite and the Ethiopic. Unfortunately it has become almost obsolete.) Counting the several variations of the Latin rite as only one, there are ten rites in this last sense, and each one is represented by a body of Catholics using it today (and, with the exception of the Latins and Maronites, by much larger non-Catholic bodies as well). Each of these bodies is also sometimes called a rite, which in this sense is equivalent to "church" and includes the manner of organization, proper canon law, customs, etc., appertaining thereto. Every child of Catholic parents belongs to one or other of these rites. If his parents differ in rite, he belongs to that of the father (a wife may adopt her husband's rite at will); if only one parent is a Catholic, the child belongs to that parent's rite. The word *rite* constantly occurs in these pages in one or other of all these senses: which one is meant should be clear from the context.

Throughout this volume I have had time and again to refer to and emphasize differences of one sort or another between the Catholic churches of the East and of the West, and to call attention to a succession of simply external things, sometimes trifling matters, because external things are the differences that

---

[1] It is rather as if an Eastern Catholic should insist on calling English-speaking Catholics "Romanists", a term that we associate with hostile polemics.

[2] In 1939 Cardinal Tisserant, then secretary of the Sacred Eastern Congregation, wrote strongly in this sense to Abbot Neuzil of St Procopius's at Lisle in the United States.

first strike our notice. This was necessitated by the nature and object of the work. But I must say, once and for all, that the differences, striking as they are, are less important than the likenesses which underlie them. I refer, of course, to accidentals. In its faith, its religious dogma and canons of conduct, there is complete oneness in all parts of the Catholic Church: there is no room for either likeness or dissimilarity—there is simply identity. But even in accidental matters—of worship, discipline, usage, mental habit—study and examination show how often the same or similar ideas, framework, origin, are behind the differing practices of East and West. And above all and in all is the same enlightening Spirit.

This does not mean that the differing characteristics of Christian East and West are confined to what is external. Every people (for that matter, each individual person) lives the immutable truths in its own way, according to its history, culture, temperament and "personality". Within the common framework of the Western church there is such variety of mind and life that we can speak, and not improperly, of a German Catholicism, a Spanish Catholicism, an Irish Catholicism, a Garden-of-the-Soul Catholicism. So, too, the East and particular parts of the East have their own traditions going back through the centuries; they have their own "spiritualities", as we say, their own theological emphases, their own ways of approaching Christ's mysteries, of living his faith. These things have determined and influenced their ways of worship and the rest, and been in turn influenced by them. The sad events of history have for centuries deprived Western Catholics of consciousness of these other traditions, and *vice versa*. No attempt is made in this book to get below the surface to these deeper, more interesting and most important things; but perhaps it may provide the elements of a background within which the interested reader may explore more deeply for himself.

My thanks for help generously given are due to many people in many lands, too numerous to name individually. All the pictorial illustrations, unless otherwise noted, are reproduced by kind permission of the editor of the *Eastern Churches Quarterly*.

D.A.

CONTENTS

Introduction to Volume I vii

I East and West Before the Separation . . 1

II The Eastern Catholics Today 15

III The Byzantine Rite: Liturgy and Customs . 38

IV Catholic Churches of Byzantine Rite . . 55

   1. The Melkite Patriarchate of Antioch . . 55

   2. The Italo-Greeks 65

   3. The Ruthenians or Ukrainians . . . 72

   4. The Podcarpathian Ruthenians or Rusins . 94

   5. The Hungarian Ruthenians 100

   6. The Yugoslavs 102

   7. The Rumanians 105

   8. The Greeks 112

   9. The Bulgars 117

   10. The Russians and Byelorussians . . . 120

   11. Other Byzantine Elements 126

V The Alexandrian Rite 128

   1. The Copts 128

   2. The Ethiopians 138

xiii

CONTENTS

VI THE ANTIOCHENE RITE 147
   1. The Syrians 147
   2. The Maronites 158
   3. The Malankarese 169

VII THE ARMENIAN RITE 173

VIII THE CHALDEAN RITE 188
   1. The Chaldeans 188
   2. The Malabarese 199

IX EASTERN MONASTICISM 209

APPENDIX 216

GLOSSARY 219

GENERAL BIBLIOGRAPHY 226

INDEX 228

LIST OF ILLUSTRATIONS

Following page 16

    Byzantine Liturgy in St. Peter's
    Byzantine church plan
    Russian church, Chevetogne, interior
       „   „   „   exterior
    Byzantine altar

Following page 32

    Byzantine church in Finland
    Byzantine Liturgy: beginning
        „   „   consecration
        „   „   communion
        „   „   altar vessels
    Melkite eikons

Following page 72

    Patriarch Maximos IV Sayegh
    Rusin church
    Rumanian church
    Church of the Russian College

Following page 88

    Ukrainian church
    Ordination of a Melkite bishop
    Metropolitan Andrew Szepticky
    Four victims of persecution

Following page 136

    Coptic church, exterior
        „   „   interior
    Patriarch Stephen Sidaruss
    Coptic ordination
    Coptic church, Fagus
    Syrian church, Bairut
    Ethiopic Liturgy

LIST OF ILLUSTRATIONS—*continued*

Following page 152

Cardinal Ignatius Gabriel Tappuni
Archbishop Gregory Thangalithil
Malankarese Syrian Liturgy
Maronite Liturgy

Following page 184

Cardinal Gregory Peter XV Agagianian
Armenian clergy
Armenian church, Bzommar
Chaldean church, Mosul
Chaldean monastery
Melkite monastery

Following page 200

The Chaldean patriarch
Maronite monk
Malabarese church
Malabarese group
Patriarch Paul II Cheikho
Patriarch Peter Paul Meuchi
Pope John XXIII and Bishop Sipovich

CHAPTER I

EAST AND WEST BEFORE THE SEPARATION

ONE of the most common misunderstandings about the Catholic Church is that it is uniform in all respects throughout the world. That is not true. The Church has unity, that is, there is only one true church and she is one in herself, and she has uniformity of faith in things divinely revealed, whether touching dogma or the principles of right conduct: these things are matters of absolute truth and therefore necessarily uniform. But beyond that, no. There is not and never has been any principle of uniformity in Catholicism that requires all Catholics to worship with the same liturgical forms, in the same language, to be subject to an identical canon law, to have the same customs and usages, the same religious temperament, spiritual approach, practical and speculative emphases. And in fact they do not.

It is easy to see how the misunderstanding has arisen. Most American and western European Catholics never assist at any Mass but the Roman Mass in the Latin tongue, or come across usages with which they are not more or less familiar, or hear of discipline or religious approach that differs from their own; pulpit, press, and private conversation all seem to assume (sometimes definitely say) that these things are and must be the same for all Catholics everywhere, And yet we have not to look very far to see that this seeming uniformity is fallacious. To mention only one thing, but the most important of all, the Mass: the prayers and observances of the Mass as celebrated by a Dominican or Calced Carmelite friar are not exactly the same as those in the Roman Missal; nor are those of the Carthusian monks, nor those used in the archdiocese of Milan and Braga and Lyons, or at Toledo; while in many churches in Yugoslavia the Roman Mass is celebrated in Slavonic.

The Mass is always and everywhere *one* considered as the Eucharistic Sacrifice: the true sacrifice of the body and blood of Christ made present on the altar, the representation and renewal of the offering made once for all on the cross of Calvary, the doing of that which our Lord at the Last Supper told us, through his apostles, to do; and that is what matters, and all that matters, essentially. But to say that in every Catholic church Mass is celebrated with the same prayers and observances is not true. The Eucharistic Sacrifice is one, the ways of offering it are many.

The varieties of the Latin Mass mentioned above are more or less closely related to and resemble the usual Roman form. But there are other Catholics, some millions of them, distinguished as the Catholics of the Eastern rites, whose Mass is altogether different in its prayers and externals from those with which we are familiar, who are subject to different canon law, who may differ from us in almost every conceivable thing—always excepting faith and morals.

For some time after all the Apostles were dead the organization and worship of the Church were fluid: she was there in her essential structure and living reality, but she had not come from Christ's hands "ready-made" and fully developed in all her parts and aspects. The unit was the local church, the community of Christians in one place, whose bishop, assisted by priests and deacons, "presided in the place of God" over the faithful of that locality, as St Ignatius of Antioch wrote about the year 107. It was not long before certain important bishops were exercising jurisdiction over other bishops, especially those whom they had themselves ordained and set over some new Christian community.[1] This was the beginning of "metropolitans" or "archbishops" and led later to the very important office of "patriarch" and the accompanying territorial division. The forms of worship and offering the Holy Sacrifice differed from church to church and were in the vernacular of the local faithful (e.g., Aramaic at first in Jerusalem, Greek at Antioch

---

[1] The principle that a bishop has jurisdiction over the bishop whom he consecrates is a very important one in ecclesiastical history, especially in the East. The pope as Patriarch of the West has the right to consecrate all bishops of the Western church (a right which for obvious reasons he does not exercise in person); the same with the other patriarchs.

and Rome); gradually these forms solidified into types or "families", those of the most important churches becoming the norms for the lesser ones associated with or dependent on them.[2]

From the earliest times a primacy of the see of St Peter in Rome was recognized by all other sees, though it was a long time before the full extent, implications and prerogatives of that primacy emerged in their fullness. The next most important bishops were those of Alexandria (whose church may have been founded by St Mark) and Antioch, where also traditionally St Peter had presided, and these were also the three chief cities of the Roman Empire. After Constantine the Great had transferred his capital to the east, Constantinople soon attained in fact the second place of ecclesiastical honour. These four cities give their names to the four chief types of Christian liturgy, which with their variants are in use today. In the early centuries the East played a preponderating part in Christian history and thought (Greek was the language of the Roman church until about the middle of the third century: Latin was first used for liturgical purposes in Africa); the Greek fathers and doctors not merely left an ineffaceable mark but were the fundamental formative influences in the post-apostolic Church; as Pope John XXIII has said, "the entire later edifice of theology in East and West rests on the mighty shoulders of St Basil, St Gregory Nazianzen and their fellows". The classical first seven oecumenical councils were all held in the East and were predominantly Eastern in their constitution. For seventy-five years in the seventh and eighth centuries almost every one of the thirteen popes of Rome was a Greek or Syrian; and there were others, over twenty Eastern popes in all.

Though, of course, the great heresies of the early days of Christianity, Arianism, Pelagianism and the rest, did not disappear without leaving a trace, only two of them are still represented by existing churches, whose origins were in the Christological controversies of the fifth century which are known respectively as Nestorianism and Monophysism.

The heresy which takes its name from Nestorius, bishop of

---

[2] In the middle of the third century Firmilian, bishop of Caesarea in Cappadocia, remarked that the liturgical variety then existing made no difference to unity.

Constantinople, maintains that in our Lord there are *two* persons, God the Son and the man Jesus, and that Jesus alone was born of our Lady and died on the cross. The controversy raged round the representative word *theotokos*, Mother of God, a title which the Nestorians, of course, refused to recognize. Diodore, bishop of Tarsus, and Theodore, bishop of Mopsuestia, rather than Nestorius, were the originators of the heresy, which was condemned in the year 431 by the oecumenical Council of Ephesus. Refusal to accept this condemnation gave rise to the separate heretical *Nestorian Church*, those members of which who have returned to Catholicity are called Chaldeans.

Twenty years later there was an even worse schism. The patriarch of Alexandria supported the false doctrine of a monk called Eutyches (d. *c.* 455), who taught that in Jesus Christ there is only one nature, his humanity being completely absorbed in and identified with his divinity and his body not of one substance with ours, which means that he was not really a man at all and his earthly life only an appearance. It arose from the opposition to Nestorianism, which was led by St Cyril, patriarch of Alexandria, upon whose death in 444 his successor Dioscoros hotly and unscrupulously took up the cause of the innovators. After six years of controversy and violence the Emperor Marcian convened a council, at which Pope St Leo I's legates presided. It met at Chalcedon and, after deposing Dioscoros who refused to submit to the "dogmatic letter" in which, two years earlier, the pope had set out the truth about the disputed matters, the bishops on 22 October 451 declared the Catholic faith to be that in the one person of Jesus Christ there are two real, perfect and complete natures, the divine and the human. Thus the Council of Ephesus was confirmed against Nestorianism, and Eutychianism solemnly condemned. Many in Egypt and Syria refused to accept the findings of the council, and so gave rise to several schismatic churches, namely, the *Coptic* in Egypt, the *Syrian Jacobite*, the *Armenian*, the *Ethiopic* and (indirectly and centuries later) the *Malabar Jacobite Churches;* minorities from all of these have since come back to Catholic unity.

These bodies are known historically as the "monophysite churches", because they are supposed to uphold the doctrine of our Lord's "one nature". But it is not so simple as that. Apart from some extremists, the so-called monophysites in fact repudiated (and repudiate) the teaching of Eutyches. What exactly they did profess, and why (apart from very powerful political and "nationalist" considerations) they rejected the Council of Chalcedon, are extremely difficult questions to which no wholly satisfactory answers have been found.[3] Such problems are not the concern of this book, and so herein the usual historical terms "Monophysism" and "monophysite" are used, without the intention of begging any questions. The important point here is that the churches mentioned above have for the past fifteen hundred years been out of communion with both Catholics and Orthodox.

For six hundred years and more after the Council of Chalcedon the Universal Church remained organized in five distinct parts, the patriarchates of Rome (or the West), Constantinople, Alexandria, Antioch and Jerusalem. The West included roughly everything west of a line from the eastern end of Crete through Macedonia (the borders, especially Illyricum, were disputed with Constantinople), with the north coast of Africa; Constantinople had Thrace, most of Asia Minor and, at the end of the period, Russia; Alexandria was reduced to the few Catholics left in Egypt and the lands south of it who were faithful to Chalcedon; Antioch ruled the similar but much larger Catholic remnant in Syria; Jerusalem had the small territory of Palestine and the Sinai peninsula. Each of these divisions was administratively independent of the other and appointed its own patriarch locally, and each had its own liturgy, discipline, and customs,[4] though after the Arab invasions what was left of the last three patriarchates ultimately became uniform with Constantinople. (In those days there was perhaps more liturgical and disciplinary uniformity in the Catholic East than in the West; Constantinople has sometimes tried to impose her own observances as a matter of principle.) The four Eastern patriarchs recognized in the bishop of Rome, as successor of St

---

[3] The best general treatment of the subject is by Maspero, *Historie des Patriarches d'Alexandrie* (Paris, 1930). Monophysite theologians often accused the Chalcedonian fathers of Nestorianism.

[4] But a man did not necessarily have the same liturgy as his patriarch, e.g., the pope ruled over Byzantines in *Magna Graecia* and Illyricum.

Peter, a primacy of jurisdiction of uncertain extent, and a final court of appeal in doctrinal matters, although the dogma of papal infallibility was not yet distinctly formulated. Appeals to Rome from the East were frequent from the fifth to the ninth centuries; and during imperial attacks on the veneration of holy images papal prestige was very high among the anti-iconoclast majority.

At that time one could speak of a geographical Eastern and Western part of the Church with more definiteness than now, and the difference was much more than geographical and ritual (as it still is). It was psychological, and there was a strong cultural division. Surprising as it may seem to us, Constantinople looked on western Europe as a land of barbarians—and not without reason. She, "the New Rome", was the heir of the glories both of Greece and of Rome and, with all her glaring faults, a worthy one; she was, too, the bulwark of Christendom, staving off to the best of her ability the Arabs, Turks and Mongols while the western countries were painfully hammering out a new order from the ruins of the western empire and the new barbarian peoples that occupied its lands.

Nevertheless, despite the unhappy rivalry that emerged, there was fundamentally less cultural cleavage between the western Europeans centred at Rome and the eastern Europeans centred at Constantinople (for they all had roots in Old Rome) than there was between both and the Asiatic Christians in Syria and farther east. From some aspects the more or less arbitrary line of division between Christian east and west should be drawn north and south through Antioch; but as ecclesiastical history, closely bound up with secular history, developed, it is an irregular course roughly from Riga through Yugoslavia to Alexandria that the line takes. Constantinople (Byzantium) was the critical point, for that was the imperial city, and quasi-sacred emperors concerned themselves very actively in religious matters. This (together with very much later national situations) has given rise in the West to frequent accusations against the Byzantine church of "Caesaropapism," the subjection of religion to the state. But in fact the ecclesiastical authorities were far from being so submissive as they have been represented; Henri Grégoire goes so far as to say that "the Byzantines

6

became accustomed to the idea that organized opposition to the imperial will in religious matters was normal and legitimate".

Tendency to friction and ill-feeling between East and West was aggravated by Constantinople's rise to ecclesiastical power, and her ambition was increased after the Arabs had overrun the other Eastern patriarchates and made them powerless. On the other hand, it is admitted that Rome did not always act with discretion and in a spirit of conciliation, though it was a perfectly legitimate political action that in some measure darkened the historical background of tension and rivalry when on Christmas day in the year 800 Pope St Leo III crowned the Frankish Charlemagne as Emperor of the West. This could be interpreted as the transference to the West of the age-long *imperium* of the Byzantine *basileus*.

Little by little Constantinople allowed herself to be led away by the idea of setting up a Byzantine universality in opposition to Roman universality and, when opportunity offered, at its expense.[5] The first stakes in this struggle were the southern Slavs and the slavonized people of Bulgaria, who were established on the borders of the two powers, and the duel, though its most important consequences did not come till later, was fought our chiefly during the ninth century. It was with a letter written at the patriarch's order by Leo, the metropolitan of the Bulgars, that the schism of Cerularius began 150 years later.

Meanwhile, temporary formal ruptures of communion had become frequent, until in the year 858 there began the "affair of Photius", who had been intruded into the see of Constantinople by the emperor Michael III: serious difficulties between Photius and Pope St Nicholas I followed. There is no need to go into all that here, but this much must be said: For centuries Photius has been regarded in the West as a great man whose insatiable ambition betrayed him into becoming the archschismatic and opponent of the primacy of the Holy See, and by the Orthodox (who keep his feast as a saint on February 6) as the great champion of Eastern independence against the encroachments of Rome. But in our own time the historical records on which these judgements were based have received new and

---

[5] As early as 586 John IV the Faster assumed the title of Oecumenical Patriarch, still borne by the patriarch of Constantinople; but *oikumene* here means no more than the territory governed by the emperor of New Rome.

intensive study from Catholic scholars, of which the result has been—not indeed entirely to rehabilitate Photius—but to produce a picture of what actually occurred different from the one hitherto rather uncritically accepted. Pope Nicholas himself called Photius "a man of great virtue and world-wide knowledge", and it has always been recognized in the West that he "was one of the greatest men of the middle ages, one of the most remarkable characters in all church history. . . . The greatest scholar of his time . . . (with) no shadow of suspicion against his private life" (Fortescue). We now know that he was not as well the unscrupulous ecclesiastic we had hitherto supposed, even though he did quarrel with the pope (and the Bulgarian question just referred to was involved in that) and make charges against practices of the Western church. All the same, the Photian troubles unquestionably did great harm, and helped to bring Greeks and Latins, East and West, into formal opposition.[6]

From the end of the ninth to well into the eleventh century was a black era in the history of the Roman church, during which many weak or totally unworthy men were elected to or forced upon the papal chair, and ecclesiastical disorder was widespread. Rome had earned the contempt of the East; but the great reform had begun, and St Leo IX was pope when the patriarch of Constantinople, Michael Cerularius, for his own reasons impugned certain Western customs as unchristian, and without provocation closed all the Latin churches in Constantinople.

The principal customs which Cerularius, borrowing from Photius, objected to were celibacy of the lower clergy (never the rule in the East), fasting on Saturdays as well as Fridays (then usual in the West), and the use of unleavened bread (*azyme*) in the Eucharist. It must be clearly understood that neither the pope nor anybody else had asked Constantinople to adopt any of these practices. There was no mention at first of the *Filioque*, but that trouble, too, was in its origins more disciplinary and liturgical than dogmatic. The East has always

---

[6] A summary, with pertinent bibliography, of the findings in this matter of Amann, Laurent, Grumel and Dvornik can be found in the *Clergy Review* (London) for November, 1938, by Andrew Beck, called "Propaganda in History: the Greek Schism". See also Fliche & Martin, *Histoire de l'Église*, tome vi (Paris, 1938); and F. Dvornik, *The Photian Schism* (Cambridge, 1948).

attached more importance to matters of discipline and ritual than the West has. At this time all their traditional usages were esteemed of directly apostolic origin and were given a textual support from Holy Scripture (e.g., for fasting, Luke 5:33-35). Also they had a great aversion for "judaizing", hence their objection to *azyme* and the Sabbatine fast.[7]

Cerularius had not the support of the emperor Constantine IX, but he was a self-confident and ambitious man; he did not want a breach with the pope, but he did want his own way, and he was popular with his people. After vain negotiations the legates sent from Rome solemnly excommunicated Cerularius and two of his prelates in the church of the Holy Wisdom on 16 July 1054. Just as the liturgy was about to begin, Cardinal Humbert of Silva Candida, Cardinal Frederick of Lorraine and Peter, archbishop of Amalfi, passed through the crowded church, entered the sanctuary, and laid the act of excommunication upon the altar. *"Videat Deus et judicet,"* they exclaimed, and departed.

It was a regrettably theatrical gesture, and recent scholarship has criticized it heavily (*e.g.* Jugie, in *Échos d'Orient*, No. 188, 1937). At the moment of the excommunication Leo IX, the pope from whom the legates received their powers, was dead, and it is arguable that those powers had accordingly lapsed; it is also arguable that Leo would not have approved their violent action; it is certain that Cardinal Humbert was extremely ill-informed about the East and the matters in dispute. In any case, though this event is commonly taken to be the definitive separation of East from West, it was long before the separation was everywhere consummated and accepted as permanent; Rome's practice today is rather to date it from 1472, when Constantinople formally repudiated the Union of Florence.[8]

It certainly appears that at the time nobody regarded these events as having anything final about them; but if it be taken simply as a conventional date, 1054 may well be regarded as the most calamitous date in Christian history. It marks the beginning of the complete parting of East and West, and no

---

[7] In modern times Eastern Catholics received without demur the definitions of the Immaculate Conception and papal infallibility, but raised endless trouble about the Gregorian calendar and the election of bishops (Melkites in 1857-60, Armenians and Chaldeans in 1867-79).

[8] An example of this is the permission given to Russian Catholics to observe the feast of St Sergius of Radonezh (d. 1392) and of other medieval Russian saints.

subsequent reconciliation has been lasting or widespread enough to make any substantial difference. The Great Church of Constantinople itself was not (and has never been) excommunicated by the Holy See, who accused her of no heresy; but she separated from Rome, and the other Byzantine patriarchates followed, thus forming what is now known as the *Orthodox Eastern Church*[9].

For long there were no continuously and unambiguously Catholic Orientals at all except the Greeks in southern Italy and Sicily (*Magna Graecia*), whose wavering allegiance to the Holy See was consolidated and strengthened at the Council of Bari in 1098, largely through the efforts of St Anselm, archbishop of Canterbury, and, after the First Crusade, the Maronites in Syria and some Armenians. There were for long men on both sides who appreciated the wickedness and folly of the situation and did their best to mend it, but the separation gradually hardened, ecclesiastical intercourse between East and West grew less and less, and the churches drifted further apart.[10] One of the biggest factors against reconciliation was, unhappily, provided by the Westerners themselves in the way they conducted the Crusades, especially the fourth. Indeed, it can be cogently argued that the Crusades, with their violence, intrigue and treachery, did more to produce a spirit of separatism between ordinary Christians of East and West than the actions of bishops such as Cerularius and Humbert could ever have done. The Greeks did not forgive and never have forgiven the Latins for sacking Constantinople in 1204, driving out their bishops, stealing their churches, and setting a Frank on the imperial throne for fifty-seven years; they resented and feared the haughty arrogance and domineering efficiency of Normans and Venetians, and wanted to have nothing to do with either them or their church. What Pope Innocent III himself thought of the heroes of the Fourth Crusade can be read in his letter to Cardinal Peter of Capua: "The Latins have given an example only of perversity and works of darkness. It is natural that (the

---

[9] It would appear that historically the epithet "Orthodox" in this connection distinguishes those Christians who accepted the Council of Chalcedon: *see* P. de la Taille in *Orientalia Christiana*, Vol. v, no. 21, p. 281. Some Byzantines in communion with Rome call themselves "Catholic-Orthodox", quite reasonably. In the *berat* which the sultan formerly gave to a newly elected Catholic Melkite patriarch he was called head of the *Rûm kathulik milleti*, of which the English equivalent is "Catholic Orthodox people".

[10] One Greek bishop was present at the eleventh oecumenical council (Lateran III) in 1179.

Greeks) should regard them as curs. These soldiers of Christ . . . are drenched in Christian blood." Unfortunately the pope himself adopted a policy that was the very reverse of pacifying. A spirit of division and particularism increased on both sides, epitomized in Petrarch's words "The Turks are enemies, but the Greeks are schismatics and worse than enemies". "Sectarian imbecility can go no further," comments Mr Patrick Leigh Fermor in *Mani* (London, 1958, p. 297).

The Greeks looked time and again to their fellow Christians in the West for help in their struggle against the oncoming tide of Islam; but it was rarely forthcoming and never effective. This was not always the Westerners' fault. But the only western "powers" helping the Greeks at the last defence of Constantinople, the city that had conserved our civilization through the barbarian dark ages, were a handful of archers sent by the pope and a few ships and seven hundred men from Genoa. When, after the Council of Florence, the news reached Constantinople that the Greek bishops Bessarion and Isidore had been made cardinals, "Better," said Duke Luke Notaras, remembering the fourth crusade, "better the turban ruling in Constantinople than the Latin mitre". The people of the city were to learn whether it was so or not.

There were, nevertheless, two attempts at complete reunion during the middle ages, in both of which political considerations (very just ones) played a decisive part. In the later thirteenth century, the pope no less than the emperor at Constantinople was alarmed by the aggressive policy of Charles of Anjou, and Michael VIII Palaeologus accordingly sought to strengthen his position by a settlement with Bd Gregory X. The patriarch Joseph I was not so willing, so the the emperor shut him up in a monastery, set up John Bekkos, who was favourable, in his stead, and sent representatives in 1274 to the Second Council of Lyons, who concluded a union with the Roman Church. There was no difficulty about it, because the emperor said that his representatives were to make the union and not argue. But the people, monks and clergy of Constantinople did not want it, it was never effective, and was repudiated by the emperor Andronicus II eight years later. The story of the Union of Florence in 1439 is somewhat similar, though with

11

more important results. John VII Palaeologus wanted help against the Ottoman Turks, who were at his very gates; he seems also to have been sincerely concerned for the unity of Christians in the Church. This time the patriarch of Constantinople, Joseph II, himself attended the council,[11] as well as representatives from other churches, and acts of reunion were at length effected on behalf of the four Orthodox patriarchs, the katholikos of the Armenians, the Coptic patriarch and the Syrian Jacobites. In the case of the last three the union was never effective, though it had important repercussions in the non-Byzantine East.

The "four points of the Council of Florence" which formed the basis of agreement with the Orthodox were their acceptance of the supreme primacy of the pope, of the validity of the use of unleavened bread in the Eucharist, of the existence of Purgatory, and of the procession of the Holy Spirit from the Father and the Son.[12] In Russia the Great-Prince Basil II refused the union at once, but it was the remote cause of the reconciliation of the Kievan eparchies at Brest in 1595. In the patriarchates of Alexandria, Antioch, and Jerusalem it subsisted only for a short time, but it seems never to have completely died out in the second of them. At Constantinople it was not well received; but at the taking of the city by the Turks in 1453 the last Liturgy was celebrated in the church of the Holy Wisdom ("St Sophia") and the last Roman emperor, Constantine XI, died in battle, in communion with Old Rome.

These efforts at reuniting Christendom failed, and not simply because some of the motives at work were insufficiently pure;[13] the time in any case was not yet ripe, the mass of Christians did not recognize the enormity of Christian division. Despite the interest of Roman church authorities, much of the West was indifferent to the matter, while in the East people and clergy as a whole were against union with Rome; in this they were led by the monks, sincere men but apt to be narrow and fanatical, who had the ear of the populace, to whom the West simply

---

[11] He died in Florence. His tomb may be seen in Santa Maria Novella.
[12] These four points were made the basis of the Rumanian reunion at Alba Julia in 1698.
[13] The Anglican scholar, the late Canon J. A. Douglas, is not the only one to have remarked that Christian disunion is too often presented as the evil fruit simply of theological perversity. Heresies (and orthodoxies) have been used as battle flags in national and social quarrels; enduring schisms have been as much the work of civil leaders and politicians as of theologians; "No one can understand the Orthodox Church today without grasping that fact."

meant foreign domination in the Norman manner. This anti-Roman feeling can hardly be a matter for surprise in view of such attitudes as that of Petrarch in Italy, whose words have been quoted above. The situation was bedevilled by politics and general inadequacy on both sides.

For the rest, the Crusades were instrumental in regularizing the Maronites of Syria in communion with the Holy See, from which they have never since swerved, and in organizing a church of Armenian Catholics in Asia Minor, most of whom afterwards fell away. From time to time Dominican and Franciscan friars were active in Armenia, Syria, Egypt and Ethiopia, and among the Nestorians, but with no solid results; obscure groups were reconciled here or there and came to an end; sometimes influential individuals were convinced but found few to follow their example. Such, for instance, were the Greek theologian Barlaam, whom Pope Clement VI made bishop of the Byzantine diocese of Gerace in Calabria, and his disciple the layman Demetrius Kydones, secretary to the emperor John VI, who was reconciled c.1355 and translated works of St Augustine, St Anselm and St Thomas Aquinas into Greek.

Twenty years after the end of the Byzantine empire, the Church of Constantinople formally repudiated the Union of Florence, in part under pressure from Constantinople's new Turkish masters. For four hundred years Eastern and Western Christians had been going their separate ways, out of communion with one another, yet unwilling formally to recognize a condition of ecclesiastical separation: the Orthodox, in the nature of things never so conscious of Old Rome as the West, had not noticed much practical difference; the Catholics for long had looked on the Orthodox, not as a "different church", but as part of the One Church temporarily out of communion— a state of affairs that had been known before. But now, in addition to the ecclesiastical disagreements, the Christian people of the Byzantine East (except the Russians) were under the civil rule of a great foreign and non-Christian power which aimed at further conquests in Europe: the Turks would not tolerate the association of the Christian church in their dominions with the Christian church of their "Frankish" enemies (the three Orthodox patriarchs in Turkish territory had been forbidden to attend the Council of Florence); that is an important aspect of the Greek schism that is often overlooked.

So in 1472 the separation became as it were definitive: Catholics and Orthodox have since in general looked on one another, not simply as erring brethren, but as members of, so to speak, quite different and separate Christian families.

It was not till the sixteenth century that permanent reunions of Orientials in notable numbers began to take place, beginning with some Nestorians in 1551. The more important of these were of the Ruthenian dioceses west of Kiev in 1595, of the Rumanians in Transylvania in 1698, and of the Melkites in 1724, all from the Orthodox. But these and other like movements were not of sufficient weight to alter substantially the separated churches of the East, and except for the continual subdivision of the Orthodox and other internal results of history, they remain as bodies today what they were five hundred years ago.

Today Eastern Catholics are a small, heterogeneous body; the non-Catholics, even more heterogeneous, outnumber them very many times. Truth does not depend on a counting of heads and the unity of the Catholic Church is indefectible, it remains formally resplendent; but materially she is maimed and weakened, lacking most of her Eastern children: the unhealed breach between Rome and the East is the saddest and in some ways the most difficult to understand among the divisions of Christendom.

BIBLIOGRAPHY

F. Dvornik, *Les Slaves, Byzance et Rome* (Paris, 1925).
———— *The Photian Schism* (Cambridge, 1948).
G. Every, *The Byzantine Patriarchate 451-1204* (London, 1947).
S. Runciman, *The Eastern Schism* (Oxford, 1955).
Y. Congar, *After Nine Hundred Years* (New York, 1959).
J. Gill, *The Council of Florence* (Cambridge, 1959).
O. Halecki, *From Florence to Brest* (Rome, 1958).

CHAPTER II

THE EASTERN CATHOLICS TODAY

WHAT would have been the statistical position today had the separation never happened or had the brief reunion patched up at the Council of Florence in 1439 been permanent? Other things being equal, there would be a very large (instead of a very small) proportion of Catholics representing the age-long Christian traditions of the East, with their own "approaches" and emphases, and their own canonical dispositions, using the liturgy of Constantinople in numerous languages, with communion in both kinds, a married parochial clergy, and all other their own customs, under their own patriarchs, subject to the pope as supreme pontiff. But the schism *did* take place, and those who became separated from Rome looked upon the Catholic Church as a West-European institution, "Latin" in its outlook, worship, and usages: as if Catholicism were synonymous with the Western church. And after the Council of Trent there was a greater and ever increasing uniformity of worship, discipline, and administration. Throughout the later middle ages it was almost true to say that in every Catholic church the Mass was the Latin, western Mass. Almost, but not quite. There remained faithful to Rome a body of Christians of Greek origin in southern Italy and Sicily who kept their Greek liturgy and customs; there was in the Lebanon the larger body of Maronite Catholics, with their Syrian liturgy and customs; and after the First Crusade there was in Cilicia a number of Christians of the Armenian rite who had returned to communion with the Holy See. This tiny minority of Catholic Easterners served providentially to preserve the material catholicity, the all-embracingness, the diversity-in-unity of the Church.

Up to the time of the separation there had never been any

idea of uniformity in the Universal Church outside the necessary uniformity in faith and morals: such a notion would have been regarded as superfluous, impracticable, improper and more than a little laughable. The rites of the East Syrian monk who gave communion to Edward I of England in France early in the fourteenth century must have been as unfamiliar to the king as they would be to us: but they did not cause him to question the stranger's catholicity and orthodoxy. After the separation, as I have said, the Church took on to all intents and purposes an entirely Western, Latin, and more uniform complexion (though it must not be forgotten that in those days the Latin Mass varied in details almost from diocese to diocese).[1] This was greatly extended by the missionary activities of the sixteenth and seventeenth centuries. But at the very time when Spanish, Portuguese and French missionaries were carrying Catholic faith and Western practices to the heathen of the New World and the Far East, bodies of Eastern Christians nearer home began to return to the pope's obedience. The first of these was led by the Nestorian katholikos John Sulaka in 1551. From that time onward there has been a continuous movement of Orientals back to Catholic unity, generally a dribble of individuals but sometimes amounting to the small wave of an "hierarchical reunion", down to the reconciliation of Mar Ivanios and Mar Theophilos in India in 1930. It is with these Catholics and their few predecessors that this book is concerned.

When these people were reconciled with the Holy See they kept their own forms of worship, church law, and religious customs. It must be clearly understood that this is not a matter of *concession* but of canonical *right*: they as Catholics have as much right to their traditional and immemorial usages as we Latins have to ours.[2] To attempt to produce a universal uniformity in these things would be artificial, unnatural, untraditional, un-Catholic; and it would not succeed. Moreover, their orders being valid, their prelates and priests were usually reinstated in the offices which they had held when separated. There were only two exceptions to this on a large scale, the

[1] During the latter middle ages there were in England and Wales alone the "uses" of Sarum, York, Hereford and Bangor, to say nothing of those of the religious orders.

[2] No doubt in the abstract the Holy See could impose the Latin rite on, say, Byzantines—and could impose the Byzantine rite on Latins. It is as likely to do the one as the other.

16

CELEBRATION OF THE BYZANTINE LITURGY IN ST PETER'S, ROME

(*See page 45*)

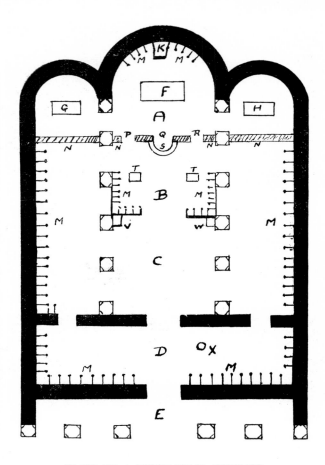

PLAN OF A BYZANTINE CHURCH

A, Sanctuary (*bema*). B, Choir (*khoros*). C, Nave (*naos*). D, Narthex. E, Vestibule. F, Altar. G, *Prothesis*. H, *Diakonikon*. K, Bishop's throne (*kathedra*), MMMM, Stalls (*stasidia*). NN, Eikonostasis. P, North door. Q, Holy doors. R, South door. S, Step (*solea*). TT, Lecterns (*analogia*). V, Pulpit (*ambon*). W, Eikon-stand (*proskynetarion*). X, Baptismal font.

By courtesy of

RUSSIAN CHURCH, CHEVETOGNE

Chevetogne Priory

RUSSIAN CHURCH, CHEVETOGNE

Left: Byzantine Altar, Seminary of SS. Cyril and Methodius, Pittsburgh (*by courtesy of Byzantine Catholic World*).

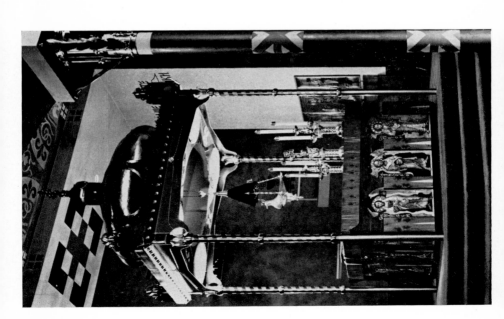

Ethiopians and the Malabarese in the seventeenth century: both were disastrous and resulted in the loss of many people to the Church. Both these tragedies were due to too close a dependence of missionary clergy on a "Catholic power" (Portugal) and to the disregard by European prelates (who were ignorant and frightened of Oriental ways) of the instructions of Rome that these people's lawful customs were not to be interfered with.

Since then the Holy See has made it perfectly clear time and again that the Church is Catholic and not specifically Latin or European. In his bull *Etsi pastoralis* in 1742 for the Italo-Greeks, Pope Benedict XIV declared that they were to keep to their own rites, recognized the ordination of the married, and ordered that no precedence was to be based on rite; certain provisions that implied privileges for the Western rite were abrogated subsequently. In the following year he addressed a decree, *Demandatam caelitus*, to the Melkites, in which he forbade them to alter their liturgy or to become Latins without Rome's express permission. In 1755 the same pope issued an encycical letter, *Allatae sunt*, to missioners in the Near East. Herein he traced the consistent attitude of the Holy See in this matter from the eleventh century onwards, and set out legislation based on the text "We desire most intensely that all people should be Catholics but not all Latins", reminding those whom he addressed that their function was to support and help the local indigenous Catholic clergy and not to boss them. Pope Pius IX emphasized the same things in his appeal to the separated Orientals, the encyclical *In suprema* of 1848.

More recently, in the encyclical letter *Orientalis ecclesiae* of 1944, Pope Pius XII wrote: Goodwill towards our brethren of the East implies "a proper respect for those traditions which are the special heritage of Eastern peoples, whether these be concerned with the sacred liturgy and hierarchical orders or with other elements of Christian life, so long as they are in keeping with the true faith and the moral law. Each and every people of Eastern rite must have its rightful freedom in all that is bound up with its own history, genius and character, subject always to the truth and integrity of Jesus Christ's teaching. . . . Let them all be fully confident that they will never be forced to

17

give up their own legitimate rites and venerable traditional customs. All these are to be held in equal respect and honour, for together they clothe our common mother the Church as with a queenly robe of many colours. Such diversity of rites and customs, each keeping inviolate what is most ancient and precious of its own, puts no obstacle whatever in the way of true and genuine unity".

In 1893 the international eucharistic congress was held in Jerusalem and at it the Eastern element predominated. It marks a new era in the history of the Catholic East, of which the first important fruit was Pope Leo XIII's constitution *Orientalium dignitas* in 1894.[3] Among other things, this emphasized that all rites are on exactly the same footing religiously and canonically. It decreed that any Western priest who should persuade an Eastern Christian to adopt the Latin rite should by that very fact incur suspension from his sacerdotal functions; without a rescript from the Holy See, no Catholic can change his canonical status from Eastern to Western, or vice-versa, and an Eastern dissident on becoming a Catholic was to adhere to the rite he had hitherto followed.[4]

But it is well known that the law in these matters has not everywhere been administered in its full rigour,[5] and that is one of the reasons why non-Catholic Easterners insist that "Rome wants to turn them all into Latins". The relative insignificance of some of the Eastern churches and the obscurity of the individuals who compose them, right and proper soil wherein Christianity may flourish, produce a result very marked among the smaller, and apparent in its degree in all, the Eastern churches—some dissidents who wish to return to Catholic unity, especially if they be persons of some culture or position, or if, on the other hand, they be extremely poor or downtrodden, ask to be, and are, allowed to join the Latin rite. Numbers of

[3] This pope did a pleasing thing in 1882. He substituted the title "titular bishop" for "bishop *in partibus infidelium*" because some of the sees *i.p.i.* again had Christian populations, though not in communion with Rome.

[4] According to the new code of Eastern canon law (II, ¶1) an Eastern Christian on being reconciled with the Church is now free to choose his rite. But it appears that this is to be applied only in certain Western lands and not in the East (*Le Lien*, Cairo, 1958, no. 2, pp. 5-6).

[5] There have been cases of most improper pressure being applied to induce Orientals to "turn Latin". The Russian exarch Leonid Feodorov (see p. 121) had to report to Rome that the Latin Catholics of Petersburg acted on their allegation that the papal directions contained in *Orientalium dignitas* were intended only for the churches of the Levant. The present writer was assured by a very high ecclesiastic in the Levant that *Orientalium dignitas* applied only to Europe. And to my certain knowledge his clergy were so instructed in the local seminary.

Orientals, whether Catholic or to be reconciled, and even bodies of non-Christians living among Catholics of Eastern rite (e.g., Alauite villages in Syria) do this. Why? Religious reasons? Undoubtedly, sometimes and in part. But there are other reasons, the existence of which Western missioners admit but do not enlarge upon: material reasons. In the eyes of some people, to belong to the Latin rite stands for civilization and influence, for attractive ideas of progress, for prestige, education, commerce, pseudo-Parisian clothes; Eastern rites are looked down on as being for mere peasants: too often Westerners accept rather than oppose such wrong views. All rites and those who belong to them are equal in the Church: but in practice they are often, accidentally, nothing of the sort—and it is the Latin rite that always gains from the misfortunes of its brethren; European missioners sometimes accept and encourage, not always overtly or even consciously, that situation. A rite, whether in the wide or narrow sense of the word, is not something arbitrary: it is the religious expression of ages of history, of particular cultures and religious orientations; and the Church as Church has never lost sight of the fact that Variety is the correlative of Catholicity. For many years now the Holy See has emphasized the desirability of people keeping their own rite, and that the adequacy of the reasons of those who desire a dispensation to change it be more strictly examined. Increasing numbers of Latins are allowed to do so in order that they may work as priests or nuns among their Eastern brethren.

It is one thing to "belong" to a rite and quite another to "frequent" it. Western Catholics are not only at liberty but strongly recommended by the Holy See to attend the churches of Eastern Catholics, and vice-versa, so that they may learn more about one another and strengthen the bond of mutual charity. Not only that, but the Code of Canon Law expressly lays down (canon 866) that a Latin Catholic may receive communion in a Catholic Eastern church out of devotion (and not merely in case of necessity). And why not? The only restriction in this matter is that "Easter duties" and the last sacraments should be received if possible in one's own rite. Marriages should be according to the rite of the groom, and the bride is free to adopt her husband's rite either permanently or until widowhood. Children follow the rite of their father (unless he be a non-Catholic), even if through error or in emergency they have been baptized by a priest and with the observances of another rite.

Several popes from Gregory XIII onwards made tentative efforts to establish at Rome some sort of congregation or permanent commission to deal with Oriental affairs. Eventually, in 1862, Pius IX set up a congregation "for Eastern Rite business", as a department of the Sacred Congregation for the Spreading of the Faith. This was found inconvenient and the association with the *Propaganda*, whose concern is primarily with the heathen, recognized to be unfortunate, and in 1917 Benedict XV set up the independent Sacred Congregation for the Eastern Church.[6] Of this congregation the prefect is always the reigning pope in person, and its personnel consists of a cardinal secretary and other cardinals, an assessor, a *sostituto*, and a body of expert consultants (a number of whom are, of course, Orientals). This congregation is competent in all matters arising out of the Eastern rites whether persons, discipline or divine worship are in question. Later legislation has extended its jurisdiction to Latin Catholics also in Egypt, Eritrea and northern Ethiopia, southern Albania, Bulgaria, Cyprus, Greece, Iraq, Lebanon, Palestine, Persia, Syria, Transjordan and Turkey, where formerly there was a double jurisdiction with the Congregation *de Propaganda Fide*.

The very first canon of the Roman *Codex Juris Canonici* says that it does not bind the Eastern churches except when it deals with matters which from the nature of the case affect them also, and in 1935 Pope Pius XI appointed a commission to draw up a code of Eastern canon law. A considerable part of this law derives from ancient sources common to the whole Church, and for this and other reasons the differences between Eastern and Western canon law are not always so great as might be supposed. With rare exceptions, Eastern Catholic law is the same as that of the dissidents on points where it differs from Western law. But Eastern law varies somewhat as between a church of

---

[6] In the *motu proprio* of erection the Pope made use of the words printed on the title page of this book.

one rite and another. Accordingly the Catholic Eastern code (the first of its kind) consists of general norms applicable to all Catholic Easterners, with provision when necessary for the particular laws operative in a particular rite. Instalments of the code were published in 1949, 1950, 1952 and 1957. In 1958 a Greek Orthodox theologian and canonist, Professor H. S. Alivisatos, wrote of the remarkable skill and theological insight with which this work had been done; he also had criticisms and questions arising from it.

In 1917 Benedict XV created the Pontifical Institute for Eastern Studies ("The Oriental Institute"), which is now one of the autonomous institutions of the Pontifical Gregorian University and is under the direction of the Society of Jesus. Its ordinary course is of three years, and it is open to all Eastern clergy and students (whether Catholic or not) and to Westerners, especially those who are going to work in the East. Its professorial body is extraordinarily strong (a dozen nationalities are represented on it) and includes eight professors of Eastern languages and one of Islamic religion. Among the learned publications of the institute are the series *Orientalia Christiana Analecta* and *Orientalia Christiana Periodica*. In 1940 Cardinal Eugene Tisserant established the Institute of St John Damascene for clergy pursuing Eastern studies in Rome; during over twenty years as secretary of the Sacred Eastern Congregation, Cardinal Tisserant served the Eastern churches with unwearying energy, immense learning and a most enlightened spirit,

The position today then is that the overwhelming majority of Eastern Christians belong to the separated Orthodox churches; a minority belong to the old heretical Nestorian and monophysite churches (their originating heresies seem now to be material only); and another small minority is Catholic. These are divided into Catholics of the Byzantine rite, organized according to nationality or origin; of the Alexandrian rite, in two independent bodies (Copts and Ethiops); of the Antiochene rite, in three bodies (Syrians, Maronites, Malankarese); of the Armenian rite; and of the Chaldean rite, in two churches (Chaldeans proper and Malabarese).

After all that has been said there should be no need to emphasize that these Eastern Catholics are as fully and completely

21

members of the Church as are "Westerners": they are not an inferior kind or sort of halfway house to Rome, but just plain Catholics, as were St Athanasius, St John Chrysostom, St Basil, St Gregory Nazianzen, St Gregory of Nyssa, St Ignatius of Antioch, St Cyril of Jerusalem, St Cyril of Alexandria, St John Damascene, St Ephrem the Syrian, St James of Nisibis, St Gregory the Wonderworker, St Gregory the Enlightener, St Theodore the Studite, St Antony the Abbot—none of whom celebrated the Roman Mass or said their prayers in Latin.

It is sometimes said that Catholics of Eastern rite have a horrid tendency to go into schism when they can't have their own way. Before making such a judgement it is desirable to acquaint oneself with the Eastern point of view and to study the traditional relationship between Rome and the East. From the very fact that they are Orientals they have never been, and are not even now, in such close touch historically and juridically with Rome as we of the West. We do not realize how many of *our* relations with the Holy See are in its patriarchal and not its papal capacity; the pope is our patriarch as well as supreme pontiff and so is bound to mean more in practice to an American or a Frenchman than to a Syrian or Russian. Some people have tried to make capital out of the fact that the Eastern bishops at the Vatican Council supported the party who regarded a definition of the pope's infallibility as inopportune. That proves nothing; a Catholic was perfectly entitled to think it inopportune; thousands did. Those bishops had solid reasons for fearing the effect of such a definition on the non-Catholic Christians of the East. Time has proved that they were right; just as time has proved that the reasons in favour of defining the pope's infallibility were right too. And what was the upshot of the council? Papal infallibility was defined to be an article of faith and was at once accepted throughout the Catholic East; it was in the West, as in Germany, that some Catholics went into schism rather than accept the decree of the oecumenical council. And as a matter of sober history some of the Eastern Catholic bodies, e.g., the Melkites, have loyally suffered as much during the past three hundred years for their allegiance to the Holy See as any one of the Western churches has been called on to do. I am not concerned to deny that there has been a number of schisms among the Orientals[7]—some of them are referred to elsewhere in this book—but they were rarely, if ever, concerned with any matter fundamental to Catholic Christianity. And, though nothing can justify the sin of schism, it can sometimes be explained, and we do well to bear in mind that these little, oppressed bodies of Eastern Catholics have centuries of neglect, persecution and inculpable separation from the centre of unity behind them; and that, to a small, depressed and sometimes ignorant people who, rightly or wrongly, think they have a legitimate cause of complaint, schism must often appear to be the only weapon of defence against a powerful and well-equipped authority. In his splendid book on the Italo-Greeks and Melkites Dr Adrian Fortescue, after pointing out what irritations and injustices have been suffered by Catholics of Eastern rite through the disregard by local Latins of the instructions of the Holy See, says, "The really wonderful thing about them is . . . their magnificent loyalty to the Catholic ideal. It is the right sort of loyalty, to an ideal, not to a person. They have no more personal devotion toward Italian cardinals and the monsignori of the Roman congregations than we have in the North. What they care for is the one united Church of Christ throughout the world, and the Holy See as guarding that unity . . ." (*The Uniate Eastern Churches*, p. 23). The Eastern Catholics are neither favourers of schism, as their Catholic critics assert, nor yet groaning under the yoke of Rome, as so many non-Catholics fondly imagine.

Of all the matters for discussion arising out of the Eastern Catholics and their customs, none are more frequently debated than those of clerical marriage and the "hybridization" of rites.

The custom of a celibate clergy has become so firmly rooted in Western Catholic consciousness, its economic, administrative and social advantages have been so amply demonstrated, and the spiritual qualities accruing from this willing deprivation are so resplendent, that we are prone to forget that it is not an evangelical precept and that it took a thousand years for it to become general in the West. In the East, whether before or after

---

[7] I do not refer to such common incidents as ecclesiastics and others becoming Catholic and then returning to schism soon after. These are easily explained by their inadequate "reasons" for reconciliation in the first instance. It is on sound historical grounds that the submission of dissident prelates to Rome is often regarded with a prudent scepticism.

the separation, clerical celibacy was never the rule for the lower clergy. There the normal law is that a married man may be ordained to the diaconate and priesthood and retain his wife; he may not be married after receiving the diaconate[8] or, if his wife dies, marry again; bishops must be single or widowers, and for that reason were formerly invariably chosen from among the monks. Of all the so-called peculiarities of the East this is the one that seems most troublesome to Westerners. I once had to read a paper on the Eastern rites to a Catholic audience, and afterwards the wife to a well-known Irish man of letters came up and told me that, as I had spoken without disapproval of married priests, I could not possible be a Catholic. I protested that I was. Not a *Roman* Catholic, then. Yes, a Roman Catholic. At last my chairman, who happened to be a bishop, persuaded her that I really was in communion with the pope of Rome and the bishop of Cork, so she said as a parting shot that "nothing would induce *her* to go to confession to a married priest". I could think of no more devastating reply than that she was not likely to be asked to[9]. Another woman of my acquaintance, of a quite different class, simple but intelligent, who had heard that there were married Catholic priests somewhere in the world, was quite distressed: that none of our clergy were under any circumstances allowed to have wives was for her apparently an ultimate proof of the truth of Catholicism. A well-known Catholic "intellectual" once admitted to me that he could not reconcile himself to the idea of a married priest; he was conscious that his attitude was unreasonable and all against his own instincts, and he must try and get over it. I think those three examples about cover the average Western reaction to this subject.

Now, we must do better than that, and help others to do better than that, if we are to produce a more sympathetic atmosphere and state of mind where Orientals are concerned. An unmarried clergy is one of the great achievements of Western Christianity and there is not the remotest chance of the Latin church altering its general law in this matter; nor, for an indefinitely long period, will the Eastern churches to any

---

[8] According to the new code of canon law for Catholics, the subdiaconate.
[9] I may note here that a Syrian priest told me that in parts of his country people did not like to go to confession to an *unmarried* priest.

considerable extent alter theirs. It may well be thought that the ideal would be general clerical celibacy among the Orientals as well, but only one Eastern body (the Malabarese) as yet has the full Western discipline,[10] and the Church is not likely to favour any *strict* application of that discipline to the East at large, for the simple reason that it would be a further barrier raised against reunion of the dissidents. We Western Catholics must realize that any and every mass reunion of Orientals will bring more and more married priests into the Church and we must face the fact that there is no essential inconsistency between holy orders and marriage. We have to admire the austerity involved in the voluntary renunciation of marriage and appreciate the heightened spirituality which this asceticism for God's sake has brought to the Western clergy; we know what an advantage celibacy has been in spreading the Gospel in foreign missions, in times of persecution and in many aspects of parochial work at home; we realize how much this selfless renunciation has done to raise the priesthood in the eyes of the faithful. But on the other hand, whatever accidental difficulties may be involved, the fact that a priest has received one more sacrament than usual does nothing to derogate from his priestly dignity. The popular Western attitude is not only unreasonable —it may easily become uncharitable. In places where there are some married Eastern Catholic clergy, America, for example, this attitude of their Latin brethren has been extremely distressing and embarrassing to those priests—and to their wives and children.[11] If we can do something to modify that attitude of mind among people in our own country we shall have done a work of charity and something that will help to encourage non-Catholic Eastern clergy toward reunion. Pope Pius XI spoke quite unambiguously in his encyclical letter *Ad Catholici sacerdotii*: "What we have said in commendation of clerical celibacy must not be interpreted as though it were our mind in any way to cast reflection on or as it were disapprove the different discipline legitimately prevailing in the Eastern church."

10 The disciplines in force among Catholics of various Eastern rites are noted in the following chapters. Before the recent disruption of the Ruthenians and Rumanians, about half of the 8,000 Catholic Eastern secular priests were married.

11 A Byzantine priest who had to minister to his people in a European city told me with tears in his eyes that his neighbours, clerical and lay, made him feel like a criminal because he had a wife and children. "And," he added, "the Holy Father himself has blessed my family."

25

"Hybridization" is the modification of Eastern liturgies, customs and modes of thought by undiscriminating adoption of foreign practices and submission to foreign influences; as these practices and influences mostly come from the West it is also called "latinization", but occasional examples of small hybridisms from one Eastern rite to another are to be met with. Another term, "uniatism", has come into use to designate this process by which Catholics of Eastern rites tend to become de-orientalized, neglecting the study of the Eastern Fathers and the early councils, adopting Western disciplinary customs, forms of popular devotion and ascetical treatises to the exclusion of their own, adapting themselves to a European or alien outlook, and accepting liturgical hybridism. In spite of the fact that the Church is opposed to this process, especially since the constitution *Orientalium dignitas* of Leo XIII, most of the Catholic Eastern churches have suffered more or less from it, some of them very badly. Sometimes it is due to what can only be called "aggression", as when in 1636 the bishop of Paphos in Cyprus descended upon the Maronite colonies in his diocese and arbitrarily insisted that they should give up using wooden altar "stones" and ministering communion in both kinds, that they should put holy-water stoups in their churches and kneel throughout the Liturgy, and other things entirely foreign to their customs. Quite often it was due to the Orientals themselves, many of whom, long subject to the Turks or other overlords, had a sense of inferiority and thought that anything from the West was essentially superior, or else they wanted to flatter and please their European benefactors. And much of it was due to the well-meaning efforts of Western missioners and nuns, who sincerely believed that a more or less tactful process of latinization was in the best interests of the Orientals: some of them apparently could not imagine that Eastern customs were best fitted to the needs of Easterners, that they were really as legitimate as those of Rome, and they seem to have thought that the popes were inadequately informed about Eastern affairs. There has been in our day a very strong, but not complete, reaction against hybridization.

And this is well, for such innovations make the most noticeable external difference between dissidents and Catholics of the same rite[12] and so come to be improperly identified with Catholicism itself, which becomes in consequence in worse odour than ever among the dissidents, who are greatly attached to their own legitimate customs and fear to lose them if they recognize the Holy See. Hybridization, so often condemned at Rome[13], is a grave stumbling-block to reunion, and it is in effect a practical identification of Catholicism solely with the Western church— the false idea that Eastern Catholicism is essentially an inferior or only half-authentic article, and that the more it is made to resemble the Latin church the more "really Catholic" it will be. Moreover, the ancient Christian liturgies are works of art, the supreme works of art, manifestations of the religious, social and cultural life of Christian communities over long centuries; to tinker with them, to spoil their integrity by borrowing from alien cultures, is not in accordance with that variety, inclusiveness, and local perfection and fittingness which are marks of the universal ark of salvation.[14]

What these external differences between West and East in worship and discipline are, will be found set out in some detail in the chapters which follow, but a few general observations may usefully be made here, especially as regards that which matters most—the Mass. And first of all, Orientals do not, in their own languages, call it "Mass". That word in its primary and original sense means the complex of prayers and ritual, words and actions, *as used in the Western church*, which, said and done with the requisite intention by a minister validly ordained to that end, effects the Eucharistic Sacrifice. Orientals

---

[12] *External* difference. What really differentiates Eastern Orthodox from Catholics has been put thus: "Eastern Christianity has a view of God, of man, of the Church, of dogma, of Scripture, of tradition, of spirituality, which frequently seems very close to Catholicism in its expression, but which is experienced in an utterly different manner. It is precisely this that makes the palpable difference between an Orthodox and a Catholic Oriental."

[13] Those occasional papal pronouncements that seem to approve "latinizing" are either due to special local circumstances (e.g., the Italo-Greeks in the sixteenth century, Kholm in 1874), or, if compared with earlier and later decrees, are seen to be advancing stages in the recovery and keeping of integral orientalism.

[14] From this point of view a case can be made out for the long-established modifications of the Italo-Greeks (and in a lesser degree of the Ruthenians), as being now assimilated and historically proper to them. Cf. the 800-year-old "latinisms" of the Armenian rite.—I refrain from enlarging here on the much-discussed matter of the adoption by Western clergy of an Eastern rite when working amongst Easterners, now a very common practice, approved by the highest authority. Undoubtedly it is in some circumstances desirable and even necessary. But there is always the danger of the external forms of one rite being used by "a person or group who remains intimately and decisively animated by the spirit of another". This objection, and others, are often voiced by non-Catholic Eastern Christians; and so it comes about that a proceeding which it is hoped will encourage closer relations between us can have just the opposite effect.

call it "the Divine Liturgy" or "the Offering".[15] Things should be called by their proper names, and so in this book "the Liturgy" means the Eucharistic Sacrifice in one or other of its Eastern forms, unless the context obviously requires the more extended meaning of the word.

Eastern Liturgies are on the whole more primitive in type than the Roman Mass: they are longer, their *tempo* is slower, their material expression more ample and their atmosphere more "mysterious" than in the Latin Mass; their language is more artless, less refined and scholarly (but not less theologically accurate); a later but very notable characteristic is a tendency to ritual purely for the sake of its symbolism; they lack the straightforward simplicity to which we are accustomed. In them the deacon has an important part, and is the only sacred minister necessary to the celebrant at a solemn Liturgy; particularly is it his business to form a link between celebrant and people by means of litanies and, especially in the Byzantine and Armenian rites, in a sense to direct the proceedings as a sort of master of ceremonies for both priest and people, so perpetuating the primitive diaconal charge of the congregation.

What we call "low Mass" is a late development of Christian worship; in the Western church high or sung Mass is the normal Mass still (though we often forget this). In the East it is not only normal but a sung Liturgy is the usual and ordinary way of celebration. All Catholic Eastern rites now provide for "low Mass" on week days, but in only some of them is the form systematized. The scriptural lessons and certain chants and verses are variable, according to the feast or time, and all of them (except the Armenian and Malabarese) have a number of alternative *anaphoras*, that is to say, different "canons of the Mass"[16], which are used interchangeably on certain occasions, somewhat after the manner of our proper prefaces. The celebrant's voice can be heard by all throughout the church, *especially* at the words of consecration, except, of course, that when the deacon or choir are chanting he speaks in a low voice.

---

[15] Cf. the Celtic languages, which have no word for *Missa*. Irish *An t-Aifreann*, Welsh *yr Offeren*, Cornish *an offeren* Scots *an aifrionn*, are all equivalent to the Greek *Anaphora* and Syrian *Kurbana*, "Offering" or "Sacrifice". Arabic-speaking people in common speech call the Liturgy of any rite *Kuddas*, "hallowing".

[16] Strictly speaking, the part of the Roman Mass from the beginning of the preface to the postcommunion corresponds to the Eastern *anaphora*.

"Low Masses" are supposed likewise to be said aloud, but this is one of the matters in which admiration for Roman prestige has often led to an unreasoning and unnecessary adoption of Roman customs.[17] Organs are not customary in Eastern churches, though occasionally they are now heard. The "Glory to God in the highest" does not figure in any Eastern Mass, and the Creed of Nicaea-Constantinople is the only one used liturgically.

Orientals have to a large extent conserved the Christian tradition of *standing* at public prayer (kneeling is proper only to penitential seasons, and sitting, to them, a sign of laziness or even disrespect), and in general there are few or no seats in their churches (except in Western countries); women, too, are often accommodated apart from men. Many Easterners assist at the Liturgy in their daily tongue; others understand the language used in varying degrees, and some make use of a quite dead language. Unless "latinized", Orientals do not genuflect but bow profoundly (as in the West until relatively lately, and still liturgically among Carthusians, Dominicans and Calced Carmelites), and all Byzantines, Catholic or not, make the sign of the cross with the thumb and first two fingers *from right to left*, as all Christians probably did in earlier times.

Other notable customs normal to the East are the use of leavened bread for the altar (as for centuries in the West), the reception of communion in both kinds (observed in the West till the twelfth century), Baptism by immersion, or involving a partial immersion (still the practice in a few Western dioceses) and Confirmation given immediately after by the priest, and the forbiddance of statues in the churches—except under Western influence, only pictures, wall-paintings and mosaics are allowed. This appears to be a backwash of the Iconoclasm controversy of the eighth and ninth centuries. On the other hand, the great veneration accorded to these *eikons* is a notable characteristic of Eastern religious life in its normal manifestations. The traditional eikon, "realistic" but not "naturalistic", seeks to express religious truths in such a way as to help the faithful to penetrate deeper into the Christian mysteries; its appeal is not primarily to the senses but to the mind and spirit, it repre-

---

[17] There is nothing intrinsically sacred about an inaudible canon of the Mass. It has been general in the West since the tenth century.

sents a universal Christian art. St John Damascene called the holy images of Christ and his saints "channels of divine grace", and they have a conspicuous part in the religious devotion of most Eastern Christians.

Eastern Catholics have a fundamental sense of religious worship as a social and corporate act centred in the Holy Sacrifice; but they had no extra-liturgical *cultus* of the Blessed Sacrament until it was introduced from the West, and the degree of it varies from rite to rite and even within the same rite. Latins are naturally surprised, even shocked, by the apparent indifference sometimes shown by Easterners in the presence of the Blessed Sacrament. The surprise is not all on one side; their veneration is directed rather toward the whole sanctuary as the holy place of God. The difference in emphasis is in part due to the fact that the East has known no heresies denying Christ's real presence in the Eucharist, and the consequent necessity to emphasize that presence. And they sometimes remind us that the efficacy of the Eucharist as a sacrifice is bound up with the act of the Mass, and as a sacrament with the act of eating with faith. We excite devotion by displaying the Blessed Sacrament, theirs is aroused by its very hiddenness. Both attitudes are permissible, both true, both Catholic; and so with other divergences that we continually meet.

While all eucharistic Liturgies are identical theologically and are fundamentally identical in structure, there are nevertheless differences between the celebration of the Mass of the West and of the Liturgies of the East that go deeper than accidental differences of language, of forms of words, of actions, of music, of ceremonial dress. But, like many deeper things, they are more easily "felt" (I do not mean merely by a comparison of resulting emotions; the mind, too, can "feel") than understood and expressed in words. One deep difference has been illustrated thus by Dr Andrew von Ivanka (*Irénikon*, vol. ix, no. 5, p. 420): "Whoever has had occasion to assist at an Eastern Liturgy, even if only in the little church of some Ukranian country parish, and has been struck by the intimate participation and inspired collaboration of even the most simple peasants in the wonders of the Liturgy, that perfect *ensemble* of teaching, prayer, and sacred action, he alone is able to estimate the treasure of doctrine, lived faith and encouragement to religion of which Catholics in the West are deprived." "Intimate participation" and "inspired collaboration" in the teaching, prayer and sacred action of the Eucharist are precisely what the "liturgical movement" is bringing back to Catholics of the West.

It is undoubtedly true that the disposition and character of peoples have profoundly affected the spirit and form of their Liturgies. We commonly take it for granted that lay people do not in any degree influence such matters. It is a mistake. Their influence is not expressed corporately or juridically, that is all. The Holy Spirit of God, concentrated in the bishops of his Church, is also diffused among *all* her members; and that Spirit is not gainsaid or without effect merely because we are unconscious or forgetful of it. For instance, the definition of the dogma of our Lady's assumption into Heaven was not the work of a body of theologians; it was the expression by proper authority of what the *whole* Church knew by faith to be true. And so the needs and natures and graces of the people at large, clergy and laity, help to mould our forms of corporate worship, even within the limits of the same technical "rite". Nobody present at a Russian Liturgy could suppose himself to be in a Greek church, or would mistake a Maronite for a Roman Mass (though their vestments and church appointments are alike); one present at Mass in Brittany or Naples could be forgiven did he not recognize the same act and form of worship he had seen in a Catholic church in a London suburb. Some Orientals, without external necessity and for purely spiritual reasons, habitually frequent Latin churches, and the reverse process is far from unknown. Such exceptions serve to emphasize the part of temperament in determining liturgy. On the other hand, liturgy also influences people, and thus there is produced a continual action, interaction, and tension—and without tension there is no human life.

The variousness of human temperament has had its profound and legitimate effect on religious life and worship no less in the East than in the West. The Oriental, for instance, in general prefers an interior process before, even at the expense of, external discipline, juridicism is foreign to him, his note is "passi-

31

vity" rather than "activity". It is significant that the sacraments may be ministered by deprecatory forms, "The servant of God N., is baptized . . . ," "May God, though me, a sinner, forgive you. . . ." Confirmation is received passively by babes, there is sometimes no explicit contract between the parties to a marriage, the monk does not "make his profession" but "receives the habit". Western man has his mystics and contemplatives, but in general prides himself on being a "practical fellow"; among the Slavs, on the contrary, preoccupation with efficiency and order is little esteemed, and mysticism, in a broad sense, is the heritage of all. Holiness to them definitely means contemplation, and the complete recluse is the practical as well as the abstract ideal of a holy man. Orientals have been accustomed in a large measure to leave the obligations of religion and morality to the individual conscience, rather than to make them the subjects of positive law. For example, the obligation of public worship. All that the old Eastern canon law has to say about it is that a Christian living in a town who absents himself from church for three Sundays running shall be deprived of communion (canon 80 of the Council *in Trullo*, canon 11 of Sardica). Catholics have now the Western legislation, together with the general principle of dispensation, which again is foreign to the East. The lack of a system of recognized dispensation does not necessarily operate in favour of the individual supplying a lax one for himself, as the following anecdote, related to me by a French priest who worked among Byzantines, shows. An old Catholic woman of that rite found the Lenten fast very trying and her parish priest offered to dispense her. "You cannot dispense me from the law of God" said she. "Then the bishop can." "No. He cannot." "Then I will go to the pope for you." "His Holiness would be better employed fasting himself than by releasing an old woman from it," was the reply. In this connexion it is to be noted that the standard of physical asceticism is far more exacting in the East than in the West.

Eastern religious temperament is indeed radically different from Western, but is not therefore in itself at variance with Catholicism, which is not tied to any one temperament or mentality. It is true that Western prestige and the Roman

BYZANTINE CHURCH AT REKOLA, FINLAND

Beginning of the Liturgy

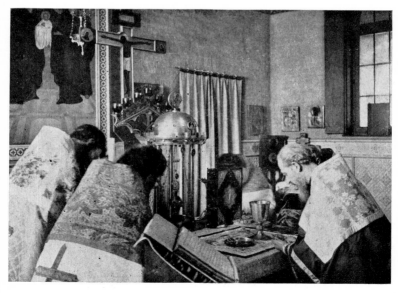

The Consecration

THE BYZANTINE LITURGY

The Communion

Asterisk, paten, lance and spoon

THE BYZANTINE LITURGY

MELKITE EIKONS
Seventeenth and eighteenth century

genius for centralization, acting often involuntarily (and contrarily to official legislation) on relatively small bodies, have tended to make of the Catholics of Eastern rite a religious and cultural hybrid. Nevertheless, these Catholics continue to display spiritual and religious characteristics proper to them as Orientals, and among the more recent groups there is a strong consciousness of the need to maintain their orientalism integrally for the Church's sake as well as their own. The Christians of both West and East have suffered and tended to develop one-sidedly through being deprived, for hundreds of years, of each other's contribution to philosophy, theology, general culture and Christian life, and the balance can never be redressed from one side only. It was " as a member of the true and venerable Orthodox Eastern or Greco-Russian church" that the great philosopher and theologian Vladimir Solovyev declared that he recognized "as the supreme judge in matters of religion . . . the apostle Peter, who lives in his successors and who did not hear our Lord's words in vain".

Catholicity, universality, is not a matter of numbers, and the whole body of Eastern Catholics, small though it be, is a very important part of the Catholic economy. Without them, the Universal Church would appear perilously like what so many of its opponents assert it to be—a product solely West-European in religious culture, disposition and history. Of all people we Catholics of the Latin rite should glory in these Catholics of Eastern rite, as Dr Adrian Fortescue said, for "they are an exceedingly important factor in our concept of the universal Church; they are our great palpable argument that the primacy of Rome is more than patriarchal rights over part of the Church. Indeed, in some ways, it is just they who save the whole situation, from our point of view. . . . The fact that vast numbers of the members of the Eastern patriarchates have gone out of the Church altogether, distressing as it is, does not affect the legal position. . . . In spite of the many heresies and schisms which at various times have robbed each patriarchate of its members, the constitution of the Catholic Church remains what it has always been, not one patricharchate with one rite, but the union of East and West, differing in rites, having in many cases different details of canon law, but united in the

profession of the same faith and in conscious inter-communion"
(*op. cit.*, pp. 27, 28). That position is safeguarded by the Eastern
Catholics.

There is another thing. It is a charge often made against the
Church, and it is a charge to which intelligent people today are
very sensitive, and rightly so, that she stretches the necessary
uniformity of revealed truth, faith and morals, to cover other
things; that she has no real regard for the variations in human
mentality, temperament and culture. The words and actions of
many individual Catholics give colour to this accusation; when
Hilaire Belloc reiterated that "the Faith is Europe and Europe
is the Faith" he was saying something which, if taken at the
foot of the letter (as people take such sayings), would make of
the Church a large European sect: on this showing, Ireland, for
instance, must be imperfectly Catholic and imperfectly civilized,
for she was never submitted to the rule of the Roman Empire or
bathed herself in the waters of the Mediterranean basin. If this
charge of desiring, or even tending, to impose an unhuman,
unnatural uniformity on the human people whom God has
made diverse were true, it would be a practical denial of the
Church's catholicity. On every page of this book it is demonstrated that the charge is false. "The Church", wrote Pope Pius XII
in his encyclical letter *Summi pontificatus*, "the Church aims at
unity, a unity determined and kept alive by that supernatural
love which should be actuating everybody; she does not aim at a
uniformity which would only be external in its effects and would
cramp the natural tendencies of the peoples concerned. Every
nation has its own genius, its own qualities, springing from the
hidden roots of its being." And again Benedict XV, "The
Church is not Latin or Greek or Slavonic; it is Catholic",
oecumenical: and Catholicity includes *everything* that is not in
any way sinful or in any way erroneous. Just as there is nothing
secular but sin, so there is nothing foreign to Catholicism but
error, ugliness and disaccord with right reason, The prevailing
Latin uniformity of the Church today is simply the result of
historical events. Catholicism is the religion of variety, the
variety displayed by two thousand million people (or however
many there may be in the world), and the best and simplest
proof of this is the variousness of divine worship as used by

Catholics, the fact that the Mass is one but the ways of celebrating it are many.

Many of the things referred to above are externals, matters of outward observance, and to them it is fatally easy to give too much importance. But the opposite mistake also must be avoided: it must not be forgotten that the sacramental principle —that which is inward and invisible signified and effected by that which is outward and visible—goes through the whole of Christian life, and is not confined to the seven sacraments that have a special place in that life. The "inner life", asceticism, worship in spirit and in truth, the quality of religion, inevitably expresses itself in outward worship, just as it inevitably expresses itself in the ordinary affairs and relations of life, "how we behave". As a man believes, really believes, so he does or tries to do; and as a man does or tries to do, so he *is*. When we say there are differences of rite between East and West, we are saying that there are all sorts of other, objectively more important, differences. And it is this inner life, this religious quality, of the Orientals that we of the West have to try to grasp and understand and learn from—for it is al part of that grand synthesis of divine truth and love and human needs and duties that is called the Catholic Christian faith. And in like manner the Orientals, whether Catholic or separated, can learn from the West.[18]

* * *

Since the above pages were first written, a quarter of a century ago, half the Eastern Catholics in the world have, as it were, disappeared. The churches of Byzantine rite in the formerly Polish Ukraine, in Rumania, in Czechoslovakia and elsewhere have been violently destroyed by communist governments, their leaders jailed and sometimes killed, and their people forcibly aggregated to the Orthodox Russian, Rumanian and other churches.

Surprise has been expressed at the spectacle of communist governments persecuting one Christian church for the "benefit"

---

[18] There is an admirable essay on Eastern worship and asceticism by Father John LaFarge in *The Eastern Branches of the Catholic Church* (see General Bibliography). And a book by an Orthodox monk called *Orthodox Spirituality* (London, 1945) tells us much that is true of Eastern Catholics as well, while underlining the fundamental identity of Eastern and Western Christianity. On the general subject of "rite", see the important article by Dom Polycarp Sherwood, "The Sense of Rite", in *Eastern Churches Quarterly*, vol. xii, no. 4 (1957-58), pp. 112-125; the author stresses Pope Pius XII's wide conception of rite. Cf. also C. Korolevsky, *L'Uniatisme* (Amay, 1927).

of another. There is no need for surprise. If a government that aims at a completely "unitary" state discovers—as the government of Russia has discovered—that Christianity is hard to get rid of, then the next best thing is to bind as many believers as possible into one church, and to bring and keep that one church so far as may be in subservience to the state; and there are several reasons why it is less difficult to force Byzantine-rite Ukrainians or Rumanians into the Orthodox Church than Latin-rite Poles or Hungarians. Moreover, not the least factor in Soviet communism's enmity towards the Catholic Church is her supranational influence and prestige. To the Eastern Orthodox Christian the force of this influence is less than the appeal of the Orthodox ethos and tradition. But Catholics of the Byzantine rite combine the two—the supranational unity of Rome with a great deal of the Orthodox tradition; and therefore the communist authorities regard this as a specially dangerous form of Christianity, even in a small minority. Hence the ruthless destruction of the Byzantine Catholic church in the Ukraine, Rumania and elsewhere. Hence, too, what many have never realized—the special bitterness with which the microscopic group of Catholics of Byzantine rite in Russia were pursued and stamped out before the last war. The agonizing death of their holy exarch, Father Leonid Feodorov, at Vyatka on 7 March 1935, meant more to the Soviet government than the simple event alone would suggest.

As a footnote to this chapter I quote the impression of a great English bishop, William Bernard Ullathorne of Birmingham, on first coming into contact with his Eastern brethren at the Vatican Council. It is quoted from his letters by Abbot Cuthbert Butler in his book on the council (London, 1930).

The orientals have sweet and clear voices, with a certain richness, especially the young and middle-aged, the older voices growing thinner. Their movements and gestures are quiet and gentle, full of dignity and self-possession. For instance, there is an Armenian archbishop, with grave but youthful features, very regular and sweet, with his coal-black hair parted *à la Nazarène*, and peaked beard, who has been twice in the ambo; and his entire presence, front face, profile,

gentle gesture, and sweet full voice, earnest without effort—
his whole man, in short, so irresistably strikes me as exactly
like our idea of our Lord . . . even to the very costume, that
I have been wonderfully captivated with this type from the
plains from which the Hebrews sprang.

BIBLIOGRAPHY

Statistica con cenni storici della gerarchia e dei fedeli di rito orientale
(S.C.O., Rome, 1932). Much of this official publication is now out
of date, but it is still very valuable for its historical sketches.
R. Janin, *Les Églises orientales et les rites orientaux*, 4th edition (Paris,
1956).
C. Gatti and C. Korolevsky, *I riti e le chiese orientali* (Byzantine only),
Genoa, 1942.
G. de Vries, *Oriente Cristiano ieri e oggi* (Rome, 1949).
A. A. King, *The Rites of Eastern Christendom*, 2 vols. (Rome and London,
1947-48).

CHAPTER III

THE BYZANTINE RITE:
LITURGY AND CUSTOMS

THE Byzantine rite[1] is the name given to the system and forms of worship and administration of the sacraments proper at first to the Great Church of Constantinople (Byzantium) and her dependencies. After the defection of the monophysites Constantinople gradually extended her own liturgy to the faithful of the other patriarchates, and by the end of the thirteenth century the Melkites of Alexandria, Antioch and Jerusalem had abandoned their own ancient usages in its favour. The Byzantine rite is therefore now used by the whole of the Orthodox Eastern Church and by many Catholics, and is the most widely spread rite after the Latin; emigration has given it an almost worldwide extension.

The Byzantine rite derives ultimately from the primitive usages of Antioch and Jerusalem, modified by other influences, especially that of eastern Asia Minor. It has not the uniformity of the Roman use of the Latin rite, even among the dissidents. Catholics observe it with varying degrees of uniformity, whose deviations from the Constantinopolitan or Russian norms seem to be in corresponding ratio to the size of their body: e.g., the little groups of Greeks and Russians preserve exact liturgical purity while the Ruthenians have sundry modifications, many of them from Western sources. The account given here follows in general the typical Greek or Russian observances, the principal modifications being noted later when dealing with the people concerned.

Church buildings. The system of building whose characteristic and essential feature is a dome covering a space which is square,

---

[1] It is often called the "Greek rite". See page 44.

38

and whose prototype is the great church (now a museum) of the Holy Wisdom ("St Sophia") at Constantinople, spread all over the Byzantine religious world, much modified from place to place by local and national characteristics. The interior appearance of a Byzantine church is sufficiently well known. Its chief characteristic is a solid screen, covered with pictures (*eikons*, and therefore called the *eikonostasis*), before the altar and hiding the sanctuary (*bema*); this is pierced by lateral and middle ("holy") doors. Greek screens are usually lower than Russian ones. Among the Ruthenians the screen is sometimes of open-work (I have seen it so in several Melkite churches).[2] The holy doors are closed and covered with curtains at certain parts of the liturgy. The *eikonostasis* or *templon* is not in its present form an ancient institution. Throughout the Church from early times there was a barrier of some sort between the sanctuary and the nave, first a low railing, then a row of columns or arches of stone or wood, but still low, open and without pictures; such screens still existed in Greece in the fourteenth century. The origin of the solid wooden screen covered with eikons seems to have been in the ninth century, after the defeat of Iconoclasm; in time hanging eikons were replaced by permanent paintings, multiplied in number and arranged according to a definite plan. The custom spread all over the Byzantine world, and its development was particularly marked in Russia.

The stone or wooden altar stands away from the east wall (apsidal), normally beneath a canopy on four columns (*ciborium*); it is square, flat and plain, with a flat crucifix, two or more candlesticks, and the gospel-book upon it; the Blessed Sacrament is reserved in a small tabernacle (*artophorion*) or hanging pyx. In Russian churches the crucifix stands behind the altar, together with a stand for seven lamps. To the north and south respectively, sometimes in separate apses, are altar-like tables, the *prothesis* and *diakonikon*. In the nave there are normally no seats, except around the walls, or statues, but *eikons*, often with a lamp, are numerous. Men and women are

---

[2] Some Catholic Byzantine churches in North America have no screen, as some in south Italy and Syria have not. The reasons given for this innovation are not always convincing. Churches of immigrant Orthodox always have an *eikonostasis;* it is really now a liturgical necessity of the rite. The times at which the holy doors are open or shut vary; e.g., the Greeks open them at the priest's blessings, Russians do not.

accommodated separately in many churches. The stalls for the choir are in front of the *eikonostasis*, though there is often a mixed choir occupying a decently screened gallery. There is sometimes an ambo on the north side in front of the screen and there is always one or more *proskynetaria*, small sloping desks on which the *eikon* of the saint or mystery of the day is exposed for veneration: the faithful cross themselves and bow three times and kiss it. The bishop's throne is in the apse behind the altar and there is as well an episcopal stall on the south side of the choir. Open "side altars" are an innovation; strictly speaking, if there is more than one altar each should have its own *eikonostasis*, etc., forming as it were a separate church (*parekklesia*). According to strict Eastern usage the holy Sacrifice may not be celebrated on the same altar more than once in a day, nor should there be more than one altar in a church: hence the *parekklesia* and the frequency of concelebration. Larger churches have a closed porch (*narthex*) extending the whole width of the west end, with ("royal") doors into the nave, containing the baptismal font.

Vestments correspond more or less to the Roman ones and have the same origins, but they have evolved into quite different shapes. The deacon wears a long, ungirdled, wide-sleeved tunic (*stikharion*), white or dark red and often embroidered; over it, his stole (*orarion*) is a long narrow strip of silk, worn over the left shoulder with the back end hanging to the ground and the front carried under the right arm and over the left shoulder (Greek) or hanging down back and front over the left shoulder (Russian). A priest puts on first a *stikharion*, plainer than the deacon's and with narrow sleeves; then the *epitrakhelion* or stole, in one piece with a loop at the top to go over the head, the *zone* (girdle), like a belt, the *epimanikia*, oversleeves or cuffs (unconnected with our maniple), and lastly the *phelonion* or chasuble, a long, full, bell-shaped garment, sometimes cut away up to the chest in front. In Catholic churches lace albs are now seen as often as *stikharia*, and among the Ruthenians the deacon's *stikharion* has usually become a "dalmatic" (under the *orarion*), worn over an alb. The vestments are usually white; there is no regular sequence of liturgical colours, except among the Ruthenians. A bishop wears the *sakkos* (rather like a

40

dalmatic) instead of the *phelonion* and a diamond-shaped ornament (*epigonation*) depending at his right side (cf. the pope's *subcinctorium*). He also wears the crown (*mitra*), the *omophorion*, like a long, wide *pallium*, once worn only by patriarchs and archbishops, the pectoral cross, and two *enkolpia* or *panagia*, round or oval medallions suspended from the neck bearing images of our Lord and his all-holy Mother. The episcopal crown or mitre is rather like the papal tiara, derived in shape from the imperial crown, and the pastoral staff, shorter than the Western crozier, ends in the form of two serpents facing one another. Other episcopal insignia are the *khazranion*, a straight ebony walking-staff, and the *mandyas*, a processional garment not unlike a blue or purple cope but longer and fastened at the lower hem as well as at the neck.

The principal articles of clerical ordinary dress are the black or dark *rason*, a loose, wide-sleeved gown, and the *kalemaukion*, a cylindrical hat about six inches high with a flat brim at the top, rather like an inverted top-hat. Minor clerics and Russian priests wear it without a brim, bishops and monks cover it with a black veil falling on to the shoulders (some hierarchs, notably the patricarch of Moscow and Russian metropolitans, have this veil white). Russian priests wear a plain pectoral cross. Byzantine bishops do not normally wear rings, but all the Catholic hierarchs do so. The beard and long hair were formerly strictly *de rigueur* for all Byzantine clergy, but the latter is going quickly out of fashion in most places and even clean-shaven bishops and priests are now not unknown, especially in America.

Liturgical books. In most Eastern rites the offices are arranged in a number of separate books, each containing only those parts required by individuals, e.g., celebrant, deacon, choir, as formerly in the West. The chief Byzantine books (by no means uniform in arrangement) are the *Typikon*, a perpetual calendar with full instructions for carrying out the office; the *Eukhologion* which is, roughly, a compendium of Mass-book, office-book and, among the Greeks, pontifical and ritual; the books of the gospels and epistles; the *Horologion*, containing the common parts of the daily offices and certain proper hymns, etc., of the eucharistic liturgy; the *Triodion, Pentecostarion* and *Parakletike*

41

or *Oktoekhos*, choir-books forming a sort of "proper of the season" of both Mass and Office; the *Menaia*, one volume for each month, have the proper parts of the Divine Office for all fixed feasts, including each day's reading from the synaxary ("martyrology"); and the Psalter.

Numerous Catholic editions of these books have been published in various places according to local requirements, the typical Greek editions at Rome. The best Orthodox editions were for long those of the Phoenix Press at Venice. The Orthodox books differ from ours practically not at all and in fact were used by some Catholics, e.g., the Russians, with such necessary modifications as the addition of the pope's name to the diptychs. A fine edition of these books according to Melkite usages is published by the Fathers of St Paul at Harissa in Lebanon. A typical Slavonic edition was undertaken at Rome, of which the *Sluzebnik* (*Eukhologion*) appeared in several formats between 1940 and 1945. It is in two separate and distinct editions, according to Russian ("vulgate") and Ruthenian usages respectively, and was followed by the *Trebnik* (Ritual of the Sacraments). A definitive edition of the Greek *Horologion* was published at Rome in 1937. All these magnificent books are printed by the monks of the abbey of Grottaferrata (see p. 68), as were the Rumanian books.

Altar-vessels and bread. These are the chalice (*poterion*); the paten (*diskos*), larger and deeper than the Western paten, with a rim and sometimes a foot; the *asteriskos*, made of two pieces of metal crossed and bent into two semicircles, sometimes with a small star hanging at the intersection, and put over the paten to prevent the veil touching the holy Bread;[3] the lance, a knife for cutting the altar-bread; the spoon, often with two small prongs projecting from the bowl, for giving communion; and a small piece of sponge (*mousa*) sewn up in red silk, used for several purposes, including that of the Western "purificator". There is a small silk veil each for chalice and paten and a larger one (*aer*) to cover them both.

During celebration of the Liturgy the altar table is covered by an *antimension*, a piece of linen or silk about eighteen inches square on which is embroidered or painted an image of Christ's

[3] A similar thing is used to cover the paten when communion is brought to the pope when he celebrates pontifically.

burial; sewn into it is a tiny bag containing relics. It must be consecrated by a bishop.[4] Strictly speaking it is not required on a consecrated altar but is now always used above a "corporal" (*eileton*) of linen. The ordinary altar coverings are a linen cloth which hangs down on all sides and a silk or velvet one above it which may be coloured and embroidered.

The Eastern thurible has shorter chains than in the West and incense is offered by swinging these chains from their ends, with one hand. The *ripidion* or *hexapterygon* is a flat metal disc, representing a cherub's head surrounded by six wings, mounted on a shaft in such a way that it can be made to revolve on its axis. These are carried in processions and on pontifical occasions; their original use was to keep flies from the holy things during the *anaphora*, but the deacon now generally waves a veil instead.[5]

Bishops make use of a hand-cross to give certain blessings, as do Ruthenian and Russian priests, and some episcopal benedictions are given with a two-branched candlestick (*dikerion*) in the left hand and a three-branched one (*trikerion*) in the right.

The Byzantine altar-bread (*prosphora*) is a flat round cake of leavened bread about 1½ inches thick, stamped in the middle with one or more square "seals" containing a cross between the letters I C X C N I K A ("Jesus Christ conquers"); on the left is a square with a triangle, called "the all-holy" because it is set aside as a commemoration of our Lady; and on the right three rows of three triangles for the choirs of angels and the saints. The portions of the Host that are to be reserved are all "anointed" with a drop of the sacred Blood; before ministration to the sick it is dipped into unconsecrated wine (not by the Ruthenians). There are other patterns of *prosphora*.

Music. The music of the Byzantine rite varies from country to country, and in some large churches polyphony of Western type is now heard. The traditional Greek liturgical chant is enharmonic, and as the modes are continually changing even in the same melody there is a singer appointed to sing the

---

[4] During World War II American chaplains of the Latin rite were authorized to celebrate Mass on an *antimension*, as being more convenient than the portable altar-stone. Large numbers of *antimensia* were consecrated for their use by the Byzantine bishops of North America.

[5] They were formerly used also in the West and have survived in the papal *flabella*.

dominant (*ison*) throughout, changing it as the mode changes. This music requires an incredible skill of voice and accuracy of ear, for it abounds in quarter-tones and other strange intervals, but the result to Western ears is not happy, until one learns to recognize its strange beauty.

In Slav churches, on the other hand, the singing is immediately attractive to Westerners. Russia is the land of harmonized church music par excellence. After a varied and complex history Russian church music came into its own during the nineteenth century. Rimsky-Korsakov solved the problem of how best to harmonize the old Muscovite chants and his work was taken up by A. T. Gretchaninov, Rachmaninov, P. P. Chesnokov, and A. D. Kastalsky, with results in which some people find a far more religiously satisfying quality than in the musically greatest efforts of the classical polyphonists of the West.

Liturgical languages. The Byzantine is sometimes called the "Greek rite", because that was its original language, but it is characteristic of it that linguistic uniformity is not required and the numbers who use it in the *koine* Greek are now a minority; among Catholics they are very few, only the "pure" Greeks and Italo-Greeks in fact. Church Slavonic ("*Staroslav*") is now its principal language, and it is also celebrated in spoken Rumanian, Magyar and Arabic.[6]

THE EUCHARISTIC LITURGY[7]

The Byzantine rite has two *anaphoras*, or rather, Liturgies, that of St John Chrysostom for ordinary use and that of St Basil for Sundays of Lent (except Palm Sunday), Maundy Thursday, Holy Saturday, the vigils of Christmas and the Epiphany, and St Basil's feast, and a Liturgy of the Presanctified Gifts (called "of St Gregory the Dialogue Writer", i.e., Pope Gregory the Great) for every day in Lent except Saturdays and Sundays; in practice this last is often sung only on

[6] And by the Orthodox in many tongues, including Japanese, Chinese and Korean. A Byzantine priest may celebrate in any of the approved liturgical languages he chooses, subject to local legislation. There is a growing use of English among some Catholic Byzantines in North America.

[7] For an excellent short account of Eastern rites of public worship in general, see I. H. Dalmais, *The Eastern Liturgies* (London and New York, 1960). D. Attwater's *Eastern Catholic Worship* (New York, 1945) provides translations of the substance of each of the eight eucharistic Liturgies.

Wednesdays and Fridays, the other weekdays of Lent (except Saturday) then having no celebration. Unlike practically all other Eastern *anaphoras*, that of Basil is probably in part the work of the man whose name it bears; the Chrysostom Liturgy resembles it closely, most of the differences in the text being in the anaphora proper (the attribution to St John Chrysostom seems to be purely honorific). Because of the widespread emigration of Byzantine Christians, these two are better known in the West than any other Eastern Liturgies.

Concelebration by several celebrants together, all consecrating the same bread and wine at one altar, is very common among Byzantines. The senior in dignity officiates aloud, the others all saying the prayers in a low voice. Any number of priests, of priests and bishops, or of bishops alone, may thus celebrate together; each one so doing offers the holy sacrifice really and truly and may accept an offering therefor.[8] Catholic Byzantine clergy celebrate "low Mass" on weekdays but there is no uniform version of the Liturgy adapted for this purpose, except to a certain extent among the Ruthenians.

There are many English translations of the text of the Liturgy of St John Chrysostom, two of which are noted in the bibliography on p. 54. The following general points may be mentioned.

The deacon's normal place is in front of the screen, his function being precisely to be a link between the celebrant and the people. If there be no deacon, the priest has to sing or say everything, with the help of a lay cantor. Among the Orthodox a priest (other than as just mentioned) never acts as deacon. As in most Eastern liturgies, the epistle at "ordinary" celebrations is read or sung by a layman, as also at more solemn celebrations when an ordained reader is not available, that is, practically always.[9]

The common ending to inaudible prayers throughout the service is by a raising of the voice, to which the singers respond "Amen". This is called an *ekphonesis*; cf. the conclusion of the "secret" in the Roman Mass.

---

[8] This practice has long gone out in the Western church, except at the ordination of priests and consecration of bishops. In the Holy Year of 1950 Pope Pius XII presided at a concelebration of the Byzantine Liturgy in St Peter's. The principal celebrant was the Melkite patriarch, Maximos IV, with 15 bishops (7 Melkite, 2 Greek, 2 Italo-Greek, 3 Russian, 1 Ruthenian), a Rumanian archpriest, 2 archimandrites (Italo-Greek and Ruthenian) and 2 other hieromonks (Melkite). The audible parts were all in Greek, in which language the pope pronounced certain blessings.

[9] In some rites the gospel is sung by the celebrant, and there are other variations.

No Catholics of Byzantine rite need sing "and from the Son" in the creed, unless its omission would cause scandal. In fact, many of them do sing it; but the words do not appear in the official Greek and Russian books printed at Rome. This need cause no surprise; the function of the liturgical creed is not to give a list of all our articles of faith.

It is Slavonic usage for the deacon (or priest) to lift up the chalice and paten (with his hands crossed) after the consecration. But the real "elevation", common to all Eastern liturgies, comes later, at the words "Holy things to the holy!" This has nothing essentially in common with the elevations at the consecration in the Roman Mass—it is rather the "little elevation" at the end of the Roman canon. The medieval errors whose propagation made the Western elevations desirable were not known in the East.

The Lord's Prayer ends with the words "For thine is the kingdom and the power and the glory, Father, Son and Holy Spirit, now and for ever, world without end. Amen". They are not a Protestant innovation as is so often supposed.

At the end of the Liturgy blessed bread (*antidoron*) is distributed. It is Greek usage to bless it formally; in most churches it is what remains of the *prosphora* after the preparation, simply hallowed by its original use. The French *pain bénit* is a similar custom but not exactly equivalent. The origin of this custom is complex and uncertain. *Antidoron* means "a gift instead of" (communion), but it was formerly called *eulogia*, "a blessing".

THE DIVINE OFFICE

The Byzantine divine office (*Akolouthia*) has eight "hours", corresponding to those of the Roman breviary, but its composition is entirely different. The psalter is sung through every week and there is a large number of rhythmic hymns. The office is exceedingly long, and when sung takes about eight hours altogether; Catholic priests are bound to recite privately only as much as they conveniently can, and this by custom rather than by law.

Mesonyktikon (midnight-office) in its ordinary form consists of the *Trisagion*, the Lord's Prayer, Nicene Creed, with psalms, prayers, and *troparia* (hymns), and a final litany. It is not sung on certain days. *Orthros* (Matins and Lauds) has in addition to psalms and hymns a litany, the *Magnificat*, the day's reading from the *Menaion*, and a gospel on Sundays and feasts, when an amplified form of "Glory to God in the highest" is sung. After this office on a great feast those present are anointed with oil from the lamp burning before the *eikon* of the day. The offices of the First, Third, Sixth and Ninth Hours each have three psalms, prayers, and hymns, and sometimes short additions called *mesoria*. *Hesperinos* (Vespers) begins the liturgical day, as with us. It is divided into three parts, of which the second contains the "hymn at the lighting of lamps", *Phos hilaron*,[10] which is the centre to which all parts of the office converge; it ends with the Song of Simeon, *Trisagion*, Lord's Prayer, the *troparion* of the day and a prayer to our Lady. Normally an office is sung in every Byzantine church on Saturday evening. *Apodeipnon* (Complin; literally "after supper") is extra long during Lent and is joined to the night-office to form the vigil service of Christmas and Epiphany. Ordinarily it consists of three psalms, Nicene creed, *Trisagion*, Lord's Prayer, and a hymn for the day.

The short hymns of this rite are called *troparia*, and they are of frequent occurrence throughout the offices. Each strophe is properly a *troparion*, of which several make up an *ode*. Nine odes, having reference to the scriptural canticles, make a *kanon* (three in Lent, *triodion*). There are numerous classes of *troparia*, e.g., a *theotokion* is in honour of our Lady, a *kontakion* refers to the feast of the day, an *apolytikion* precedes the dismissal, that at the end of Orthros and Hesperionos serving a somewhat similar purpose to that of the antiphon to the *Magnificat* and *Benedictus* in the Roman office; and so on.

THE SACRAMENTS[11]

Baptism. After three exorcisms, renunciation of Satan is made and the Nicene creed said by the sponsor, the effect of which is to make the child a catechumen. Then the priest incenses the

---

[10] There is a good translation by Keble of this lovely hymn in *Hymns Ancient and Modern*, No. 18. The melody given to it there is good, too.

[11] The word "mystery" is used for "sacrament" throughout the East.

baptistery, the deacon says a litany, and after several prayers the priest blesses the water and oil. Then he anoints the child on the forehead, chest, back, ears, hands and feet, and afterwards plunges it three times into the font, saying, "The servant of God N. is baptized in the name of the Father, and of the Son, and of the Holy Spirit. Amen". Psalm 31 is sung three times and a hymn, while the priest puts the baptismal garment on the child. He then proceeds to confirm it.

Confirmation. The child is anointed with chrism (*myron*) on the forehead, eyes, nostrils, mouth, ears, chest, hands and feet with the words "The seal of the gift of the Holy Spirit. Amen" at each anointing. Priest and sponsor with the child then walk around the baptistery, singing, "You who have been baptized in Christ have put on the garment of Christ. Amen". An epistle (Rom. 6:3–11) and gospel (Matt. 28:16–20) are read, and the rite ends with a short litany.

Penance. Standing before an eikon of Christ, the priest says certain prayers, in which the penitents join. Then each one approaches the priest and, standing or kneeling (or even sitting, in Greece), confesses his sins. The priest exhorts him, imposes a penance and, laying the end of his stole on the penitent's head, absolves him in one of several deprecatory forms, e.g., "May God, through me, a sinner, forgive you. . . ." But among the Slavs the form is "May our Lord and God Jesus Christ through the goodness and depth of his love for men forgive you all your sins, my child N. And I, an unworthy priest, by the power that he has given me forgive you and absolve you from your sins in the name of the Father. . . . Amen". Many Catholic Byzantines have approximated this office more closely to the Roman usage, and minister the sacrament in a confessional-box. The new Slavonic books print an alternative shorter version of the rite.

Eucharist. After the communion of the celebrant and ministers the holy doors are opened and the deacon (or priest) lifts up the chalice covered with its veil, exclaiming, "Draw nigh with fear of God, with faith and with love!" Each lay communicant, standing before the priest with hands crossed on the breast, receives a particle of the holy Body steeped in the precious Blood, drawn from the chalice in the spoon, which is put into his mouth. The words of administration are: "The servant (handmaid) of God, N., receives the precious and all-holy body and blood of our Lord, God and Saviour Jesus Christ for the forgiveness of his (her) sins and everlasting life. Amen." At solemn celebrations sometimes each communicant at once receives a draught of ordinary wine and a piece of blessed bread (cf. newly made priests in the Roman rite of ordination). See also pages 63, 90.

Anointing[12] theoretically requires the ministration of seven priests, one for each anointing, but the sick must usually be content with one, who gives them all. Seven candles are lit, the priest incenses the room and those present, and blesses the oil. The sick person is anointed on seven parts of the body, each anointing being preceded by an epistle, a gospel, a short litany and a long prayer; each is accompanied by another long prayer, which begins: "Holy Father, physician of souls and bodies, you sent us your only-begotten Son, our Lord Jesus Christ, to cure every sickness and save us from death: heal your servant N., from every bodily and spiritual ill that afflicts him and fill him with healthy life by the grace of your Christ." A shorter version of this very long rite has been approved for the Slavs and Rumanians.

Orders. The orders of the Byzantine rite are reader, subdeacon, deacon, priest, bishop. For the ordination of a deacon the candidate is led to the altar before the communion during the Liturgy. The bishop blesses him, and then, whilst the candidate kneels with his forehead leaning against the altar, lays the right hand on his head, invoking the Holy Spirit: "The grace of God that always strengthens the weak and fills the empty, appoints the most religious subdeacon N. to be deacon. Let us then pray for him that the grace of the Holy Spirit may come upon him." The bishop continues the prayer, and afterwards vests him with the *orarion* and cuffs and hands him the *ripidion*, exclaiming *Axios*!, "He is worthy!" which the assistants repeat, three times. The ordination of a priest is similar, he being vested in the stole, girdle and chasuble; this takes

---

[12] This is the Eastern name for what we call Extreme Unction. Our name is misleading. *Extreme* here means the *last* anointing we receive (i.e., after those at Baptism and Confirmation), not one to be received when *in extremis*: it is supposed to be ministered before that. Dissident Orientals sometimes err the other way, by giving it to those who are not sick at all.

place after the great entrance, and the new priest concelebrates with the bishop. The episcopate is likewise conferred by laying on one hand and invoking the Holy Spirit; two co-consecrators are, of course, required. It is to be noted that there are no anointings in any of these ordinations.

Some deacons remain in that order all their lives (deacons of office), and Eastern archdeacons are properly deacons, not priests. The subdeacon has no liturgical office, and this holds good for most Eastern rites.

Marriage. This office varies but little from country to country and has strongly influenced the corresponding services in non-Byzantine churches of the East.

Before they leave their homes, bride and groom are blessed by their parents with *eikons* of our Lord and his all-holy Mother. The wedding rite consists of two parts, the betrothal and the blessing, The groom waits near a small table set before the *eikonostasis* and the bride comes to him up the church, preceded by a boy carrying an *eikon*. Having ascertained their free consent, the priest gives each party a lighted candle, censes and blesses them, and a litany is sung for them. The priest takes the rings from the altar and puts one on the hand of each party, saying "The servant of God N., joins him(her)self with the servant of God M., in the name of the Father . . . for ever. Amen." The betrothal ends with a long prayer referring to the rings.

The couple retire to the end of the church and, while Psalm 127 is sung, the priest leads them back to the table. After another litany and several very long prayers, he brings two crowns of metal and precious stones from the sanctuary. These he puts on their heads, saying, "The servant of God N. is crowned for the servant of God M., in the name of the Father," etc. A passage from St Paul's letter to the Ephesians (cap. v; cf. the Roman wedding Mass) is read and the gospel of the wedding at Cana, and, after a litany and the Lord's Prayer, the married couple drink thrice from a cup of blessed wine. The priest joins their hands, which he covers with his stole, and leads them in procession three times round the cross and gospel-book on the table, while the choir sings hymns. The rite ends with a prayer that invokes the memory and virtues

50

of Abraham and Sara, Isaac and Rebecca, Jacob and Rachel. Some Eastern marriage rites require an explicit declaration of contract from the parties, others do not.

Calendar. The reformed annual calendar put forward by Pope Gregory XIII in 1582, and at once adopted by most of western Europe except England and Wales, Scotland and Ireland, took a long time to get any foothold in the East. None of the dissident Orthodox churches began to accept it before 1924, and few Eastern Catholics before the beginning of the nineteenth century. Even now, though most of the different Catholic bodies have received it, a majority of the individuals are following the old Julian calendar because that is the custom of the numerically superior Ruthenians. According to the Julian reckoning, fixed feasts fall thirteen days after the corresponding day by the Gregorian reckoning, and the two Easters and feasts depending thereon coincide about one year in every three.

The Byzantines have no liturgical cycles corresponding to those of the Roman church year, but the period from the Sunday "before Septuagesima" to the Saturday after Whitsunday (*triodion* of Lent and *triodion* of Easter) stands apart from all the rest in importance. Many Sundays are named after the gospel which is read: Sunday "of the Prodigal Son" (Septuagesima), "of the Paralytic" (third after Easter), etc. Certain feasts are preceded by vigils, of which the "greater vigils" extend over several days (e.g. five before Christmas), and there are likewise periods corresponding to the Western octave, which last from three (e.g., Sunday "of the Man Born Blind"—fifth after Easter) to nine days (e.g., Epiphany). An interesting observance is the feast called a *synaxis*, assembly, when the people meet together to honour those saints connected with the mystery celebrated on the previous day, e.g., of St Joachim and St Anne on the day after the feast of our Lady's birthday. The ecclesiastical year begins on September 1.

Feasts. These may be divided into "great", "lesser", "little", and what we should call "commemoration". Easter stands all by itself; and Sunday, the commemoration of the Resurrection, always has precedence over all feasts except those of our Lord. The feasts of saints celebrated of course vary from country to country; e.g., the calendar used by the Melkites has about 100 ancient feasts of all sorts in common with the Roman church, some of them on different dates. The traditional Slavonic calendar naturally has a number of Russian and other saints little known elsewhere (the feasts of about thirty earlier ones have been admitted to Catholic observance), but also includes such great Western names as Irenaeus, Ambrose, Augustine, Benedict, Leo, Gregory, Jerome, Martin of Tours. To these, Catholic usage adds Francis of Assisi (deeply venerated by some Russian Orthodox), and, of course, the more recently recognized Eastern martyrs, St Josephat Kunsevich (see p. 74, and note), the Armenian Bd Gomidas Keumurgian (June 5), the Maronites BB. Francis, Abdulmuti and Raphael Masabki (July 10), and the Ethiopian Bd Gabra Michael (August 28). The chief more recent modifications among most Catholics are the addition of Corpus Christi and the Sacred Heart, and increased solemnity given to St Joseph (on the Sunday after Christmas) and to the Child-begetting of the Mother of the Mother of God, i.e., the Immaculate Conception, on December 9.

Among the special Byzantine observances are the feast of Orthodoxy (first Sunday in Lent), celebrating the triumph of orthodox veneration for holy images over Iconoclasm in 842, the Three Holy Hierarchs (SS. Basil, Gregory Nazianzen and John Chrysostom), on January 30, Mary the Protectress (October 1), and many feasts of the just of the Old Dispensation (Joseph, David, Elias, Joshua, the Three Children, Job the Great Athlete, the Ancestors of the Messiah, etc., and a general feast which includes Adam and Eve). The Exaltation of the Cross on September 14 is a specially solemn day. The number of "holy days of obligation" varies.

Penitential seasons. Eastern fasting, like many other of their religious usages, is the observance proper to monks gradually extended to the people at large (but by custom more than by law), and it is notoriously severe. For centuries the pious faithful made it a point of honour to keep the fasts, and many still do; but conditions of modern life make it increasingly difficult to do so. Amongst Catholics, new conditions have been met in some places by canonical legislation, generally approximating to Western observances; in others, local customs are in process of evolution.

There is only one word, *nesteia*, to designate both fasting and abstinence and it is rather difficult to distinguish between them. Among the Greeks, fasting involves one meal only and that after sunset; strict abstinence forbids meat, milk, eggs, fish, oil and wine; mitigated abstinence allows oil and wine, and sometimes fish; this is according to the old canons and customs, which envisaged strict fasting every Wednesday and Friday and in Lent, and abstinence on from 50 to 90 other days. But for the Catholic Melkites, for example, the second synod of Ain Traz in 1835 directed that fasting should consist of complete abstinence from food, drink and tobacco until noon; afterwards anything might be eaten without limit of quantity, except meat, eggs and milk. Their fasting days were five before Christmas, four before Epiphany, all Lent except Saturdays and Sundays and the Annunciation, and three other days. The same synod defined abstinence to extend to meat, eggs and milk. It was obligatory for ten days before the fast of Christmas, twelve days before SS. Peter and Paul, fourteen days before the Assumption, on the solemnities of the Beheading of St John Baptist and Holy Cross, and every Wednesday and Friday. But there is no fasting or abstinence during paschal-time and at certain other seasons, and the above regulations are modified from place to place (cf. p. 63).

General observations. The Catholic Byzantines have taken up the use of Western "devotions", rosary, stations of the cross, etc., in varying degrees.[13] Among their own observances is the Akathistos Hymn, an office in honour of our Lady which is sung publicly at certain times and used privately as well. Holy water (*hagiasma*) is solemnly blessed in the baptismal font (and sometimes in rivers or the sea) at the Epiphany, in commemoration of our Lord's baptism. On Good Friday a shroud bearing the image of our Lord is laid on an ornamental bier (*epitaphion*) with flowers, spices and grave-clothes. In the evening it is carried in procession round and out of the church, sometimes through the streets (the "Burial of Christ"); and

---

[13] Here and elsewhere any specifically Western practice adopted by Eastern Catholics does not apply to dissidents unless expressly stated to do so.

then laid in the middle of the church while mourning *troparia* modelled on the last five verses of Matthew 27 are sung. On a dozen chief feasts there is at the end of Vespers a procession (*Litia*) during which the Song of Simeon is sung, and five loaves of bread, wheat, wine and oil are blessed (*Artoklasia*). The bread is distributed to the faithful, who are anointed on the forehead with the oil. This blessing of food, being associated with a vigil, may be the remnant of an evening meal.

It has been wittily observed that "visitors from the West commonly find Byzantine services interminable for the simple reason that they never stay to the end".

BIBLIOGRAPHY

P. de Meester, *The Divine Liturgy of . . . John Chrysostom* (London, 1926). Greek text and translation.

C. C. Englert, *The Byzantine Liturgy* (Fordham, N.Y., 1956). Russian use.

F. Mercenier et al., *La prière des Églises de rite byzantin*, 3 vols. (Chevetogne, 1951-53).

Ordo celebrationis Vesperarum, Matutini et Divinae Liturgiae iuxta recensionem Ruthenorum (Rome, 1944).

A. Couturier, *Cours de Liturgie grecque-melkite*, 3 vols. (Paris, 1912-30).

F. J. Moreau, *Les liturgies eucharistiques* (Brussels, 1924).

H. Holloway, *A Study of the Byzantine Liturgy* (London, 1934).

N. B. Gogol, *The Divine Liturgy* ("meditations"), (London, 1961).

Eastern Churches Quarterly, vol. vii, nos. 3, 5, 7 and viii, 2 (1947-49). Divine Office.

V. McNabb, *The Akathistos Hymn* (Oxford, 1947).

Translations of other Byzantine offices have been published by Williams and Norgate (Ernest Benn Ltd., London).

A. Stoelen, *L'année liturgique byzantin* (Amay, 1928). Russian use.

I. M. de Vries, *The Epistles, Gospels and Tones of the Byzantine Liturgical Year* (Ramsgate, 1954).

L. A. Hamilton, *Byzantine Architecture and Decoration* (London, 1956).

D. T. Rice, *Byzantine Art* (Penguin, 1954).

L. Ouspensky and V. Lossky, *The Meaning of Icons* (Boston, Mass., 1952).

C. Cavarnos, *Byzantine Sacred Art* (New York, 1957).

H. J. W. Tillyard, *Byzantine Music and Hymnography* (London, 1930).

E. J. Wellesz, *A History of Byzantine Music and Hymnography* (Oxford, 1960).

Chants grecs de la Liturgie de St Jean Chrysostome (Chevetogne, 1951).

A. Couturier, *Syllitourgikon* (Paris, 1925). Responses and other chants in European notation.

Music for the Liturgy of St John Chrysostom (Tournai, 1937). Russian.

CHAPTER IV

CATHOLIC CHURCHES OF BYZANTINE RITE

I. THE MELKITE PATRIARCHATE OF ANTIOCH

AFTER the Council of Chalcedon the Monophysites in the patriarchates of Alexandria, Antioch and Jerusalem dubbed the orthodox Catholics "Melkites", from Syrian *malok*, "king", because they professed the orthodoxy of the emperor. The name stuck and is often used without qualification to designate the Catholic Byzantines of Syria and Egypt, though the dissident Orthodox are equally Melkites.[1] After the Arab invasion in the seventh century the Melkites of all three patriarchates came for a time more and more under the ecclesiastical domination of Constantinople, and by the end of the thirteenth century they had abandoned their own liturgies to the Monophysites and adopted that of imperial Byzantium.

There was another important change after Chalcedon, in the *personnel* that made up these patriarchates. Alexandria was originally Greco-Egyptian, Antioch and Jerusalem Greco-Syrian. Today, the Orthodox of Alexandria are Greek and Syrian, those of Jerusalem are Palestinian-Arab under a Greek ecclesiastical caucus, those of Antioch are almost entirely Syro-Arab. The Catholic Melkites are fundamentally Syro-Arabs, racially more or less one with the Syrians and Maronites, but they have received more Greek influence.

Though numerically small, the patriarchate of Antioch is still of great historical interest and ecclesiastical importance because of the number of its patriarchs and bishops who were

---

[1] In the popular speech of the Levant the word "Catholic" primarily means "Catholic Melkite", for of the half-dozen Catholic rites represented in Syria, Palestine and Egypt, the Melkites are hierarchically the "authentic local Catholics". The Orthodox are called *Rúm*, Roman, for Constantinople was the New Rome whilst a Western Catholic is simply a *Lateen*.

in communion with Rome between the Byzantine separation[2] and the definite emergence of two hierarchies, Catholic and dissident Orthodox, in 1724. When the Crusaders captured Antioch in 1098 they acknowledged the Catholicity and jurisdiction of its patriarch, John IV; but after the death of the papal legate Adhemar du Puy, their attitude altered and they treated John so badly that he fled to Constantinople.[3] It was this that started the series of absentee Melkite patriarchs in the imperial city, which helped to strengthen the spirit of opposition to Rome. But Theodosius V signed the act of union at Lyons in 1274 and resigned his see rather than repudiate it; others must have followed his example, for Saracen writers of the fourteenth and fifteenth centuries make a clear distinction between the Melkites who submit to the pope of Rome and the other Christians (Jacobites, etc.) who do not.

The patriarch of Antioch, Dorotheos I, accepted the union of Florence, and there is reason to think that the three Melkite patriarchs did not wholly relapse into schism again until the Turks cut off Syria from the West in 1516 and the Greeks seized the patriarchal throne of Jerusalem from the Syrians in 1543. But again in 1560 Joachim V was apparently a Catholic, and in 1585 the retired patriarch, Michael VII, and with the seventeenth century there began a strong movement toward definitive reunion. The patriarchs Athanasius II, Ignatius III, Euthymios II, Eutychios, Makarios III and Cyril V, and the bishops Euthymios Saifi of Tyre, Gregory of Aleppo, Gerasimos of Saidnaia, Parthenios of Diarbekr, and others, all made formal profession of allegiance to the Holy See between 1600 and 1720; Western missioners, indeed, seem to have recognized all Melkite bishops in Syria as the legitimate ordinaries of their rite.

When the Orthodox patriarch Athanasius III died in 1724, a nephew of Euthymios of Tyre who had been educated in

---

[2] The contemporary patriarch, Peter III, implored Cerularius not to separate himself and his church from Rome and the West. There have been some Catholic patriarchs of Alexandria, too, since the thirteenth century, and two are reported at Jerusalem in the seventeenth.

[3] Thereupon the Crusaders instituted that anomaly, a Latin patriarch of Antioch. It was this playing fast and loose with Eastern sees and their holders (to say nothing of such things as their sacking of Constantinople in 1204) that made the name of crusader—and consequently of Catholic —stink in the nostrils of pious Orientals. The current *Annuario Pontificio* records titular Latin patriarchal sees of Constantinople, Alexandria and Antioch, but names no holders of them; the resident Latin patriarch of Jerusalem (a see restored in 1847) is simply an archbishop with patriarchal precedence; the pope is the only real patriarch in the Western church.

Rome, Seraphim Tanas, was elected in his place; he took the name of Cyril VI. Thereupon those who were not in favour of communion with Rome (and some who were) selected a Cypriot candidate, Silvester, and sent him off to Constantinople, where he was consecrated and put forward as the true patriarch of Antioch.[4] Silvester had the support of only five bishops out of fifteen, but he obtained the favour of the Turkish government first and Cyril had to take refuge in a remote Maronite monastery in Lebanon.

THE CATHOLIC MELKITES

For a time there was a violent persecution of the Catholics, and even when it died down the reign of Cyril continued to be troubled; he fell foul both of the Jesuits and the Maronites, and Pope Benedict XIV had to send a severe instruction that the Maronites were not to induce Melkites to join their rite and that Melkites were not to call Maronites heretics. Cyril VI Tanas resigned in 1759, but the state of the Catholic Melkites continued to be disturbed. For example, a synod at Karkafah in 1806 published a number of "acts" which later had to be condemned by the Holy See for their "conciliarism," there were quarrels between the patriarch Agapios III and the metropolitan of Beirut, and from 1817 till 1832 there was a bloody persecution at the hands of the Turks—nine Melkites were murdered out of hatred of the faith at Aleppo in 1818.[5]

The rule of the great Maximos III Mazlum (1833-1855) was a period of reform and progress, culminating in his obtaining from the Turkish government complete civil autonomy for his people under their patriarch. In the time of his successor, Clement Bahath, there was for three years a small but very noisy schism caused by the imposition of the Gregorian calendar in place of the Julian. Gregory II Yusuf (1864-1897) was another energetic and far-seeing patriarch. He suggested the formation of the seminary of St Anne at Jerusalem, and at the epoch-making international eucharistic congress held in

---

[4] From this time on there are two lines of patriarchs, one for Catholics, one for dissidents. The Catholic patriarch is the historical as well as the spiritual successor of St Evodius, St Ignatius the God-bearer and the Flavians. The Orthodox have contested the validity of the election of Cyril VI, but the synod of Constantinople itself admitted it by claiming to depose him.

[5] Earlier martyrs were David the Greek (1660) and Ibrahim al-Dallal (1742).

that city in 1893 Gregory was the outstanding figure. He had assisted at the Vatican Council and was well known to the West. There has been a remarkable extension of his church in the regions of Tripoli, Galilee and Jordan in recent years.

PRESENT STATE

Patriarch. The supreme head under the sovereign pontiff of the Catholic Melkites is the "Patriarch of Antioch and of All the East"; since the days of Maximos III each holder has had the personal privilege of adding the titles of Alexandria and Jerusalem.[6] His jurisdiction extends to all the faithful of his church in what was in 1894 the Turkish empire and Egypt, with a certain oversight of emigrants everywhere. He is elected by all the bishops, diocesan and titular, of the patriarchate gathered in synod. If the person elected be not already a bishop, the choice must be confirmed by the Holy See before he is proclaimed, enthroned and enters on his duties. If an election is not made within fifteen days, appointment lapses to the Holy See. Among the patriarchal rights are the ordination, transfer and canonical deposition of his bishops, the appointment of titular bishops at will, the erection, division and suppression of dioceses, the consecration of chrism (*myron*) for his whole church, the convening of a plenary synod, as well as certain civil rights in respect of his flock. He confers the *omophorion* (the Eastern *pallium*[7]) on each bishop at ordination. The patriarch is assisted by a synod of four of the other bishops, chosen, for five years, two by the patriarch and two by the rest of the bishops. The principal patriarchal residences are at Cairo and Damascus.[8] Kyr Maximos IV Sayegh was elected patriarch in 1947.

[6] On solemn occasions he is "The most blessed, holy and venerable chief and head, Patriarch of the great cities of God, Antioch, Alexandria and Jerusalem, of Cilicia, Syria and Iberia, of Arabia, Mesopotamia and the Pentapolis, of Ethiopia, Egypt and all the East, the lord N., Father of fathers, Shepherd of shepherds, High priest of high priests, and Thirteenth Apostle." "The East" is the Roman prefecture *Oriens.*

[7] The pope confers the *pallium* on a newly elected patriarch in recognition of communion with him. The *pallium* has, however, no ancient historical significance in the East and was unheard of there before the time of Pope Innocent III, during the Crusades.

[8] None of the five governing patriarchs (Catholic Melkite, Syrian and Maronite, Orthodox Melkite, and Jacobite) who have the title of Antioch live there. "Antikiya" is now a poor little town, mostly Moslem, a mere section within the ruined walls of the ancient "great and God-protected city".

Bishops. The sees are Damascus (the patriarchal eparchy[9]), Tyre, Akka, Aleppo, Bairut, Bosra (Hauran), Homs, Baalbek, Paneas, Petra (Amman), Sidon, Tripoli and Zahleh. The first seven of these are metropolitan according to the old lists, but all the bishops are called archbishop and are subject directly to the patriarch. A diocesan bishop is elected by the patriarch and other bishops in synod. The choice must be confirmed by the Holy See, but if the name of the elect figures on a list of persons already approved at Rome as suitable, no further confirmation is necessary. The authority of the patriarch of Antioch was extended to the Melkites of the patriarchates of Alexandria and Jerusalem in 1778; he has vicars (who are titular bishops or archimandrites) in Egypt and at Jerusalem, Damascus, Khartum, Baghdad and Constantinople.

Each bishop is the sole judge of ecclesiastical cases in his own eparchy, and acts to a certain extent as judge in some civil cases as well; for this purpose he usually appoints a tribunal. The Melkite patriarch and bishops live as simply as do their parish clergy and most of the members of their flocks; they are fathers in God whose contact with their children is very close and familiar.

Parochial clergy. Before the days of Maximos III practically all the parishes were served by monks, who still have charge of some of them. A seminary was founded in 1811 at Ain Traz in Lebanon, a great Melkite centre where three plenary synods have been held. Its career was chequered and not very successful, and it was closed in 1899, but it has recently been reopened for "late vocations" and the training of married clergy. After the Crimean War the Turkish government presented to France, as a *baksheesh* for her part in the campaign, the crusaders' church of St Anne in Jerusalem. Here in 1882 Cardinal Lavigerie, at the suggestion of the patriarch Gregory II, opened a general seminary for Melkites under the direction of the White Fathers.[10] By the end of its first fifty years this institution had produced eight bishops, 126 priests, and three permanent

---

[9] *Eparchy* is the Byzantine term for what in the West we call a diocese. Tyre is the Melkite protothrone, i.e., the first see after the patriarch's; but the term is sometimes used for the patriarchal see itself.

[10] The Society of Missionaries of Africa, founded at Algiers by the cardinal in 1868. Lavigerie played an important part in the abolition of the slave trade, and his society worthily carries on the tradition of his genius.

deacons, of whom Mgr Lagier says, "Their modesty, un-worldliness, cultured wide-spiritedness, and dignity of soul make up a priestly *ensemble* that is surpassed nowhere in the Catholic Church". All the St Anne's priests voluntarily accept celibacy, but there is also a number of married priests among the Melkite clergy, who are hard-working and highly respected men. A few aspirants are sent to the Greek College at Rome. There are junior seminaries at Rayak in Lebanon and at Nazareth.

Archimandrite[11] and sometimes other titles are conferred as titles of honour, the holders of which affect certain distinctions of dress. The clergy wear the traditional Byzantine *rason* and *kalemaukion*.

Religious institutes. For two hundred years the monks were the mainstay of the Catholic Melkite church. In 1708 Euthymios Saifi of Tyre built a monastery at Masmuseh, near Sidon. He put its members under the "rule of St Basil", but his object was to form a congregation more on the lines of the clerks regular of the West; nevertheless they are canonically reckoned as monks. His foundation prospered and grew, receiving the name of *Salvatorian* Basilians from its mother-house "of the Saviour", Dair al-Mukhallis; this house still flourishes. The *Shuwairite* Basilian monks were founded about the same time at Shuwair by two hieromonks from the Orthodox monastery of Balamand ("Belmont"), near Tripoli. Their organization was more strictly monastic than that of the Salvatorians, but they also were soon engaged in parochial and mission work. Almost from the beginning there was friction between the Shuwairite monasteries in the Lebanon mountains and those of Aleppo, which was ended in 1829 by the formation of a separate congregation of *Aleppine* Basilians (the others are sometimes called Baladites, i.e., rustics).

These three congregations all developed under Western influence, principally of the Jesuits and Capuchins. Nevertheless, their members are an indigenous product, and cannot be mistaken for anything other than they are—Eastern religious who have developed in certain conditions and in response to

---

11 Any bishop may confer this title on any priest he pleases within his own eparchy. The White Father Abel Couturier, that "ghost from the *lauras* of Pharan", was in 1927 named archimandrite by the patriarch Cyril IX Mogabgab.

a particular demand. On account of the shortage of secular priests the Melkite Basilians have throughout their history been principally engaged in serving parishes, and the value of the service they have done for the faithful of their rite is incalculable. To a monk of Shuwair, Abdullah Zahir, was due the establishment of the first Arabic printing-press in the Ottoman empire, early in the eighteenth century.

According to the categories of the new code of Eastern canon law, these Basilian religious constitute a "non-monastic religious order". Each of the three congregations has a superior general (*archimandrite*) at its head, who appoints local superiors (*hegumenoi*) and can transfer monks from one house to another at will. There are fifteen principal monasteries and the majority of the monks are priests (*hieromonks*), some of them serving parishes. They wear the traditional Byzantine monastic dress.

After he retired from the see of Baalbek in 1894 Germanos Muakkad[12] founded the society of *Missionaries of St. Paul*, at Harissa in the Lebanon. They do a great work in giving missions and retreats and running a polyglot printing establishment.

All three Basilian congregations have convents of nuns affiliated, totalling over 180 members, whose life till recently was strictly contemplative and the most traditionally Eastern of any nuns in the Catholic Church, being entirely free from foreign influence. It is still partly so, but since 1941 the nuns of the Salvatorian branch have been a missionary congregation. When he was archbishop of Bairut, Patriarch Maximos IV founded a congregation of missionary and teaching nuns, the *Sisters of our Lady of Unceasing Help*. Since their beginnings in 1936 these religious have rapidly increased in numbers and effectiveness. Their mother-house is at Harissa. There are some Melkites among the Maryamat (see p. 164), and a few convents of other sisters.

The Faithful. There were in 1960 about 220,000 Melkites in the patriarchal territory (Lebanon 107,000, Syria 42,000, Egypt 30,000, Israel 20,000, Jordan 15,500, and some other groups; 12,000 were refugees from Israel. The dissident Orthodox of the three patriarchates total some 430,000). In Lebanon

[12] Dr Adrian Fortescue said of him, "I have rarely met any man who gave the impression of being a saint as did Germanos Muakkad".

and Syria a good many, and in Egypt all, of them live in the towns, and form prosperous communities whose social and religious prestige is high; in the rural districts of Syria and Jordan increasing numbers of peasants become Melkite Catholics. By blood these claim to be pure Arabs of the Hauran, especially of the Banu Ghassan, originally from the Yemen in southern Arabia, and descended from Solomon and the Queen of Sheba—a common Oriental boast. In some of the more remote parts religious education is insufficient, and in the towns the influence of returned immigrants has sometimes been rather harmful.

In Palestine the course of history has brought about a predominance of Latin influence and the formation of a local clergy and laity of the Roman rite, but in recent years Melkite influence has increased in Galilee and Jordan. The former atmosphere of rivalry between Latins and Byzantines was very regrettable, and indeed there has not always been among the Catholic bodies of the Near East in general that accord, good feeling and mixing with one another that one would wish to find. Their rivalries were of old standing, and kept alive particularly by some of the laity and lower clergy.

OTHER JURISDICTIONS

North America. There has been emigration of Melkites to America for the past seventy years, but many of them were lost to religion. Their first priest in the United States, where they call themselves Syrian Greek Catholics, was a monk, Father Abraham Bashawata, and the first church was at Brooklyn. There are now about 40,000 faithful, with 26 churches in the United States and one in Canada, at Montreal. Many of the parishes are around New York and in New England, and in 1954 a seminary was opened at Methuen, Mass.; it is directed by Salvatorian Basilian monks.

Elsewhere. There are said to be nearly 100,000 Melkites in various parts of *South America*, especially in Brazil and Argentine; it is difficult to get particulars of them, but they certainly have commodious and handsome churches in Rio de Janeiro and São Paulo, especially the latter. In other countries they have churches at Marseilles (founded in 1821), Paris (Saint-Julien-le-Pauvre), Sydney, Brisbane and Mexico City. Those in Brazil now have a bishop, who is a vicar general of the archbishop of Rio de Janeiro.

Particular Customs

The Melkites are jealous for the good observance of their rite. The Byzantine liturgy and other offices are celebrated normally entirely in Arabic, and have been modified only in small points, chiefly of externals; amongst the emigrants there is a beginning of the use of local vernaculars in some places, including English and Spanish. Their chant is in substance that of Constantinople. Baptism is ministered by seating the child in the font and pouring water over it. A number of the smaller churches are too poor to have an *eikonostasis*.

The use of the traditional spoon for giving holy communion is being more and more superseded by the practice of dipping the holy Body in the sacred Blood and ministering them by hand. The Melkites accorded a degree of external *cultus* to the Blessed Sacrament before any other Catholics of Eastern rite. An Arabic *Pentekostarion* of so early as the end of the seventeenth century was found at Damascus containing an office for Corpus Christi, and since the plague was stayed at Aleppo in 1732 the feast has been observed with increased solemnity. Benediction with the Blessed Sacrament, with a completely different ceremonial from that of the West, has been introduced into some eparchies, as has the unnecessary innovation of giving absolution by the Western indicative formula (in Arabic, of course).

One or two Western devotions are practised among the Melkites, e.g., the rosary, but there are no statues in the churches, only eikons. In addition to their old observance of Corpus Christi, the feasts of SS. Augustine, Jerome, Maro, Cyril and Methodius and Josaphat of Polotsk have recently been added to their calendar. Holy days and rules of fasting vary from one eparchy to another, pending agreement for uniform observance between the different rites in the Near East.

Close relations are maintained between the Catholic Melkites and their Orthodox brethren; more than one recent Catholic patriarch has publicly declared his willingness to resign his office in favour of the Orthodox patriarch should the latter bring back his people to unity with Rome.

BIBLIOGRAPHY

C. Charon, *Histoire des Patriarcats melkites*, 2 vols. (Paris, 1911). Unfinished; one volume covers institutions, hierarchy etc; the other, history, from 1833 to 1855.

J. Devreesse, *Le patriarcat d'Antioche depuis la paix de l'Église jusqu'à la conquête arabe* (Paris, 1945).

A. Fortescue, *The Uniate Eastern Churches* (Italo-Greeks and Melkites) (London, 1923).

J. Hajjar, *Le patriarche Maximos III Mazloum* (Harissa, 1957).

P. Gorra, *Sainte Anne de Jérusalem; Séminaire grec-melkite* (Jerusalem, 1932).

H. Ayrout, *Transjordanie melkite* (Louvain, 1935).

O. Kerame, *Unionisme, Uniatisme, Arabisme chrétien* (Bairut, 1957).

A. Couturier, *Cours de Liturgie grecque-melkite*, 3 vols. (Paris, 1912-30).
——————— *Syllitourgikon* (the chant in Eastern and Western notation) (Paris, 1926).

A. Sayegh, *Mélodecte: Recueil de chants byzantins* (Cairo, 1956).

J. Raya and J. de Vinck, *Byzantine Missal* (Birmingham, Ala., 1958). Melkite use.

N. Edelby, *Liturgicon* (Bairut, 1960). Melkite missal in French.

Eastern Churches Quarterly, vol. ix, nos. 4-7 (1952). Melkites in U.S.A.

2. THE ITALO-GREEKS

THE Italo-Greeks, more accurately called now Italo-Greek-Albanians, or even Italo-Albanians, are the only Orientals who have been continuously in communion with Rome since before the Eastern separation; they therefore have an historical interest out of proportion to their numbers and present importance.

For several centuries before the birth of Christ Hellenic colonists had made Sicily and southern Italy predominantly Greek: the provinces of Calabria and Apulia are known historically as *Magna Graecia*. From at least the second century after Christ there were Christian communities in these parts, and the present inhabitants regard their churches as apostolic foundations (Acts 28:11-14).[13] The first seven hundred years of their ecclesiastical history are full of difficulties, but it seems certain that, after the superseding of Greek by Latin in the liturgy at Rome about the middle of the third century and the crystallizing of different liturgical rites, Roman and Byzantine usages existed side by side in southern Italy and Sicily, and that all bishops of these Christians were under the direct jurisdiction of the bishop of Rome.[14]

About the year 732 the Iconoclast emperor Leo III the Isaurian began forcibly to subject these Greek districts which Justinian had joined to the Eastern empire to the patriarch of Constantinople, and metropolitan sees were erected at Naples, Syracuse and elsewhere. To avoid disputes the popes accepted the situation. But the conquest by the Normans of southern Italy, begun in 1017, and then of Sicily (at that time in Saracen hands), removed the possibility of these Greek churches

---

[13] Pope St Agatho (d. 681) was a Sicilian Greek, and Pope St Zachary (d. 752) a Calabrian Greek.

[14] Liturgical rite has essentially nothing to do with patriarchate. The notion that all subjects of the same patriarch should have his rite is partly a result of "uniformizing" by Constantinople. The Pope was patriarch of Byzantines in Illyricum as well as metropolitan of those in *Magna Graecia*. The great archbishop of Canterbury, St Theodore, was a Greek monk of Calabria; when Pope St Vitalian appointed him to England in 664 he had to "change his rite"—and his style of hair-dressing (see Bede's *Ecclesiastical History*, iv, 1).

following Constantinople into schism, and they came again under the immediate jurisdiction of the pope, as they have ever since remained.[15]

The influence of the Normans and the increasing Latin element was not favourable to the Greek Catholics; several of their eparchies (dioceses) were suppressed, whole parishes turned Latin, the numerous monasteries became decadent. By the beginning of the fifteenth century the Byzantines were on the verge of extinction. But there was an influx of refugees from Constantinople after 1453, and then for a hundred years there came colonists and mercenaries from Albania, following the alliance of Skanderbeg with Ferdinand I of Naples. Some of the immigrants were Latins, some Byzantines; these last saved their dying rite in Italy[16], and account for the Italo-Greeks of today being mainly of Albanian descent. Nevertheless the decay continued, and the last Byzantine bishopric disappeared at the end of the sixteenth century; some of the monasteries hung on much longer. From before 1600 the Byzantines were subject to the local ordinaries, who encouraged and urged them (to put it mildly) to join the Latin rite; in consequence, the Byzantine rite was given up altogether in Apulia and Terra d'Otranto, and greatly decreased elsewhere. (To the average Western bishop of those days, Eastern subjects were a nuisance, and at least suspect of heresy all the time. That Orientals have as much right to their "peculiarities" as Latins have to theirs did not occur to them: the popes, indeed, seem to have been the only ones who never lost sight of this.)

Moreover, there was difficulty in recruiting and training their clergy, though the Greek College at Rome was open to them. An Oratorian priest, George Guzzetta, started an Albanian community at Piana in Sicily in 1716 and a seminary at Palermo in 1734; during the century or so of their existence these Byzantine Oratorians did much good work but were handicapped by their insistence on the Western principle of clerical celibacy; the seminary is still in being. There was a seminary for Calabria at Ullano from 1732 till 1860. Pope

[15] At a council held by Pope Urban II at Bari in Apulia in 1098 certain Italo-Greek bishops threw doubt on the procession of the Holy Spirit from the Son ("*Filioque*"). They were answered by St Anselm, archbishop of Canterbury.

[16] Pope Clement XI (1700-21) was a descendant of one of these Albanian families, which had settled in the Papal States.

Clement XII authorized the consecration of a bishop, who should ordain priests but have no jurisdiction, for Byzantines in Calabria, and one for those of Sicily was appointed by Pius VI.

Meantime, in 1742, Pope Benedict XIV issued the constitution *Etsi pastoralis*, which was a sort of compendium of canon law for the Greeks and Albanians: their rites and customs are to be kept, their privileges are confirmed, no Latin ordinary is to interfere with their lawful usages or invite them to become Latins, and a Byzantine vicar general must be appointed; the Latin rite has no precedence as such over the Byzantine: "before God there is neither Greek nor Jew nor barbarian nor Scythian, for all are one in Christ." The effect of this was to restore self-respect to the Greco-Albanians and put a brake for the time being on their cultural and ecclesiastical decay; moreover, *Etsi pastoralis* paved the way for other and more far-reaching papal pronouncements on the true place of Orientals in the Church.

PRESENT STATE

Italy. In 1919 Pope Benedict XV constituted a separate eparchy for the Byzantines of Calabria, with its see at Lungro. It has twenty village parishes. Though it is not in this jurisdiction, mention must be made of the church built for the Greek colony at Leghorn in 1605; the parishioners are mixed Melkites and Italo-Greeks.

Sicily. The Byzantines of Sicily have eight parishes, and these were made into a separate eparchy in 1937, with its see at Piana dei Greci. This town, near Palermo, has seven Byzantine places of worship.

Parochial clergy. These two dioceses (which are immediately subject to the Holy See) have about seventy churches and chapels, served by sixty priests. They make their studies in the junior seminary at the abbey of Grottaferrata, at the seminary founded by Father Guzzetta, transferred to Piana in 1951, and at the Greek College in Rome. (see page 112) The Italo-Albanian priests retain their right to marriage before ordination and a few are married. The use of the traditional Greek clerical costume has been restored for formal occasions; most rectors of churches call themselves protopopes, i.e., archpriests.

Religious institutes. Both in the earlier and later middle ages the centres of Byzantinism in southern Italy were the numerous monasteries. To arrest their decline, Pope Gregory XIII in 1579 united them all into a congregation on the model of the Benedictine one of St Justina of Padua; unfortunately it was also joined to the Spanish Basilian order, a purely Western institute (founded 1559; now extinct), and this hastened the decay in Italy by a prolonged process of voluntary latinization; the houses were Greek almost only in name. Rodotà, the first ordaining bishop for Calabria, could still speak in 1758 of forty-three struggling monasteries "where once there were about a thousand"; today there are none left at all, with the distinguished exception of Grottaferrata and its dependencies.

About the year 980 a Greek abbot, St Neilos of Rossano, and his monks fled before the Saracen raids on Calabria, and having long enjoyed Benedictine hospitality at Monte Cassino, established a monastery at Grottaferrata in the Alban hills in 1004. It was within the domain of the turbulent lords of Tusculum, and frequently figures in the history of the Papal States, as when that disgraceful pope Benedict IX retired there to spend his last years in penitence. Pope Pius II made the Greek cardinal Bessarion its abbot *in commendam*, and he did much for Grottaferrata. But his successor, Cardinal Julian della Rovere (afterwards Pope Julius II), rebuilt it as a fortress ("Uomo di spiriti bellicosi," as the monastic chronicler justly observes), and later commendatory abbots—and others—did much harm. These gentlemen, whose sensitive classicism was such that it could not bear the barbarous Latin of office hymns, destroyed or hid much beautiful Greek work of the middle ages, plastering it ("plaster" is the right word) with the riotous intemperances of baroque. Not all the monks took this lying down, and their chronicler remarks drily that whereas Cardinal Guadagni is commemorated above the church door in *stone*, the angels venerating our Lady's eikon within the church are only *stucco*.

The commendatory abbots did not end till 1824, and the life and worship of the monastery continued to suffer. Further decay was stopped by Pope Leo XIII in 1881, who ordered a rigorous reform and restoration of its Byzantine integrity, which was carried through with gratifying results. And in 1937 the Holy See made it an abbey *nullius* (*dioecesis*), that is, the people of the surrounding district are ecclesiastically subject to the abbot as their ordinary.

These monks have always had a reputation for learning, and their library contains valuable manuscripts, including a famous *Typikon* of the eleventh century, on which their editions of the Greek liturgical books are based. The monastery has a school of illumination and Greek palaeography, and a specialty is made of the repair of old and decayed manuscripts. Greek frescoes and mosaics, pushed out of sight by renaissance taste, have been brought back to light, and in 1907 Archimandrite Arsenios Pellegrini established a museum of antiquities.

For nearly nine hundred years, then, there have been Greek monks at the very gates of Rome, the capital not simply of the Latin but of the Catholic world. Their byzantinism has not always been above reproach; but that reproach has now been taken away, and they are a living witness at her heart that the Catholic Church is not solely a West-European institution. After visiting Grottaferrata, Professor Karolidis, of the University of Athens, wrote in a Greek newspaper that "Here is an oasis of Hellenism right at the centre of Latin civilization".[17] And this Byzantine monastic community goes back unbrokenly and organically through the ages to the time before the tragic separation of Eastern and Western Christians had taken place.

The community has fifty hieromonks and monks, mostly Italo-Albanians. In addition to a junior seminary for their rite, they conduct a printing establishment and an orphanage. In 1920 they took over the old monastery of Mezzoiuso in Sicily and made it a novitiate for the training of monks for apostolic work, while in 1932 a daughter-house was started near Lungro. In 1935 the missionary College of St Basil in Rome was entrusted to them.

There are Byzantine sisters of several congregations engaged in teaching and other good works in Calabria and Sicily.

The Faithful. Of the places in Italy and Sicily where the Greek

17 Some Orthodox Greeks are rather proud of Grottaferrata and sympathetic toward its monks, because it was founded before the separation and has not lost its Greek tradition.

observances are maintained the chief are Lungro, San Demetrio Corone, Piana dei Greci and Palazzo Adriano. The people are all peasants, rather poverty-stricken in Italy, a little more prosperous in Sicily. There are 40,000 of them in the one country and about 24,000 in the other, of whom a fair proportion (here and there whole villages) speak a somewhat debased Albanian as their usual language. A Greek dialect is still spoken in certain villages of Terra d'Otranto; there is evidence that it is derived primarily from the Greek of ancient times and not from later Byzantine colonies.

OTHER JURISDICTIONS

United States. There were emigrations of Italo-Greeks at the end of the nineteenth century, mostly to the states of New York and Pennsylvania. Many of them were lost to the Church for lack of priests of their rite. The first priest was sent from Palermo in 1904, and he opened two churches in New York. There are no statistics of their number in the United States today. Thirty years ago they were said to be 20,000, but there has been a tendency to overestimate the number of Catholic Orientals of some rites in America. In any case the great majority of the Italo-Greeks frequent churches of Latin rite, as at present they have no clergy of their own. There is reported to be 10,000 of them in Brazil.

PARTICULAR CUSTOMS

As their history would lead us to expect, the liturgy of the Byzantines underwent very serious modifications during the course of time in southern Italy, but in Sicily it was much better observed. These innovations have to a considerable extent been corrected and in most churches the Greek rite is now observed with a very fair degree of fidelity. They use the excellent books printed at Rome. But as the churches are nearly all too poor to afford *eikonostases*, and as statues, side-altars, etc., have been admitted into them, there is not much to distinguish them from the Latin churches. The Italo-Greeks adopted the Gregorian reckoning with the Catholic West in 1582, the first Easterners to do so. They have modified the Constantinopolitan calendar by celebrating certain feasts (e.g., All Saints, All Souls, St Joseph) on their Roman as well as their Byzantine dates and by the addition of more modern feasts, e.g., Corpus Christi, the Sacred Heart, St Antony of Padua. Confirmation is separated from Baptism and conferred by a bishop, and absolution is given in the Roman form. Pope Benedict XV restored the duty of confirming to priests in the eparchy of Lungro; in practice the bishop himself often baptizes, and confirms immediately after.

Their church music is a traditional version of that of Constantinople, and in some churches Albanian hymns are still sung. As is natural, Benediction with the Blessed Sacrament (in a form of their own) and all the "popular devotions" of the West have long been known among them. A curious local observance in some churches is for men to receive communion standing (according to their rite) but women kneeling.

BIBLIOGRAPHY

A. Fortescue, *The Uniate Eastern Churches* (Italo-Greeks and Melkites) (London, 1923).

P. Buccola, *Badia di Grottaferrata* (Grottaferrata, 1913).

H. Gaisser, *I canti ecclesiastici italo-greci* (Rome, 1905).

C. Rossini, *Canti tradizionali delle colonie italo-greco-albanesi* (New York, 1924). The melodies are made chromatic.

3. THE RUTHENIANS OR UKRAINIANS

"Ruthenian" is the official ecclesiastical term distinguishing certain bodies of Catholics of the Byzantine rite found in Eastern Galicia, Podcarpathia, Hungary and Bukovina, with colonies in North America and elsewhere. They all belong in origin to one people. The land that lies between Vilna in the north and the Carpathian mountains in the south was part of Poland from about 1350 to 1793 and again from 1921 to 1939; in Russian history the territory is known as "The Western Lands", and it includes the provinces of Eastern Galicia, Volhynia and Polesia. It has a very mixed population, consisting mostly, in order of numerousness, of Ruthenians (or Ukrainians), Poles and White Russians. There are many more Ukrainians and White Russians to the east, but these are no concern of ours at the moment.

The Ruthenians are Slavs and their homeland was the original nucleus of Russia. After the fall of their great city of Kiev in 1240 to the Mongols the centre of state power gradually shifted to Moscow, and eventually the Muscovites reserved for themselves the name of Great Russians and called the others Little Russians.[18] Each of these three elements, Great Russian, White Russian and Ruthenian, has its own language, descended from a common tongue that was spoken by them all before the twelfth century.

During the nineteenth century considerable cultural and political self-consciousness arose among the Ruthenians or Little Russians, which by the end of World War I developed into an acute nationalism. That is no concern of mine here, and I mention it for only one reason: a manifestation of this nationalism was to refuse the name Ruthenian, because that is what their foreign governors, Poles, Hungarians, etc., called

---

[18] In the West the Russians were first called Ruthenes and then Muscovites. The White Russians are better called Byelorussians, to distinguish them from the other "White" Russians, so called because they opposed the "Red" revolution.

MAXIMOS IV SAYEGH

Patriarch of Antioch and All the East,
and of Alexandria and Jerusalem

RUSIN CHURCH IN PODKARPATSKA RUS

CATHEDRAL OF ORADEA MARE, RUMANIA

CHURCH OF THE RUSSIAN COLLEGE, ROME

them. The majority call themselves Ukrainians.[19] However, so far as the Catholics are concerned "Ruthenian" is still their official *ecclesiastical* designation, and so I employ it in this book, varying it by "Ukrainian" when it seems convenient to do so: I use both terms without any political significance whatever.

GENERAL ECCLESIASTICAL HISTORY

St Vladimir, the first Christian prince of Russia, was a Northman and his capital Kiev, "the God-protected mother of Russian cities", was the heart of what is known now as Ukraine. For two hundred and fifty years it was the political and ecclesiastical centre of Russia, and the chief hierarchs continued to call themselves metropolitans of Kiev for two hundred years after they had resided at Moscow. Accordingly, for all the time from 989 until the Metropolitan Isidore had to flee from Moscow in 1443 after promulgating the Union of Florence, the religious history of the Ruthenians was much the same as that of the Russians in general (see pp. 120-121).

In 1458 Pope Pius II nominated a monk called Gregory to be metropolitan of Kiev, and by arrangement with Casimir IV of Poland he was allowed to exercise jurisdiction over the eight eparchies of the Kiev ecclesiastical province that were then under the control of Poland and Lithuania.[20] This lasted only till the beginning of the sixteenth century, when they slipped back into schism. During the second half of that century the Jesuits came to Vilna, Yaroslav, Polotsk and elsewhere and at once set themselves to work for the definitive reunion of the Ruthenian bishops and their flocks, the leading spirits being Father Peter Skarga (d. 1612) and Father Antony Possevino (d.1611). At length in 1595 Michael Ragoza, metropolitan of Kiev, and the bishops of Vladimir, Lutsk, Polotsk, Pinsk and Kholm met at Brest-Litovsk in Lithuania and petitioned the Holy See to admit them to its communion, and on December 23 the reunion was solemnly proclaimed in Rome. Only the bishops of Lvov[21] and Peremyshl stood out.

[19] Historically, this is the less significant name of the two. *Ukraine* only means the "borderland" or "marches".

[20] All White Russia and Ukraine west of Kiev was under the suzerainty of Poland and Lithuania from the middle of the fourteenth century till 1772-1795.

[21] This Russian spelling is the easiest for English-speakers. *Lviv* is Ukrainian, *Lwow* Polish, *Lemberg* German, and *Leopolis* Latin.

Just as the Eastern schism was brought about largely through political, social and cultural considerations, so these had their part in the Union of Brest. Among them were the desire of the Polish crown to unify the peoples of its dominions, the wish of the Holy See to consolidate a Christian *bloc* against the Turks, and the hope of some of the Orthodox leaders to raise the moral and intellectual level of their clergy to that of the Western clergy. The secular factors contributed much to the bitterness of the struggle that followed. The enemies of the union, led by the above two bishops and Prince Ostrozhsky, began a violent opposition; but Ragoza (d. 1600) was succeeded by two energetic and capable prelates, the second of whom was an outstanding figure in Ruthenian church history, Joseph Benjamin Rutsky, a convert from Calvinism. While he occupied the see of Kiev (1614-1637), the bishop of Polotsk, Josaphat Kunsevich, was slain out of hatred of the faith in November, 1623; fourteen years later his chief opponent Melety Smotritsky himself became a Catholic.[22]

In 1620, encouraged by the patriarchs of Constantinople and Jerusalem and after very many difficulties, a dissident hierarchy was set up side by side with the Catholic one, and eventually in 1632 the attacks of the Zaporozhsky Cossacks of the Dnieper forced the Polish king, Ladislaus VII, to recognize it; in the following year the city of Kiev was lost to the union, the famous Orthodox theologian, Peter Mogila, becoming its metropolitan. There followed a period of pressure and persecution from Orthodox Cossacks, Lutheran Swedes and Moslem Tartars that ended only with the election of John Sobieski to the throne of Poland in 1674. In 1692 the bishop of Peremyshl brought his flock into the Church, in 1677 the bishop of Lvov had done the same, and by 1702 schism had practically disappeared from Polish territory. The metropolitan continued to have the title of Kiev but lived at Radomysl, in Ukraine.

At this time the Ruthenian Catholics must have numbered about twelve millions, but during the seventeenth and eighteenth centuries practically the whole of the nobility and the bigger

---

[22] St Josaphat was canonized in 1867 and his feast extended to the Western church by Pope Leo XIII in 1882. We keep it on November 14. The Jesuit St Andrew Bobola was barbarously murdered by Cossacks near Pinsk in 1657. But the violence was not all on one side: an Orthodox abbot too, Athanasius of Brest, gave his life for conscience sake in 1648.

landowners (*boyary*) became polonized and passed to the Latin rite, in spite of a decree of Pope Urban VIII in 1624 that forbade them to do so. This divided and greatly weakened the faithful, many of whom had been reduced to serfdom by the Poles, for the trials that were to come.

Some writers do not scruple to represent the Galician Ukrainians since 1595 as "groaning under the yoke of Rome", held in unwilling submission to the Holy See by the governments and subservient prelates of Poland and Austria. It may be freely admitted that at the time of the Union of Brest methods were sometimes used by both sides that would not be tolerated by enlightened Christians today. But that these Ruthenians as a whole were sincere in their Catholicity their subsequent history shows; the loving flock of Andrew Szepticky were not unwilling Catholics longing for separation: there was unrest among them—but the sources of it were not to be found in Rome.

From early in the eighteenth century Russia began more and more to interfere with the internal affairs of Poland, and in 1772 there began that process known as "the partition of Poland", the earlier part of which was concluded in 1795.[23] The fate of the Ukrainians varied according to the power into whose hands they fell. Russia eventually got back all the territory in which there were any Ukrainians, except Galicia, and it soon became apparent that the government's intention was to obtain control over and then suppress those Catholics who were not Latins. Catherine II and Alexander I reduced the Ruthenian episcopal sees to three, monasteries were closed, and churches handed over to the Orthodox. Many of the Byzantine Catholics quietly accepted the new state of affairs; they could hardly see the difference—the church services were practically the same, and that was the main thing for them. But many others resisted, and after the Polish insurrection of 1830 more repressive measures were taken. An unfaithful Catholic, Joseph Siemashko, was nominated to the episcopate by Nicholas I and, on the death of the faithful Metropolitan

---

[23] To much of the territory acquired at this time (White Russia, Volhynia, part of Ukraine) Russia made a claim for which a case could be made. What happened in 1815 was quite another matter. The Russian statesmen themselves distinguished sharply between the "Western Lands" and "Congress Poland", and at first treated them quite differently from each other.

Bulgak in 1838, this man induced the two remaining bishops to sign, and over 1300 clergy to assent to, an act of union with the state Church of Russia. The czar had a medal struck to commemorate the occasion; it bore the inscription, "Separated by violence, in 1596, reunited by love in 1839". This was hardly in accordance with the facts, for the remaining clergy and very many of the lay people refused to follow them, so the government resorted to open force. Catholic baptisms and weddings were forbidden and Orthodox priests intruded into the churches; all religious houses were shut and their goods confiscated; those who resisted were flogged or exiled to Siberia, and 160 priests were degraded and imprisoned in remote monasteries. The Ruthenian Catholic church was dead in Russia. Only in the Kholm district, which was ceded by Austria in 1815 and was less severely dealt with, did it linger on till 1875 and even a few years longer.[24] When Nicholas II granted religious toleration in 1905 over 300,000 of these former Catholics and their children returned to the Church, one-third of whom were *Uporstvujushchie*, "Obstinates", old people who for thirty years and more had refused to attend the Orthodox churches; but as Catholic Byzantines were still illegal they had to become Latins.

THE GALICIAN RUTHENIANS

The story of the Ukrainians of Galicia, who came under the sway of Austria, was a less unhappy but far from satisfactory one. There were (apart from Kholm, which was to go to Russia in 1815) two episcopal sees, Lvov and Peremyshl; the Holy See in 1807 made Lvov an archbishopric, uniting with it the old metropolitan see of Galich, which had been revived a few years before. Two of the occupants of this see have been raised to the cardinalate, Michael Levitsky in 1856 and Silvester Sembratovich in 1895.[25] It was not till 1885 that the huge eparchy

[24] This grievous persecution was not primarily religious, but arose from the notion that every subject of the Russian state must be a member of the Russian church. The Latin Catholics of Poland also were persecuted, but their Catholicism was not regarded as so iniquitous because they were not Russians or regarded as "perverts from Orthodoxy". Nevertheless that Russia did not otherwise or in general oppress the Ukrainians is shown by the fact that, while Jews, Poles, Lithuanians and Great Russian sectaries emigrated wholesale, Ukrainians did not. Later Ukrainian emigration was from Austria-Hungary.

[25] Very few Orientals have been made cardinals. The office is radically in relation to the local church at Rome: that is why they are called "Cardinals of the Holy Roman Church".

of Lvov was reduced in area by forming a new one from it, Stanislavov.

Under the rule of the Austrian emperors the Ruthenians had full religious liberty; serfdom was abolished in 1848 and in 1860 Galicia was given a measure of civil autonomy and its own assembly. The Ruthenians, having lost their natural leaders by polonization, were all peasants, but from the middle of the nineteenth century a cultured and enterprising middle class began to develop and an *intelligentsia* made its appearance. For this they had to thank their married clergy, from whose children this new class was chiefly recruited. The Ruthenians were jealous of their former overlords the Poles, and the ill-feeling of the Poles was aggravated by the later policy of the Austrian government, which favoured the Ruthenians in order to counterbalance Polish influence and fostered the "Ukrainian movement" as a political move against Russia. On the other hand, the Ruthenians themselves were not of one mind politically: at the time of the outbreak of war in 1914 they were divided into five parties.

Their subsequent troubles did much to unite them. First they were suspected of pro-Russianism, and many were interned with considerable brutality, including 300 of the clergy. General Brusilov captured Lvov on 3 September 1914 and again many were interned or deported to Russia, this time on suspicion of being pro-Austrian and to conciliate the Poles. Among those deported was their archbishop, Andrew Szepticky. Full liberty was given to Orthodox clergy to cross the Podhorze and the Bug and do what they could with the Catholic Ruthenians. In circumstances in which there was so much, humanly speaking, in favour of schism, the solid Catholicity of the Ruthenians was well vindicated. Only twenty-nine priests turned Orthodox, and of these, twenty-seven were chased from their cures by their flocks; among the 1800 Ruthenian parishes of Galicia the state Church of Russia was able to establish only about one hundred temporarily in communion with itself.

At the end of 1917 a Ukrainian republic was proclaimed at Kiev and in October 1918 a Western Ukrainian republic at Lvov, whereupon Poland assumed sovereign authority over the whole of Galicia. From November 1918 the Ukrainians and the Poles were at war and the struggle was pursued with detestable bitterness and unscrupulosity on both sides. It is difficult to avoid the conclusion that a deliberate attempt was made by the Polish government to cut off the supply of Ukrainian clergy and cripple the resources of Ukrainian culture: but such misfortunes have overtaken both sides since then that it is better to be silent about the excesses of those days when these two peoples, both Slav and both Catholic, were at each other's throats. Ukrainian resistance was short-lived; and eventually, in 1923, in consideration of a promise (never fulfilled) by the Poles to give the Ukrainians an autonomous constitution, the Conference of Ambassadors confirmed Eastern Galicia as a province of Poland.

It is not difficult to imagine the results of these events—two deportations, two military invasions and a civil war—on the Ukrainian people and the Ruthenian church; their marvellous recovery was due in the first place to the activity and ability of Metropolitan Szepticky, who laboured day and night under the most trying difficulties both of the situation in itself and of obstacles deliberately put in his way. Andrew Szepticky was not only the greatest Eastern hierarch of his time, he was also one of the outstanding figures in the whole Church. He was only thirty-five when, in 1900, he was appointed to the see of Lvov and the primacy of the Galician Ukrainians. During the forty-four years of his episcopate his influence spread in a most remarkable way: he was recognized as the moral leader of Catholic Ukrainians abroad as well as at home, the Rusins of the Podkarpatska Rus looked up to him with love and reverence, many Orthodox Ukrainians and even Russians came under his spell—the spell of goodness, gentleness, sincerity and fearlessness. People sought his spiritual counsel from so far away as France and Holland and England, and the Holy See sent him on a visitation of the Ukrainians of the United States and Canada.

One who knew the Metropolitan Andrew intimately tells us that he humbly aspired to martyrdom. And in a real sense the last thirty of his eighty years of life were one long martyrdom. Persecuted and oppressed first by the Russian and then by the Polish government from 1914 to 1923; the great works of the

78

following constructive years—the monastic foundations, the seminary so carefully watched over, the tireless visitations, the great pastoral letters, the undertakings for the conservation and advancement of Ukrainian culture—all thrown down and trampled on when the Soviet army entered Lvov in 1939 and imprisoned him in his house; then the Nazis, and then the Russians again; the grinding sufferings of his children and neighbours, Ukrainians and Poles; and his own personal ill-health, which became almost complete physical paralysis and continual pain. But his great mind and noble spirit never failed.

Andrew Szepticky died on 1 November 1944.[26] His death marks the end of an epoch in the religious history of the Galician Ukrainians, an epoch that began with the Union of Brest-Litovsk in 1595 and the martyrdom of St Josaphat Kunsevich in 1623: it closes with this other martyr—and yet others. There ends, too, the troubled era, with its sad history of Ukrainian-Polish disagreements and mutual excesses, that in Galicia followed the restoration of Poland in 1919. For within a few months of the passing of the "Father Metropolitan" (as he liked to be called) the great political powers recognized the annexation of certain territory—"The Western Lands"— by the U.S.S.R. And Galicia is a part of this territory.

When the Russians occupied Galicia in 1939 Metropolitan Szepticky, his brother Abbot Clement, the aged Bishop Gregory of Stanislavov, and others were confined to their residences; a large "contribution" in money was imposed on the primate and the archiepiscopal properties were confiscated. Other ecclesiastical buildings were either heavily taxed or seized outright. All three diocesan seminaries were forcibly closed and turned into barracks, as well as the Studite and many of the Basilian monasteries and numerous convents of nuns, whose schools were taken from them. Clergy and religious were forbidden to enter schools, hospitals, orphanages, barracks, etc., and many were imprisoned. Printing-works, libraries and archives of ecclesiastical bodies were seized, church holidays suppressed, and a campaign of vilification of the clergy began. These measures were not enforced with equal rigour everywhere, and in country districts depended on the temper of the local in-

---

[26] The cause of his beatification has been introduced at Rome.

habitants. In general the staunchness of the faithful under these trials was superb, and indeed is said to have impressed the invaders. These were in due course driven out by the German counter-invasion; there were then more oppression, deportations and shootings, which did not intimidate Metropolitan Szepticky from denouncing Nazi persecution of Jews. And then the Russian armies returned—this time to stay.

Andrew Szepticky's successor was Joseph Slipy, who had been the metropolitan's archdeacon and rector of the Lvov seminary. He had been, like Joseph Bocian years before, secretly ordained bishop during the Soviet occupation in 1939, and narrowly escaped execution by the Russians when they were driven out by the Germans in 1941. At first the Russian attitude to the new metropolitan was somewhat conciliatory; he was even told that he was at liberty to communicate with the Holy See. But this was at the time when, with the permitted election of a patriarch, the official relations between church and state authorities in the U.S.S.R. were beginning to approximate in some respects to those of tsarist days; and consequently there developed in the Western Lands a religious situation analagous to that after the partitions of 1772-1795. Particularly in this: Latin Catholics may perhaps be tolerated, but Ukrainian Catholics of Byzantine rite—no. It would be hopeless for the Russians to try and convert Poles to Russian Orthodoxy, but the Polish Ukrainians are another matter—they already share in the Slav-Byzantine culture. Obviously it is desirable from the Soviet point of view to detach as many people as possible from ultimate allegiance to a religious leader outside the U.S.S.R.—the pope—and from membership in a closely-knit supranational church. They see this as clearly as did the imperial Catherine II, Alexander I and Nicholas I.

And sure enough, within a few weeks of Metropolitan Szepticky's death, the Orthodox Metropolitan Nikolay was sent by the Soviet government to Lvov to organize an attempt to bring the Galician Ukrainians into the Russian Orthodox Church. The degree of his success was little, and a few months later there was a development that showed how little: the Soviet police arrested Metropolitan Slipy of Lvov and his auxiliary, Bishop Niketas Budka (formerly exarch of the

Ruthenians in Canada), Bishop Gregory Chomyshyn of Stanislavov and his auxiliary, Bishop Ivan Latyshevsky, Bishop Nicholas Czarnecky and a large number of priests and deported them into the interior of Russia. The third diocesan bishop, Josaphat Kochylevsky of Peremyshl, despite the fact that he was still domiciled in Poland, was arrested also, together with his auxiliary, Bishop Gregory Lakota. Thus at one stroke the Catholic Ukrainians were deprived of their bishops.

The Soviet authorities found some tools for their work among the Catholics themselves: an "initiative group for the reunion of the Greek Catholics with the Russian Orthodox Church" was formed in 1945, and in it were certain priests representing each of the three dioceses, the chief being the archpriest Gabriel Kostelnyk. If we may judge from a manifesto signed by these men, Ukrainian nationalist passions helped to lead them astray.

In March 1946 this group, calling itself "the Synod of the Uniate Church in the Western Ukraine", reported to Marshal Stalin that the Union of Brest was revoked and that the Byzantine Catholics of the Western Ukraine had returned to the Russian Orthodox Church. In fact, only a handful of the clergy had followed Archpriest Kostelnyk and his fictitious "synod", and the laity remained faithful to Catholicity in overwhelming majority.

The alternative put before the people was rejection of Catholicity or deportation into the depths of the U.S.S.R., and in fact many tens of thousands were deported. Of nearly 3,000 diocesan priests (including those in Podcarpathia; see p. 95), 1,400 were jailed or deported, and 500 escaped abroad; presumably most of the rest have now succumbed to pressure— and that pressure must have been specially bitter for the many who were married. All monasteries, seminaries and convents of women were closed and their members scattered. And a large number of Ukrainians in the Polish part of the diocese of Peremyshl were forcibly "repatriated" in order to bring them under this tyranny.

In every respect this is a more brutal and unscrupulous repetition of the events of 1800-1875. No doubt it will be a long and difficult process to detach the hearts of Galician Ukrainians from their allegiance; but, deprived of their religious leaders and guides and of normal religious institutions and means of teaching, and cut off from the centre of unity at Rome, resistance cannot but weaken as the present generations pass away—unless some unpredictable change comes about in the situation. The section that follows must therefore be regarded in part as past history, a record of the situation in September 1939; and as a memory of the biggest and most important of the contemporary Catholic Eastern churches and of the greatest and best-beloved of its shepherds, the God-pleasing bishop Andrew Szepticky, and of his fellow bishops, of their clergy and of their flocks who were faithful, many of them at the price of life.[27]

STATE IN 1939

Organization. The Ruthenians or Ukrainians of Galicia formed a single ecclesiastical province containing, in spite of their numbers, only three eparchies, viz., Lvov, Peremyshl and Stanislavov. The archbishop's full style was "Archbishop of Lvov, Metropolitan of Galich and Bishop of Kamenets, Primate of Lodomeria", and his metropolitan powers were very extensive. Each see had a chapter of canons, an institution which the Ruthenians imported from the West.

Parochial clergy. The seminary of Lvov was founded in 1783 and had a very fruitful career; it entered on a new phase which seemed of much promise and importance in 1931, when it was erected into an academy of theology in fulfilment of the university aspirations that it had always had. In 1939 there were in the seminary about 220 theological students and 120 juniors. The other two eparchies also had seminaries, both established at the end of the eighteenth century. The Ruthenian College at Rome was founded in 1897, Emperor Francis Joseph of Austria providing a generous subsidy. It was first confided to the direction of the Ruthenian Basilian monks in 1904. It houses about 50 students. Of the 2150 secular priests in 1939, 77 per cent were married, but the celibate ideal was beginning slowly to gain ground; this had an important economic aspect, for while, as has been said, a married clergy has in the past been

---

[27] Of the seven bishops named above, all had died in durance by 1960, except Archbishop Slipy, who in the previous year was given another savage sentence.

a source of strength to Ukrainian religion and culture, never-theless the burden of a family was often very grievous to pastors in the poor rural parishes that predominated.

Religious institutes. The most interesting monastic body not only in Galicia but among all the Catholic Eastern churches is the *Studites*, of whom a brief account will be found on pages 211-212. They were, however, less in the public eye than the more numerous and old-established "Basilians", to whom the Ruthenians owe so much. At the time of the Union of Brest there was a number of monasteries among the Ruthenians, and within the next twenty years St Josaphat Kunsevich and Joseph Benjamin Rutsky had inaugurated a reform at the monastery of the Holy Trinity at Vilna. In 1617 this was organized as a congregation, with a superior general and a form of organization based on that of the Society of Jesus—already the monastic idea was being superseded. Before the suppression by Emperor Nicholas I in 1832 there were 96 Basilian monasteries in Lithuania, Russian Poland and Ukraine, and by 1882 what little remained of the Order of St Basil in Galicia was in dire need of reform, after having been for long the backbone of the Ukrainian clergy. In that year Pope Leo XIII entrusted the work to the fathers of the Society of Jesus, who carried it out with efficiency and thoroughness, beginning at the monastery of Dobromil. But the Ukrainian Basilians became in the process exactly like a Western religious congregation and, beginning as monks, have now become, in fact if not in name, clerks regular, though they are bound to choir-office. They take vows, tem-porary or solemn, and each religious is either a priest or a lay-brother; the last named must know some useful trade. In this capacity the Basilians have done a very great pastoral and educative work among the Catholic Ukrainians, especially in the country districts, and have carried their activities overseas to the Americas and elsewhere.

They had 36 houses, 182 priests, 220 scholastics and 213 lay-brothers in 1939, in several countries, but their numbers are now of course much reduced. They are known officially as *Basilians of St Josaphat*, and their abbot general (*protoarchi-mandrite*) resides in Rome. They have abandoned the traditional monastic dress of the East and wear a black tunic with hood, belt and cloak (*mandyas*), and their choir-office is recited, not sung. There were a score of monasteries in Galicia. At Zovkva the communists shot thirty-six out of thirty-eight monks, and the printing-house and library were partly destroyed and partly carried off to Kiev.

In 1913 Metropolitan Szepticky introduced some *Redemptorists* from Belgium into his eparchy, from whom have sprung a Byzantine vice-province of that congregation.

There were about a thousand Ukrainian nuns in Galicia, all engaged in active works of charity (except a few Studites). Three hundred of them were Basilians, and the rest belonged to local congregations.

The Faithful numbered about 4 million in Galicia and neighbouring territories. Some 90 per cent of them were peasants, and people of outstanding intelligence, cultural activity and farming ability among the huge block of peasant peoples that stretched from the Pindus Mountains to Danzig and from the Black Sea to Tirol. They remained faithful to communion with Rome throughout the generations of subjection to Polish and polonized Ukrainian landlords under the Polish and Austrian kingdoms, and during the difficult years under the Polish republic after World War I. What will be their future, God alone knows.

Bukovina. There were some 70,000 Catholic Ukrainians in Bukovina, all of which territory was part of the Rumanian kingdom after 1918. In 1930 they were organized separately under an episcopal vicar of the Rumanian bishop of Maramures. In 1940 the U.S.S.R. annexed the northern part of Bukovina, where most of these Catholic (and many more Orthodox) Ukrainians live.

THE EMIGRANTS

UNITED STATES OF AMERICA. From 1879 there have been emigrations of Ruthenians to the United States, both from Galicia and Podcarpathia. The first priest to be sent was Father Ivan Valansky, who in 1886 opened the first Catholic church of the Byzantine rite in America, at Shenandoah, Pennsylvania. The number of immigrants increased rapidly and in 1907 Pope

Pius X appointed a bishop of their rite for them, not, however, as ordinary at first but as an auxiliary to the local Latin bishop; he was Soter Ortynsky, the first Eastern Catholic bishop in America.

The arrival of numerous Byzantine Catholics in the country was naturally fraught with difficulties. Not only did they bring with them their own political and national rivalries (e.g., between Galicians and Podcarpathians)—this was perhaps to be expected; but they also had a bad reception, or none at all, from their Latin brethren in the United States. It is difficult to write of this matter in measured terms, so I quote the words of the late Andrew Shipman, of New York: "These Ruthenians have continued to practise their ancient Greek-Slavonic rites and usages . . . strange to the Catholic accustomed only to the Roman rite, and (they) have made (the Ruthenians) objects of distrust and even active dislike." Those words were written fifty years ago, and there has been a considerable change since then. A greater knowledge of our Eastern brethren, fostered by numerous publications, by the work of St Michael's Guild, and by such things as the annual conference on Eastern rites sponsored by Fordham University, has led to better understanding and therefore to better relations. Ignorance, however, is still not entirely a thing of the past.

The question of a celibate secular clergy was for long one of the chief difficulties. The bishops of the United States found the presence of married priests embarrassing, and a Roman instruction of 1890, confirmed by the apostolic letter *Ea semper* of 1907, decreed that only celibate Ruthenian priests should be admitted to or ordained in North America. This, and other innovations in their customs, was strongly resented, the Orthodox made the most of them, and 10,000 Ruthenians joined the dissidents. Eventually the Holy See did not enforce the prohibition of married priests in the United States (though no married men may be ordained there) and otherwise modified *Ea semper*, but further legislation by the decree *Cum data* in 1929 again caused trouble and more defections.[28]

In 1924 the Ruthenians were put under the direct jurisdiction

---

[28] An excellent article on this subject was written by Father Desmond A. Schmal in the *Ecclesiastical Review* (Washington, D.C.) for November, 1937. For Shipman and his fine work, see Pallen's *Memorial of Andrew J. Shipman* (New York, 1920).

of two bishops of their rite, one for the Podcarpathians and the other for the Galicians.

PRESENT STATE

Organization. In 1958 the Ruthenians from Galicia, Ukrainians, were given a regular hierarchy. The metropolitan see is at Philadelphia, with a bishopric at Stamford in Connecticut. Bishop Constantine Bohachevsky was named archbishop, and his auxiliary, Bishop Ambrose Senyshyn, was appointed to Stamford (The latter, a Basilian monk, was the first Eastern Catholic bishop to be consecrated in the New World).

Parochial clergy. In 1960 these eparchies had 286 diocesan and regular priests. A senior seminary was opened in Washington, D.C., in 1941, and there is an old-established junior seminary at Stamford.

Religious institutes. There is an American province of the *Basilian* monks, whose provincial superior resides in New York City. They have a house of studies at Glen Cove, L.I., and an important establishment in Chicago, with the fine church of St Nicholas. The Franciscan *Friars Minor* have Byzantine communities at New Canaan, Conn., and Sybertsville, Pa., and the *Redemptorists* of Byzantine rite a house at Newark, N.J. All these religious are engaged in missionary work. The *Basilian nuns*, who teach in schools and conduct orphanages, have their provincial house in Philadelphia, with a women's college at Fox Chase Manor, Pa., and a house of studies in Washington, D.C. The *Sisters Servants of Mary Immaculate* also teach in schools and have homes for the aged. These sisters were founded in Galicia in 1892, by Hieromonk Jeremias Lomnitsky.

The Faithful. There are in 1960 about 312,000 Catholic Ukrainians in the United States, the biggest concentrations being in Pennsylvania, New York, New Jersey, Connecticut and Massachusetts. They now have an assured place in American religious and social life, with great promise for the future.

CANADA

Ruthenian emigration to Canada began in the nineties of the past century, chiefly from Galicia. The first church, SS.

Vladimir and Olga's, was opened at Winnipeg in 1900, with a Slovak pastor, Father Damascene Polivka, but the dearth of clergy was so chronic for so long that many of the immigrants associated themselves with one or other of the Protestant bodies. The first priests to come to the rescue, at the instance of Mgr Langevin of St Boniface, were French-Canadians and Belgian Redemptorists (Father Achille Delaere was their moving spirit), who soon were allowed to adopt the Byzantine rite. In 1912, at the instance of Metropolitan Szepticky, the Holy See appointed a bishop as exarch with personal jurisdiction over the Ukrainians of Canada; but the shortage of clergy continued to be so great that the religious state of the people was still far from satisfactory. The rule against married priests meant, practically, that only widowers and monks could be sent from Europe, and the supply of American-born priests was insufficient. For a time, too, the attitude of Canadian Latins towards Eastern Catholics was as unhelpful as in the United States.

PRESENT STATE

Organization. After a gradual increase in the number of bishops, a regular hierarchy was set up in Canada in 1956. The metropolitan see is as Winnipeg, with bishoprics of Edmonton, Saskatoon and Toronto. These bishops have jurisdiction over Ukrainians and all other Ruthenians in Canada, whatever their country of origin.

Parochial clergy. Of the numerous parishes and missions in Canada, only a minority have resident priests; the remainder are ministered to at regular intervals from missionary centres. The total clergy numbered 267 in 1960. Bishop Basil Ladyka established a junior seminary, and senior students prepare for the priesthood in various Latin seminaries and those of religious orders.

Religious institutes. The headquarters of the Canadian province of *Basilian* monks is at their large establishment at Edmonton in Alberta, and they have another big monastery, with the novitiate, at Mundare in the same province. The monks have residences in a number of other places.[29] The

[29] The Basilian monks in Canada must not be confused with members of the Western-rite Congregation of St Basil, whose headquarters is at Toronto.

Byzantine-rite *Redemptorists* form a Canadian province, whose provincial house is at Winnipeg, with a seminary at Waterford, Ontario. They have important centres at Yorkton and Ituna in Saskatchewan and Roblin in Manitoba, and are responsible for numerous mission-stations. There are also two Byzantine *Oblates of Mary Immaculate*, that congregation to which the whole Church in Canada owes so much. An important college at Yorkton is conducted by the *Christian Brothers*.

At Woodstock in Ontario there is a small monastery of contemplative *Studite* monks. They represent the tiny remnant of Metropolitan Szepticky's famous foundation in Galicia (see p. 211), who after many vicissitudes arrived in Canada in 1951. They are under the jurisdiction of the Benedictine abbot of St Procopius's at Lisle, in the United States.

As elsewhere, the *Sisters Servants of Mary Immaculate* conduct schools, orphanages, hospitals and homes. Their mother-house for all North America is at Toronto, and they play an indispensable part in building up their church in the New World. The *Missionary Sisters of Charity* were founded by the hieromonk Mark Romanovich at Grimsby, Ont., in 1946.

The Faithful number 221,000 in 1960, mostly farming in Alberta, Saskatchewan and Manitoba, though there are numbers in Winnipeg, Montreal and other cities. Seventy years ago there were no Ukrainians in Canada; today they hold an acknowledged and respected position in their new home. Both in Canada and the United States those who have been able to avail themselves of "higher education" have done so well as strongly to confirm the high opinion of Ukrainian abilities that is current in Europe. Except for the smaller bodies mentioned below, the Ukrainians and Rusins of North America are the only Catholic Ruthenians left leading a normal free life in a free country, and with their ecclesiastical organization unimpaired. Theirs is a great responsibility, to uphold before the world and in the Church the great traditions of Slav-Byzantine Catholicity.

OTHER COUNTRIES

The few thousand Ukrainians scattered in other parts of the world before 1939 were unprovided with churches, except

UKRAINIAN CHURCH OF ST NICHOLAS, CHICAGO

ORDINATION OF A MELKITE BISHOP

Patriarch Maximos IV invests Bishop Elias Zoghby with the enkolpion

METROPOLITAN ANDREW SZEPTICKY

(*See page* 78)

Fr P. Maluga

METR. JOSEPH SLIPY
(*See page* 80)

BP THEODORE ROMZA
(*See page* 95)

Fr S. Eiletz

BP JOHN SUCIU
(*See page* 108)

EXARCH LEONID FEODOROV
(*See page* 121)

at Brussels and Vienna, where there is the fine baroque church of St Barbara, taken from the suppressed Jesuits in 1775 and made the chapel of an ecclesiastical college for Ruthenians and Rumanians by Empress Maria Teresa. It became a parish-church for Byzantines in 1784 and has had a very eventful history. A seminary was attached thereto from 1852 till 1892. It is now served by Basilian monks, who are establishing a monastery, house of studies and parish there. As a result largely of the war of 1939-45 Catholic Ukrainians and other Ruthenians are now found in considerable numbers in the following countries.

England and Wales. Ukrainians resident in England and Wales number about 20,000. Their first church (1947) was that of St Theodore of Canterbury in Saffron Hill, London, and they now have churches in Manchester, Rochdale, Bradford, Nottingham, Wolverhampton and Bedford. In some other places the Liturgy is celebrated in Latin-rite churches. A convent of Sisters Servants of Mary Immaculate has been opened at Bradford. In 1957 the archbishop of Westminster was appointed ordinary of these immigrants, for whom he has a vicar general of their rite.

France. There are some 40,000 Ukrainians and Rusins in France, where there is an episcopal exarch at their head.

Germany. The 18,000 Ukrainians and others in Germany form an exarchate, with a bishop of their rite whose residence is at Munich. The visitor apostolic appointed during the last war to look after Ukrainians deported to Germany, the greatly-loved Father Peter Werhun, died in a labour camp in Siberia in 1957.

The rest of the Ruthenians in western Europe are in the charge of a visitor apostolic, who is resident in Belgium.[30]

Argentine. There are said to be over 100,000 Catholics of Eastern rites in this country, many of them Ruthenians. Their ordinary is the archbishop of Buenos Aires, who has an auxiliary bishop for them.

Brazil. There are said to be another 130,000 such Catholics in Brazil. Their ordinary is the archbishop of Rio de Janeiro, who

---

[30] At the time of writing he is Archbishop John Buchko; he was an auxiliary bishop of Archbishop Slipy at Lvov, but escaped deportation in 1945 through being in Italy at the time.

has a Byzantine auxiliary bishop for the Ruthenians, who first settled in the state of Parana. Many of the clergy are Basilian monks, who form a Brazilian province of their order.

There are another 30,000 or so Ruthenians in *Paraguay* and *Uruguay*, subject to the local bishops.

Australia. There is a Byzantine episcopal exarch at Melbourne for the Ruthenians in Australia, New Zealand and Oceania. They are nearly all very newcomers, and number about 30,000 altogether.

PARTICULAR CUSTOMS

A number of modifications have been introduced into the Byzantine liturgy and customs by the Ruthenians in the past three hundred years. While none of these innovations were necessary, and some of them are definitely undesirable, it is to be noted that some points of divergence from standard Russian usage so far from being innovations are precisely those observances which were swept away by the patriarch of Moscow, Nikon, in the seventeenth century, whereby the great schism of the Starovery was caused.[31]

Apart from certain differences in the text, the following are among the changes made (particularly by the Synod of Zamosc in 1720); but they are not universal or uniform in all Ukrainian or Rusin churches: the amice and alb are worn in place of the *stikharion*; a large paten and purificator are used instead of the *diskos* and sponge, and ripidia have disappeared; after the *proskomide* the holy doors of the *eikonostasis* are opened and so remain throughout the Liturgy; the order of some of the chants is altered; the words *i ot Syna* (*Filioque*) are added to the creed and reverences are made at "his only Son" and "was made man"; at the consecration and elsewhere a small bell is rung; hot water is not put into the chalice before communion, nor blessed bread distributed; the people receive the Blessed Sacrament in both kinds from a spoon, but usually kneeling; washings of the fingers have been introduced; the vessels are left on the altar till the end of the Liturgy; and there is a sequence of liturgical colours for vestments, elsewhere unknown

---

[31] Metropolitan Szepticky reconciled a number of these "Old Believers" to the Catholic Church, and gave them a small church at Lvov wherein all their traditional rites and customs were observed.

in the East. A deacon is rarely seen assisting at the Liturgy except in cathedral and monastic churches, and then he is often a priest. Concelebration tends to take place only on certain pontifical occasions, with the result of the appearance of side-altars in large churches.

The eikon of the feast is displayed on a small flat table (*tetrapod*) which also bears a crucifix and candles, and stands before the middle of the *eikonostasis*. But some churches in America and other places have no *eikonostasis*, and even allow the presence of round statues. The herding of the people into pews has led to a certain "stiffening" of public worship in many places.

The ordinary dress of bishops is the same as in the West, and other clergy wear a plain black cassock; the characteristic Ruthenian round cap is still occasionally seen. Practically all the clergy are now clean-shaven (even the monks), and the conferring of Roman honorific titles on distinguished priests has led to the wearing of the corresponding costumes.

In the bull *Apostolatus officium* by which Pope Benedict XIII confirmed the acts of the Synod of Zamosc there was a note of warning against spoiling the integrity of the Byzantine liturgy, and in approving the *typikon* (constitutions) of the Studite monks in 1923 the Sacred Eastern Congregation declared: "It is the wish of this Congregation that the monks observe the Byzantine rite in all its purity, getting rid of all alterations whatever in use among the Ruthenian people and sanctioned by the Synod of Zamosc." Ruthenian "hybridization" is continually used as an argument to prove that "Rome does not really respect the Eastern rites" and to dissuade dissident Orientals from returning to unity. In fact, the new edition of the service books prepared in Rome provides for the abandonment of these peculiarities where the people wish it; but many of the clergy and people are attached to the old ways as "our tradition", and in any case small immigrant congregations are often handicapped by limited resources. But that is no reason why their churches should sometimes be almost indistinguishable from Western churches which the "liturgical movement" has not yet reached.

For the ministration of the sacraments (especially Penance)

and other rites, the Byzantine offices have been here and there interpolated with elements and prayers translated into Church-Slavonic from the Roman books, without a shadow of necessity. In the wedding rite emphasis has been put on the mutual consent and hand-clasp to such a degree that the crowning has lost its traditional place of importance. An Eastern usage that the Ruthenians might well have got rid of they have preserved: the Julian calendar. Their objection to going to a Latin church even when no other is available is unhappily largely due to their historical relations with the Poles, which have tended to make them suspicious and hostile toward all Latin Catholics. Such an attitude, whether among Easterners or Westerners, shows an insufficient understanding of what Catholic Christianity really means.

A number of less ancient Western feasts have been introduced, sometimes with altered date: e.g., Corpus Christi, the Holy Trinity, the Sacred Heart, Christ the King. Among the holy days are St Josaphat of Polotsk, St Vladimir and his two sons, SS. Boris and Gleb. Habits of fasting have been modified. Ukrainians have happily ensured the preservation of their lovely church music; in Galicia their distinctive church buildings, many of them in wood, were of great interest and beauty. Like most Catholic Orientals the Ruthenians now use the Western rosary, but their version of the Hail Mary is different and includes a mention of the mystery pertinent to each decade. They also have the stations of the cross and other devotions.

BIBLIOGRAPHY

O. Halecki, *From Florence to Brest* (Rome, 1958).

A. Guépin, *Saint Josaphat et l'Église gréco-slave*, 2 vols. (Paris, 1897-98).

E. Unger-Dreiling, *Josafat, Vorkämpfer und Märtyrer* (Vienna, 1960).

S. Konovalov, *Russo-Polish Relations* (London, 1945).

M. Korczok, *Die griechisch-katholische Kirche in Galizien* (Leipzig, 1921).

C. Korolévsky, *Le métropolite André Szeptyckyj* (Grottaferrata, 1920).

A. Delaere, *Mémoire sur les tentatives de schisme . . . des Ruthènes de l'Ouest canadien* (Quebec, 1908).

A. Dmytrievsky, *L'union des églises et les persécutions polonaises en Ukraine* (Brussels, 1939).

White Book on the Religious Persecution in Ukraine (Rome, 1953).

Eastern Churches Quarterly, vol. vi, no. 6 (1946), English translation of Pius XII's encyclical letter "Orientales omnes", on the 350th anniversary of the Union of Brest and the current persecution; vi, 8 (1946), the Ukrainians in U.S.A.; xii, 5 (1958), the Ukrainians in Canada.

A. Senyshyn, *Christ with Us* (Stamford, Conn., 1954). The Liturgy of St John Chrysostom, Ukrainian use; text, transliteration and translation.

Directory, Byzantine Rite Province of Philadelphia (Philadelphia, Pa., 1960).

4. THE PODCARPATHIAN RUTHENIANS
or RUSINS

Probably since the year 1339, certainly since the middle of the fifteenth century, there has been a settlement of Ruthenians and Byelorussians on the southern side of the Carpathians, at the eastern end of Slovakia. This district has been called by various names—Ruthenia, Subcarpathia, Podcarpathia, Podkarpatska Rus, Zakarpatskaya; Rusins is a convenient appellation for the people who live there. They early came under Hungarian rule, and they had ecclesiastical contacts with both Transylvania and Constantinople.

In 1646 a number of Rusin clergy and laity returned to Catholic communion, the Union of Uzhorod (Ungvár), and the movement spread, very slowly, to all the people. A bishop for them was named in 1651; but he and his successors were simply vicars apostolic, very troublesome conflicts of jurisdiction arose with the Latin primate and bishops of Hungary, and there were constant difficulties. Eventually these were resolved in 1771 when Pope Clement XIV, at the request of Queen Maria Teresa, re-established the Ruthenian eparchy of Mukachevo (Munkács), suffragan to the primate of Hungary. The first bishop, Andrew Bachynsky, was an outstanding figure in Rusin church history. With the liberal help of the empress-queen he built up and equipped the diocese; it was he who fixed the episcopal residence at Uzhorod and established the seminary there, and his personal character was as attractive as his public work was effective. Another see was set up in 1818, at Preshov in Slovakia.

During the nineteenth century the magyarizing and latinizing policy of the Hungarian government caused much discontent among the Rusins, and, especially after a Russian missioner, Father Alexis Kabaluk, arrived among them in 1910, some of them left the Church. The Hungarians tried to stop this movement by force; in 1913, for example, thirty-two Rusin peasants were sent to prison on the occasion of their professing dissident Orthodoxy.

In the course of World War I the Hungarian government was even more oppressive to the Rusins, on the ground that they were pro-Russian; consequently, when after the war Hungarian authority was removed and the Podkarpatska Rus became part of Czechoslovakia, all was set for schism. It broke out seriously in 1920, and was fomented for political ends by elements in the Czech government. The leading Orthodox missioner was a Russian monk of Pochaev in Poland, Father Vitaly, who had founded a monastery and book-publishing house in Slovakia. Within three years seventy villages, involving 100,000 people, had turned Orthodox. The cause was, as so often, fundamentally racial and cultural. The Rusins were very conscious of their affinities with the northern Slavs, and their experience was that the policy of the local Catholic authorities, civil and ecclesiastical, was to make them Magyar or Slovak; moreover their clergy, often trained in Hungarian seminaries, had got culturally and socially out of touch with their peasant flocks.

Very few of these clergy took part in the separatist movement, and after a time the schism was to a considerable extent mended. But it left a deep wound. It is an excellent example of an unresolved "social conflict" being at the bottom of religious separatism.

There is no need to go into the political manoeuvres as the result of which the U.S.S.R. annexed the Podkarpatska Rus during World War II. It is sufficient to say that the religious position of the Catholic Rusins there is the same as that of their brethren in Galicia: all schools, monasteries, convents and the like were closed, churches seized, other property confiscated, and the faithful subjected to the strongest pressure to enter into communion with the Russian Orthodox Church.

In 1947 the bishop of Mukachevo, the holy Theodore Romza, met his death in circumstances that pointed to murder by the Soviet authorities. Soon afterwards the persecution spread to Slovakia, and Bishop Paul Goydich of Preshov (Eperies) and his auxiliary, Bishop Basil Hopko, were thrown into jail; the death there of the first named took place in 1960. The death of

Father Alexander Chyra, said to have been secretly ordained bishop by Bishop Romza, appears to have been deliberately compassed. Clergy and people stood out solidly against their oppressors, but the liquidation of the Rusin Catholic church was officially announced in 1950.

STATE IN 1939

Organization. There were two eparchies, Mukachevo (with residence at Uzhorod) and Preshov. Both cathedrals had chapters of canons. Before 1939 it had been projected to make the Rusins a complete ecclesiastical province, under a metropolitan with one or more suffragans.

Parochial clergy. These were trained in the college of their rite at Uzhorod or in Latin seminaries. They were mostly married, and a French observer who knew them well characterizes them as "well-instructed, kindly, of a real Christian spirit . . . worthy of all respect, of simple habits free from pretensions and 'bossiness' "; but the priesthood tended to pass from father to son and as it were to form a sacerdotal caste.

Religious institutes. There were three monasteries of *Basilians* (see p. 83), and two small houses of Byzantine *Redemptorists.*

The Faithful are nearly all peasants, very self-sufficient and particularist, but sincerely religious. They have been called the "poorest peasants in Europe", but under the Czechoslovak government they fared considerably better than many minorities in other countries and their state was improving. Unfortunately there was something of a gap, social and cultural, between them and their better educated clergy. They numbered over half a million in 1939.

THE EMIGRANTS

UNITED STATES OF AMERICA

The first Rusins appeared in America at about the same time as the first Ukrainians from Galicia; but whereas in Europe the Catholic Ukrainians outnumbered the Rusins by some seven to one, the numerical difference in the United States is not nearly so great. This is in part due to the fact that in the

United States the Rusin organization includes the Slav-Byzantine Catholics who originate in the plain of Hungary and Yugoslavia as well as those who come from Podkarpatska Rus and Slovakia. The Rusins were subject to the same difficulties and played a conspicuous part in the troubles that disturbed the first fifty years of the Ukrainian immigration, as narrated above. There was considerable ill-feeling between various groups and interests concerned, and after the decree *Cum data* of 1929 a number of Rusins seceded and formed a schismatic body in communion with the Orthodox. These troubles were of an extremely complex nature, involving not only questions of rite and discipline but also political, social, economic, psychological and personal considerations.

A decisive step in restoring order was taken in 1924, when the Holy See appointed a special bishop-in-ordinary for the Rusins in the United States. Bishop Basil Takach had a long and difficult episcopate (he died in 1948), and the present flourishing American Rusin church owes a very great deal to his labours.

PRESENT STATE

Organization. The Rusins and other non-Galician Ruthenian elements in the United States form an exarchate, whose bishop resides at Pittsburgh and has an auxiliary bishop. The present exarch is Bishop Nicholas Elko, appointed in 1955.

Parochial clergy. In 1960 these numbered about 210, and there were 190 parishes, of which a large proportion are in Pennsylvania. The fine seminary of SS. Cyril and Methodius was opened in Pittsburgh in 1950.

Religious institutes. There is a *Basilian* house at Uniontown, Pa., and a priory of Byzantine *Benedictines* at Butler, Pa.; the latter was established from Lisle Abbey in 1948. There are also Byzantine *Friars Minor* ministering in the exarchate. *Basilian nuns* conduct schools, orphanages and homes. Their mother-house at Mount St Macrina is a place of pilgrimage to our Lady of Perpetual Help. A congregation of *Benedictine nuns* for work in the exarchate is in process of formation. A secular teaching institute, the *Sisters of Christ the Teacher*, was started in 1960.

The Faithful numbered 221,000 in 1960.[32] They are becoming highly americanized; as a Rusin priest has put it: "What Roman-rite Catholics fail to realize when they speak of our Byzantine rite is that we are slowly but surely being transformed into the American Byzantine rite." That can involve things both good and less good, and the process calls for much tact and imagination in the clergy and a high standard of religious education in the laity.

Canada. The Podcarpathian Ruthenians of Canada are organized with their Galician brethren (cf. pp. 86-87). The same is the case in other countries.

PARTICULAR CUSTOMS

The particulars already given of the modification of the Slav-Byzantine rite in Galicia apply also to the Podcarpathian Ruthenians with but small differences. The Rusins have always been noted for general congregational participation in the liturgical singing, their traditional music being a variation of that of the Galician Ruthenians. The wooden churches of the Podkarpatska Rus, especially those built in the Boiko and Hucul styles, are extremely attractive: certain features are, curiously enough, reminiscent of Far-Eastern architecture; others, less curiously, remind one of the timber churches of Scandinavia.

It is in accordance with what has been said above that Rusins in the United States should be more in favour of an English liturgy than are some Eastern Catholics there. On the other hand, the surprising borrowings from Western custom witnessed in some of their churches are less easily defended; they are not an aspect of legitimate americanization. But no doubt the seminary chapel at Pittsburgh may be taken as an augury of better things.

BIBLIOGRAPHY

J. B. Heisler, *Carpatho-Ukraine* (London, 1946).

M. Lacko, *Unio Uzhorodensis Ruthenorum carpaticorum cum Ecclesia catholica* (Rome, 1955).

[32] In America they are now generally called simply Ruthenians in distinction from the Ukrainians.

B. Pekar, *De erectione canonica eparchiae Mukacoviensis* (Rome, 1956).

Fr Vassily, "The Podcarpathian Schism" in *Pax*, nos. 147 and 150 (Prinknash Abbey, 1934).

Eastern Churches Quarterly, vol. vi, no. 8 (1946). The Rusins in North America.

The Divine Liturgy of St John Chrysostom (Lisle Abbey, Ill., 1942). Rusin use.

J. P. Hanulya, *The Eastern Ritual* (Cleveland, O., 1942). Rusin use.

5. THE HUNGARIAN RUTHENIANS

The so-called Hungarians of the Byzantine rite are in fact Ruthenians from the Carpathians and some Rumanians who, living in the great Hungarian plain, have lost their own languages and become almost completely magyarized. For long they were divided between five Ruthenian and Rumanian eparchies, till in 1912 Pope St Pius X, to the satisfaction both of the faithful concerned and of the Hungarian civil authorities who feared the influence of foreign bishops, united them all into the new eparchy of Hajdudorog. After the war of 1914-1918 over half of the parishes concerned were returned to the jurisdiction of Rumanian bishops on the formation of the kingdom of Greater Rumania.

Since 1945 the faithful have shared the oppression of their fellow Catholics in Hungary but up to the present (1960) they have maintained a precarious exstence as an organized church. The well-known Basilian monastery and shrine of our Lady at Mariapocs have been forcibly closed by the communist government.

PRESENT STATE

Organization. The bishop of Hajdudorog is a suffragan of the Latin archbishop at Esztergom. His cathedral is at Hajdudorog, but he lives at Nyiregyhaza where he has another episcopal church, with a chapter of canons. Aspirants for the priesthood were trained in the general Ruthenian seminaries; some of the clergy are married. According to the *Annuario Pontificio* of 1960 there are still three religious houses of men and three of women in the diocese.

The Faithful. Even since the dismemberment of the eparchy in 1919 its subjects are still numerous, 195,000, mostly peasants, in 1948. The groups of Rusins round Miskolc are organized separately. In the United States Hungarian Ruthenians are included with the Rusins.

PARTICULAR CUSTOMS

The Byzantine rite is used according to the version of the Ruthenian liturgical books. But having lost their own language, the people of Hajdudorog found difficulty in maintaining their congregational singing in Slavonic, and a movement arose in the middle of the nineteenth century to substitute Magyar (Hungarian) as their liturgical language. From 1896 there was a long and complicated controversy on the subject, in which the policies of the civil authority were engaged; and in 1912 Rome imposed the use of Greek for all liturgical services and three years were given for the change to be effected. For several good reasons this did not take place (e.g., Greek—and Byzantine chant—was even more difficult for clergy and people to learn than Slavonic); accordingly, Magyar came more and more into use. In the 1920 edition of the Liturgies the Greek text of the anaphoras was printed parallel with the Magyar; but it was not used, and under Pope Pius XI the vernacular speech was recognized as the liturgical language in practice.

A Magyar version of the Liturgy of St John Chrysostom appeared so long ago as 1795; that of St Basil and other texts followed after 1850, but a complete translation of the Byzantine liturgical books has not hitherto been effected.

BIBLIOGRAPHY

C. Korolevsky, *Living Languages in Catholic Worship* (London, 1957), pp. 15-18, 23-45.

101

6. THE YUGOSLAVS

The small body of Catholic Yugoslavs of the Byzantine rite is made up of a nucleus of croatized Serbs to which other elements have been added. When Matthias Corvinus, king of Hungary, recaptured Bosnia from the Turks he established on the border military colonies of refugee Serbs (Uscochi, "refugees") of the Orthodox Church. They nominally came into communion with Rome but it was not made real until 1611, when their bishop, Simeon Vretanjić, was recognized by Pope Paul V as Byzantine vicar of the bishop of Zagreb. Simeon's profession of faith was received by St Robert Bellarmine, and he lived at the monastery of Marča, a centre for Serbian reunion, of which there was some talk at this time, many Serbs having fled into Hungary from the Turks (nine individual bishops were reconciled between 1596 and 1704). Other episcopal vicars followed, but the period was troubled and in 1739 Marča was burnt down by brigands at the instigation, it is said, of an Orthodox bishop. The Catholic Serbs of Croatia were given a diocesan bishop by Pope Pius VI in 1777; his see was at Križevci, under the primate of Hungary.

During the eighteenth century there was a migration of Podcarpathian Ruthenians to the southwest, and another of Galicians to Bosnia and Slavonia at the end of the nineteenth; there are also some Rumanians and Bulgarians from Macedonia in this heterogeneous collection, held together by the Catholic faith and their common Eastern rite.

PRESENT STATE

Organization. The bishop of Križevci, who is now a suffragan of the Latin archbishop of Zagreb, has jurisdiction over all Catholics of Byzantine rite in Yugoslavia. These Catholics share in the oppression to which Christians in that country are subjected; in 1945 Bishop Janko Šimrak was committed to prison by the partisans of Marshal Tito; in consequence of hardships then suffered he died in the following year. But the diocese does not seem to have been wholly disrupted, and is at present (1960) in charge of an episcopal administrator.

Parochial clergy are formed in the seminary of Zagreb (founded 1685), directed by Basilian monks. The parishes are arranged in archpresbyterates or deaneries. Most of the clergy are married. There is a cathedral chapter of four canons.

Religious institutes. There are, or were, *Friars Minor* of the Byzantine rite working in this eparchy, and several houses of *Basilian nuns.*

The Faithful total 56,000 souls, among whom Ruthenians are most numerous and the Serbs next. The last-named call themselves Croats and speak Serbo-Croat; the other elements conserve in a measure the language of their respective countries of origin. The people are nearly all peasants. Their principal centres are in upper Croatia, the Backa, Slavonia and Bosnia. A few have emigrated to North America, notably Cleveland and Chicago, where they are included with the Rusins. In Yugoslavia most Croats are Catholics of the Latin rite and the Serbs are Orthodox.

The common liturgical language of these people is Church Slavonic. They observe the Byzantine rite and usages in, on the whole, a high degree of purity.

Mention can be appropriately made here of a most remarkable man who, in the seventeenth century, devoted his life to the cause of the political union of all the Slavonic peoples under the leadership of Russia and their religious union under the leadership of Rome. This was Yuri Krizanić (1618-1683); he was a Croatian Catholic priest, of the diocese of Zagreb, whose attitude to the problem of the reconciliation of East and West anticipated much that is often regarded today as contemporary development. His eventful life and learned writings were forgotten till the nineteenth century, when they were rediscovered by the Russian "slavophils"; William Palmer wrote of him in *The Patriarch and the Tsar* (1871-1876). A sympathetic account of this man and his prophetic ideas by an Orthodox writer can be read in the *Eastern Churches Quarterly*, Nos. 7-8 of vol. iv (1941).

THE CHRISTIAN CHURCHES OF THE EAST

BIBLIOGRAPHY

G. Marcović, *Gli Slavi ed i Papi* (Zagreb, 1897), vol. ii, caps. 11-15.

J. Šimrak, *Graeco-catholica ecclesia in Yugoslavia* (Zagreb, 1931).

7. THE RUMANIANS

The Rumanians are in part descendants of the "veterans of Trajan", colonies of Romans chiefly from Illyria and Italy planted by him in the province of Dacia at the beginning of the second century of the Christian era; fusing with the Thracian natives, overrun by Visigoths, Gepids, Slavs and others, they gave rise to a new people, predominantly Latin in language and characteristics but modified by Slav and other influences.[33]

The first Dacian Christians were of the Latin rite (according to some, St Niketas of Remesiana was one of their evangelizers), and so remained until they were conquered by the Bulgars. Then in the ninth century they were subjected to Byzantine bishops, who imposed their own rite, and in due course the Rumanians were drawn into the schism of Constantinople. For long the Rumanians were dependent on the prelates of the Bulgarian and other churches; it was not till the fourteenth century (when Rumanian principalities independent of Turks, Hungarians and Poles began to be formed) that three separate metropolitans were given to Valachia and Moldavia. Damian, the Moldavian metropolitan, signed the act of union at the Council of Florence, but it was not acceptable to most of his church and he and his successor had to seek refuge in Rome.

In accordance with a decree of the Fourth Lateran Council, the Rumanians of Transylvania (Ardeal), which had been conquered by the Hungarians in the eleventh century, should have been given vicars of Byzantine rite by the Latin bishops of the conquerors; this was not done, however, and they gradually fell away. After the Council of Florence St John of Capistrano rallied 30,000 of them to union, but it lasted only about 25 years. The Protestant Reformation wrought havoc in Transylvania both among Latins and Orthodox, who became "Calvinist by creed, Eastern by certain externals". There was even a

[33] Rumanian is almost an Italian dialect, with a considerable foreign element in its vocabulary.

Calvinist "superintendent" for the Orthodox, and resisters were persecuted by their Hungarian and German masters. But in 1687 the Emperor Leopold I of Austria drove the Turkish overlords from this province, and the Jesuit chaplains of his army set themselves to deal with the religious situation.

THE CATHOLIC RUMANIANS

In 1697 the Orthodox metropolitan of Alba Julia, Theophilus Szeremy, moved by the reasoning of Father Ladislaus Baranyi, s.j., called a synod which signed an act of union with Rome. Within a few weeks Theophilus was dead, not without suspicion of having been poisoned. In the following year Athanasius Anghel Popa was consecrated bishop for Transylvania at Bucarest, where he was solemnly warned by the Orthodox patriarch of Jerusalem, Dositheos (who was visiting Rumania), of the dangers of Protestantism. Athanasius took the advice to heart—but not in a way Dositheos intended. On arrival at Alba Julia he got in touch with Father Baranyi, and in a few weeks had signed, together with thirty-eight protopopes (rural deans), a profession of faith and a declaration of desire to become "members of the holy Catholic Church of Rome".[34]

The bishop and archpriests had stipulated that their "discipline, church ritual, liturgy, fasts and customs remain unchanged; if not, neither do our seals bind us". Assurance was given of this, and in 1701 the union was finally confirmed at Vienna and Athanasius solemnly enthroned.[35]

The Calvinists were furious and the Orthodox no less; there was an outbreak of violence. For a time the union was in danger, but the Jesuits came to the rescue and the neo-Catholics were eventually stabilized. It was not till 1735-1751 that foreigners, Serbs mostly, stirred up the discontent which reduced the Catholics by half, from which are descended the dissident Orthodox in Transylvania today. Some of the effects of this were modified and the Catholics greatly strengthened and

[34] It must be noted that this reunion was not entirely inspired by disinterested conviction of the truth of "Roman claims" and abhorrence of schism: not entirely, and perhaps not even primarily. Fear of Protestantism and need of protection therefrom were apparently the principal motives of both Theophilus and Athanasius. Such unsatisfactory features have been at the root of many "reunions", and must be faced and taken into consideration. Sometimes the reunion is spoiled thereby *ab initio;* at other times, as in the case of the Rumanians, the reunion nevertheless works out well and becomes permanent.

[35] The theological basis of this reunion was the acceptance of the "four points" of Florence see p. 12).

encouraged by the activities of their fourth bishop, the holy Peter Paul Aron (1752-1764).

In 1721 the Latin bishop of Ardeal invoked canon 9 of the Fourth Lateran Council against the successor of Athanasius, John Pataky, claiming that Pataky was simply his "ritual vicar". Pope Innocent XIII replied by a declaration that Pataky was the bishop-in-ordinary of the Catholics of his rite, but that he should reside at Fagaras instead of Alba Julia; future bishops would be appointed on the presentation of the Austrian emperor. Empress Maria-Teresa obtained the erection of a second episcopal see in 1777, and two more followed in 1853, when Fagaras became an archbishopric.

A curious abuse, shared with the Orthodox, persisted among the Catholic Rumanians until the middle of the last century; namely, the granting of decrees of complete dissolution of marriage in cases of adultery.

On the establishment of the kingdom of Greater Rumania in 1919 the Byzantine Catholics found themselves for the first time under a sovereign of their own nationality; they were officially accorded the position of a "minority national church", and the period between the world wars was one of progress and prosperity. But in 1948 came ruin. After denouncing the concordat then in force with the Holy See, the communist government engineered a movement in favour of joining the Byzantine Catholics with the Rumanian Orthodox Church, which was supported by a small group of aggrieved Catholic priests; coercive methods were used in an endeavour to get others to follow them. The papal representative in Bucarest, Mgr Gerald O'Hara, and the whole Catholic hierarchy protested to the government; soon after, all six Byzantine bishops were arrested one by one. On December 1 a government decree was issued declaring that the Byzantine Catholic church in Rumania had ceased to exist.

It was Galicia and Podkarpatska Rus all over again. Since 1948, over fifty priests have been killed, 200 others are dead or disappeared, 200 are in prison, 200 at forced labour; lay people who are openly recalcitrant are discriminated against and coerced. Monastic communities of men and women were forcibly dispersed and their goods confiscated; seminaries and other institutions were closed, and churches handed over to the Orthodox. There are numerous moving records of faithfulness and selfless opposition among people of all kinds and degrees; as elsewhere, the Church lived on, underground, and the holy Mysteries were celebrated in secret.

In all this process the Orthodox patriarch at Bucarest, Justinian Marina, took an active and unworthy part, but in general the Rumanian Orthodox disapproved of what was going on. It is said that at one time over seventy of their priests were in jail for refusing to take over Catholic churches; and both at home and abroad prominent Rumanian Orthodox spoke out on behalf of their persecuted brethren, Archimandrite Stephen Lucaciu, for instance, and Professor Mircea Eliade.

By 1960 four of the Byzantine bishops had died in confinement, John Suciu, Valeriu Frentiu, John Balan and Basil Aftenie; two were still alive, Alexander Rusu and Iulu Hossu, but not at liberty. Among the other victims may be named Father Vladimir, of the ancient and noble family of Ghika. At the age of eighty he died in prison near Bucarest, after spending fifty years in the devoted service of his people. The Latin church in Rumania, whose members are mostly of foreign descent, Hungarian and German, still exists as an organization, but it, too, is subjected to bitter persecution; according to the *Annuario Pontificio*, only one of its five dioceses now has a bishop.

STATE IN 1948

Organization. The Catholic Rumanians of Byzantine rite formed an ecclesiastical province, consisting of the metropolitan see of Fagaras and Alba Julia (residence at Blaj), with the four suffragan sees of Gherla and Cluj, Oradea Mare, Lugoj and Maramures (residence at Baia Mare). The archbishop of Fagaras had jurisdiction over the small minority of Catholics of his rite who lived in the "Old Kingdom", including Bukovina. All five bishops were *ex officio* senators of the realm. Representatives of all the clergy had an advisory voice in the selection of the metropolitan, who had almost patriarchal powers. The cathedrals had chapters of canons.

Parochial clergy. These numbered 1,800, of whom some

90 per cent were married. There were seminaries for their training at Blaj, Oradea Mare and Cluj, a Rumanian College was erected at Rome in 1930, and a faculty of Catholic theology was granted in the national University of Bucarest in 1932. The parishes were arranged in deaneries, of which the deans, called "protopopes", had considerable powers, constituting an ecclesiastical court of first instance.

Religious institutes. For long there were no monks or nuns left among the Catholic Rumanians;[36] but by 1948 the *Basilians* had an important monastery at Bixad, with a much-frequented shrine of our Lady, and four smaller houses. In 1930 the *Conventual friars minor* opened a college at Oradea Mare for Byzantine candidates for their order. The *Assumptionists* had a vice-province of the Byzantine rite in Rumania, and in 1938 they transferred their Institute of Byzantine Studies from the shores of the Bosporus to Bucarest. They opened a special house for the formation of clergy at Blaj (the *Casa Domnului*, "Lord's House"), and were entrusted with the direction of the old-established *Pavelian* school at Beius, and other works.[37] The *Jesuits* provided for Byzantine candidates in their novitiate at Satu Mare, and there were *Brothers of the Christian Schools* at Oradea.

The Assumptionists opened Eastern convents of their Oblate sisters, and a teaching and nursing congregation, the *Sisters of the Holy Mother of God*, founded by Metropolitan Suciu, in 1921, had several houses.

The Faithful formed the second largest body of Catholic Orientals, over $1\frac{1}{2}$ million (the Latin Catholics are about $1\frac{1}{4}$ million), whose prestige and influence were out of all proportion to their numbers, especially in Transylvania, where the Orthodox had only a bare majority. The rural Rumanians are a pious people, and, in spite of the secular submission to foreign powers, the Rumanian professional classes in Transylvania were the elite of the country; the Catholic clergy laid the foundations of Rumanian literary and academic culture in the past century. Relations between Catholics and Orthodox were on the whole

[36] Thanks to Emperor Joseph II. He would allow only Hungarian monasteries in Transylvania, so Rumanian aspirants had either to turn Latin or Orthodox.

[37] Things had changed a lot since the days (1875-1888) when a seminary had to be taken from the charge of a certain Western congregation because all the best subjects were being enticed to become Latins and join it.

good, and strong opinions in favour of reunion were expressed by Orthodox clergy and publicists from time to time.

THE EMIGRANTS

United States. The first Catholic Rumanian church was opened at Cleveland in Ohio in 1906, due to the labours of Father Epaminondas Lucaciu. The faithful now number more than 5,000, with 17 parishes and churches, mostly in the neighbourhood of the southern end of Lakes Michigan and Erie. They are under the jurisdiction of the local Latin bishops. Since 1951 there have been a few Rumanians in *Canada*, centred at Montreal.

There are a few hundred Rumanians scattered about *Italy*. In Rome itself they have had the church of the Holy Saviour "alla Coppelle' since 1914; the Pontifical Rumanian College is now the headquarters of a society for Rumanian higher studies and also of the Institute of St John Damascene (see p. 21). The 500 or so Rumanians in *France* have a centre in Paris, with a church and parish. There are also small numbers of recent immigrants, with a few clergy, in Austria, Germany, Spain, Argentine and Brazil, and a handful in England. A visiting and ordaining bishop for Rumanian Catholics of Byzantine rite in exile was appointed in 1960.

PARTICULAR CUSTOMS

The Rumanians keep their Byzantine rite in a high degree of purity, some of the few small modifications being shared by the Orthodox. The Gregorian calendar was adopted by both in 1924 for the celebration of fixed feasts only; Easter is therefore still observed according to the Julian reckoning. The liturgical language is Rumanian, which began to take the place of Slavonic in the seventeenth century. In Transylvania there is a traditional church music, derived from the chant of Byzantium, but the national architecture has been almost ousted by the neo-classic in that province; *eikonostases* reach nearly to the roof. In the country districts, however, there is a charming local style of building in wood.

BIBLIOGRAPHY

N. Jorga, *Histoire de Transylvanie* (Bucarest, 1940).
C. Kormos, *Rumania* (Cambridge, 1944).
Eastern Churches Quarterly, vol. viii, no. 3 (1949). Two articles on the Catholic Rumanians.
P. Gherman, *L'Âme roumaine écartelée; Faits et documents* (Paris, 1955).
———— *Ten Years Ago* (Youngstown, Ohio, 1958).
A Manual of Prayers and Services (Cleveland, Ohio, 1946). Includes the eucharistic Liturgy in Rumanian and English.
Romanian Catholic Church Almanac (Cleveland, Ohio, 1960).

8. THE GREEKS

Before the rise of Constantinople to civil and ecclesiastical power the country now called the Kingdom of the Hellenes was, as part of the Roman prefecture of Illyricum, within the patriarchal jurisdiction of the Roman pontiff. But eastern Illyricum became part of the Byzantine empire, and the patriarch of Constantinople claimed jurisdiction over it. The question was a source of never-ending dispute between Old Rome and New Rome until what is now Greece was definitely involved on the side of Constantinople, and was part of its separated patriarchate, sharing its political and religious history until the establishment of the modern Greek state in the early part of the nineteenth century. Then, in 1833, the Greek assembly declared the national church autocephalous and it was so recognized by Constantinople seventeen years later.

After the Greek-speaking lands fell into the hands of the Turks, Pope Gregory XIII, in 1576, founded the Greek College at Rome, primarily for refugees from Greece who wanted to study for the priesthood; but, although there were many individual Greek bishops, priests and others who returned to unity during the seventeenth and eighteenth centuries,[38] it was not found possible to form a Catholic community of Byzantine rite among the Greek people, so the college was utilized for others of that rite, especially Ruthenians.

For this and for other reasons, less easy to understand, the long history of the college has been very chequered and at times troubled. Despite this it has produced a remarkable number of great men. There may be mentioned Leo Allatius (d. 1669), a Greek of Khios, whom Fortescue refers to as "perhaps the most learned Greek since Photios", a man as distinguished in profane as in sacred learning; Josaphat Azales

[38] Cyril Kontaris, patriarch of Constantinople, in 1638 entered into communion with the Supreme Pontiff. He was dethroned, imprisoned at Tunis, and there murdered by the Turks in 1640. The cause of his beatification as a martyr was introduced at Rome, but has never been finished.

(d. 1621), who tried to reconcile the monks of Athos with Rome; Demetrios Kyriakos, a famous hellenist in the seventeenth century; Peter Arcudius (d. 1633), a most learned theologian; and Peter Rodotà, the eighteenth-century historian of the Italo-Greeks, whose work can never be superseded as a source.

Upon the foundation of a special college at Rome for the Ruthenians in 1897, the Greek College was reorganized and confided to the care of Benedictine monks; it is now a charge of those of the Chevetogne monastery (see p. 213). Since then many of the anomalies and drawbacks of the college in the old days have disappeared, and the students are now principally Greeks and Italo-Greek-Albanians, with a few Melkites and occasionally other elements.

THE CATHOLIC GREEKS

In 1829 the sultan Mohammed II emancipated his non-Latin Catholic subjects from the civil authority of the dissident patriarchs, and a body of Greek Catholics of the Byzantine rite came into existence. The leading spirit in its formation was a Latin priest from Sira, Father John Hyacinth Marango, who in 1856 started work at Constantinople with the object of persuading the Orthodox to return to unity. The results were hardly commensurate with his enthusiasm and energy,[39] but by 1861 he had a small nucleus at Pera, in whose direction he was succeeded in 1878 by Father Polycarp Anastasiadis, a former student of the Orthodox seminary at Halki. In 1895 Pope Leo XIII invited the French Assumptionists to go to Constantinople, where they organized a seminary and two parishes of the Greek rite, and began those learned studies of Oriental religious matters whose fruits are so valuable to scholars.

Pope St Pius X gave these Greeks a bishop as ordinary (exarch) in 1911, in the distinguished person of Isaias Papadopoulos, who had led a Catholic movement in the Thracian village of Malgara and suffered much for the faith. He was called to Rome in 1917 and his place was taken three years later by Kyr George Kalavassy, who in the face of great hardship and difficulties established himself and part of his flock at

---

[39] Nevertheless, it was due to him that two contemporary Orthodox bishops, Meletios of Drama and Benjamin of Neapolis, died Catholics.

Athens. In 1932 those at Constantinople were made a separate exarchate, with Kyr Dionisios Varoukhas as bishop. The Catholics of Malgara and Dandeli emigrated to near Salonika. Bishop Kalavassy was a hierarch of outstanding ability, energy and goodness; he had a long series of fine works to his credit, and he handled his difficulties with the Orthodox and civil authorities tactfully and with dignity, so that at his death in 1957 he was mourned on all hands.

PRESENT STATE

Organization. The two exarchates of Greece and Turkey are subject to the Sacred Eastern Congregation at Rome, which appoints the bishops; but the Constantinople group is very small and has had no bishop since the death of Kyr Dionysios in 1957.

Parochial clergy. These are all voluntarily celibate and are united in a society ("of the Most Holy Trinity"), but it is not a religious congregation. There is a clerical school at Athens, preparatory for the Greek College at Rome. The clergy are responsible for a boys' orphanage and a printing-press in Athens.

Religious institutes. The *Sisters of the Theotokos Pammakaristos*, founded by Bishop Kalavassy and Mother Magdalen Photiadou, conduct schools, an orphanage, a hospital and students' hostels. This small body of highly trained and educated nuns particularly distinguished itself by its work during the last war and its aftermath.

The Faithful. They number only about 2,500. Those who emigrated to Athens in 1923 have had to suffer a good deal of harsh treatment at the hands of their dissident brethren, for Catholics of Eastern rite were not known in Greece (there are 64,000 Latins, mostly of foreign origin but many now completely hellenized) and they were accordingly accused of dishonest propaganda. A law of 1938, rigorously curbing the activities of non-Orthodox religious bodies, was probably aimed particularly at the Byzantine Catholics and at a certain Protestant body: it gravely increased the difficulties of both of them.

These Catholics, whether Latins or Byzantines, are the only

people who can properly be called "Greek Catholics".[40] There is now a Byzantine church on the island of Sira.

In 1929 some of the Greek community in *Lyons*, dissatisfied with the ministration of their bishop for Western Europe, asked to be received into the communion of the Catholic Church. A priest was sent to them from Athens by Bishop Kalavassy.

OTHER JURISDICTIONS

There are two tiny groups of Greek Catholics separate from the above, which should be mentioned here rather than with the Italo-Greeks as is usually done.

Corsica. When the Turks conquered Greece seven hundred people fled from Oitylos in the Morea in 1675 and the Genoese Republic gave them a home in Corsica. They settled first around Paomia and then at Ajaccio, and eventually recognized the jurisdiction of the Holy See. In 1770 the first French governor, Count de Marbœuf, built for them the township of Cargese, which their descendants still in part occupy. They number some 400 souls and, though they have nearly lost their Greek language, they still keep their Greek rites, only a little modified by Western practices. They have one church. A colony from Cargese went to Algeria in 1875 and founded the village of Sidi-Maruan, but they have ceased to exist as a colony.

Malta. When the Knights of St John of Jerusalem occupied Malta upon being driven from Rhodes by the Turks in 1522, a church was built at Valletta for those Greeks who accompanied them. That community exists to this day, though now numbering hardly a score of souls, and till 1942 used the same church, which was handsomely furnished. In that year it was destroyed during an air raid. The church was dedicated in honour of our Lady of Damascus, named for an eikon brought from Rhodes; this eikon was saved, and set up again in the new church which has been built.

The Catholic Greeks of Greece and Turkey use the Byzantine rite and customs, in Greek, according to pure Constantinopolitan usages, without any admixture or addition of specifically Western observances.

---

[40] The name is nevertheless often used in popular speech of and by the Catholic Melkites, Ruthenians, and others, especially in North America. The Hellenes are sometimes distinguished as "Pure Greeks".

BIBLIOGRAPHY

P. L. Fermor, *Mani* (London, 1958), pp. 99-111 (on Cargese).
Eastern Churches Quarterly, vol. v, no. 5-6 (1943). Malta.

9. THE BULGARS

The Bulgars are in origin a nomad Turanian people (completely slavonized long ago) who established an independent kingdom in their present country and its borders during the seventh century. About the year 865 their ruler Boris, largely for political motives, accepted Christianity from Constantinople and imposed it on his people. But Boris wanted his church to be independent, and turned to Pope St Nicholas I, asking him to give Bulgaria a patriarch. Nicholas sent two bishops. This precipitated a long contest for jurisdiction over the Bulgars, both Rome and Constantinople claiming that they were in their patriarchate. The Slavs, too, had a hand in the conversion of the Bulgars. When the Germans made things impossible for the missionary followers of St Methodius in Moravia, a number of them fled into Bulgaria about the year 885 and evangelized the heathen there. Their leader St Clement and four of his clergy, together with SS. Cyril and Methodius, are venerated as the Seven Apostles of the Bulgars.

The Emperor Basil II ("the Bulgar-slayer") conquered Bulgaria in 1018, and the ecclesiastical province of Okhrida was eventually involved in the Byzantine schism. But it continued to be an autonomous church till 1767, when it was reduced to complete dependence on the patriarch of Constantinople, together with its sister church of Trnovo. A century later the Bulgars were demanding ecclesiastical freedom from the Greeks, and political freedom from the Turks.

THE CATHOLIC BULGARS

At the beginning of their struggle with Constantinople there was an influential minority of Bulgars who sought ecclesiastical independence of the Greeks by means of reunion with Rome. Assured by the Catholic Armenian archbishop of Constantinople, Antony Hassun, that their rites and customs would be respected, they sent a deputation to Rome in 1861, where Pope Pius IX himself consecrated their leader, the archimandrite Joseph Sokolsky, as prelate of the Catholic Bulgars of the Byzantine rite.

But the movement was spoiled in an unforseen way. The growth of Catholicism in the Balkans was obnoxious to the political aims of Russia and, diplomacy having failed, a month after his return to Constantinople Sokolsky was kidnapped, taken to Odessa, and interned for the remaining eighteen years of his life in the monastery of the Caves at Kiev.[41] Then the Russian diplomats set themselves to encourage the Turks to favour an independent Orthodox Bulgarian church, whose establishment killed the Romeward movement.

At this time there were over 60,000 Bulgars reunited with Rome.[42] They were given another prelate, and Augustinians of the Assumption and other Western congregations were sent to help them. But by 1872 three-quarters of them had returned to Orthodoxy, and most of the remainder lived, not in Bulgaria, but in Macedonia and Thrace. Accordingly, in 1883, Pope Leo XIII appointed them a vicar apostolic in each of these districts. After the Balkan war of 1912-1913 the Orthodox Bulgars of Macedonia again contemplated reunion with Rome, and again were frustrated by political forces. This war brought ruin to both vicariates; parish after parish was destroyed, many of the faithful massacred, others forced into the Orthodox Church, at the hands of the Greeks and, to a lesser degree, the Serbs. After the European war of 1914-1918 what remained of the Catholic Bulgars sought refuge in their own country.

PRESENT STATE

In 1950 the Byzantine Catholic Bulgars numbered about 7,000 souls, under an exarch whose residence was at Sofia. They were mostly peasants, but with good communities in Sofia, Burgas and Varna, and they formed a flourishing little

---

41 That Sokolsky connived at his removal and reverted to Orthodoxy has been asserted, but not proved.

42 One of the most remarkable among them was the aged monk Panteleimon, who tried to introduce frequent communion among the monks of Mount Athos. He became a Catholic in 1863 and founded three monasteries, two for men and one for women. They failed after his death in 1868.

church, which owed much to the labours of the Augustinians of the Assumption. There were two junior seminaries and a convent of enclosed Carmelite nuns, as well as houses of "active" sisters.

In 1952 the communist government arrested and sentenced to death the Latin bishop of Nikopolis, Mgr Eugene Bossilkov, and three priests, among them the head of the Byzantine seminary at Plovdiv, Father Kamen Yonkov. At the same time the exarch, Bishop Cyril Kurtev, was turned out of his house, and four years later he was arrested. He was subsequently released; but Christian schools and other institutions had already been declared closed by the civil authorities, and it appears that the Catholic Byzantine church has almost ceased to exist as an organized body.

The women's Carmel referred to above was the first in the world of Byzantine rite, it was founded at Sofia in 1935.

The Bulgarian liturgy is the Byzantine according to Slavonic usages, and innovations are avoided; even the Julian calendar is in use. Church music is either an adaptation of the Greek chant or Russian polyphony. The Bulgars are not in origin Slavs, but the use of Church Slavonic as a "national custom" seems to have begun soon after their conversion, when the followers of St Methodius from Moravia introduced the practice at the court of Boris, who adopted it as a sign of independence of Constantinople.

BIBLIOGRAPHY

L. Canisius, *Aux avant-postes du monde slave* (Louvain, 1931).
P. Kristov, *Pantéléimon* (Paris, *c.* 1929).
I. Sofranov, *Histoire du mouvement bulgare vers l'Église catholique au xixe siècle* (Paris, 1960).

10. THE RUSSIANS AND BYELORUSSIANS

The Russians date their conversion to Christ from about the year 989, when St Vladimir, grand-prince of Kiev, gave the new religion to his people. Russia received the faith from both Northmen and Greeks, but the second influence was soon preponderant: her rites of worship, her canon law, her earlier metropolitans came from Constantinople. And since this was the period of Cerularius, she was given anti-Western ideas as well. In the circumstances of the times it is impossible that the fact and significance of communion with the Holy See of Rome can have had much importance in their religious consciousness. Greek influence was predominant in their church and, in the words of Father Paul Pierling, S.J., "One looks in vain for an exact date or outstanding event that can be registered as the point of departure for the separation between Russia and Rome. It came about by implication, without shock or apparent reason, simply because of Russia's hierarchical submission to the patriarch of Constantinople."

There were, however, contacts and normal relations between Russia and the West until the middle of the thirteenth century, when the Mongol invasion isolated her for a hundred and fifty years. When full liberation from that yoke at length came, the Russian Church had become a self-sufficient national institution, and the idea of Catholicity was associated with enemies and rivals on her western borders. At the Council of Florence Russia was represented by a Greek, Isidore, metropolitan of Kiev (Moscow), who was in favour of reunion. Pope Eugenius IV created him cardinal (and the great Bessarion of Nicaea as well) and sent him home as legate to confirm the union, but the grand-prince of Muscovy, Basil II, and his other bishops would have none of it and Isidore had to escape to Rome.

In 1589 the patriarch of Constantinople, Jeremy II, acknowledged Russia as a separate patriarchate of the Orthodox

Church, with its patriarchal see at Moscow ("The Third Rome"). Six years later took place the union with Rome of the metropolitan of Kiev and other bishops under the rule of Poland, whose people included those whom we call White Russians or Byelorussians (cf. pp. 72, 76). Peter the Great abolished the patriarchal office in 1700, and set up a "Holy Governing Synod" to rule the Russian Church in concert with the civil power (1721). This lasted till the revolution of 1917, when a patriarch of Moscow was again elected. At that time the number of Russian Orthodox Christians was about 110 millions (including sects).

THE RUSSIAN CATHOLICS

During the centuries after the Council of Florence there were very few Catholics indeed under Russian rule until the partition of Poland in 1772-1795.[43] Towards the end of the nineteenth century, largely under the influence of the great philosopher and theologian Vladimir Solovyev, began a movement in favour of Russians who became Catholics keeping their own rite. Such a thing was legally impossible—a Byzantine *had* to be Orthodox—even after 1905, when Nicholas II issued an edict of religious toleration.[44] But from that time groups of Russian Catholics of Byzantine rite were formed here and there (a few converts from the sect of *Starovery*, "Old Believers"). In 1917 the Ruthenian archbishop of Lvov, Andrew Szepticky, in whom Pope St Pius X had recognized plenary powers over the Catholic Byzantines in Russia, appointed Leonid Feodorov to be their exarch. The provisional government of that year gave official recognition to them, with Father Leonid at their head, but after the outbreak of the Bolshevist revolution he was imprisoned at Solovky and his small flock scattered. Father Leonid died after great sufferings at Vyatka on 7 March 1935. He had spent fourteen of his twenty-two years of priestly life in jail: first under the czars as a Byzantine Catholic; then under the bolsheviks as a Christian. The cause of the canonization of this very remarkable man is to be introduced at Rome.

[43] Before the revolution there were some two million Latin Catholics in Russia (excluding Poland and Lithuania), many of them Byelorussian and hardly any of them Great Russian.
[44] There were in fact Catholics of Eastern rite before 1905. Solovyev himself made his profession of faith before Father Nicholas Tolstoy, a Byzantine priest, in 1896 at Moscow; and there was Father Alexis Zerchaninov, who was exiled to a monastery—the bolshevists sent him to Tobolsk.

Among his flock were the twenty-five nuns who had been founded by the heroic Mother Anna Abrikosova, the wife of a priest. They followed the rule of the Third Order of St Dominic, adapted to their rite, and did much good work in Moscow, deeply impressing their Orthodox neighbours; most of them were sentenced to varying periods of detention in Solovky, Siberia and elsewhere, a religious congregation being looked on as a "counter-revolutionary activity". Three of these young nuns were Poles, who had given up their own rite to work for reunion and therefore were specially obnoxious to the Soviet authorities.

Mother Anna died in the Butyrky prison at Moscow, and the chaplain of the nuns, Father Nicholas Alexandrov, met his death as a confessor of the faith in the fearful penal camp at Solovky. Mention must also be made here of Father Potapy Emelyanov, a monk of Pochaev and parish priest of Bog-danovka, near Kharkov. Led by him, his parishioners asked to be received into Catholic communion in 1918, and as a consequence they were bitterly ill-treated, first as "bolsheviks" by Ukrainian separatists and then as "renegade Russians" by the bolsheviks. Father Potapy was arrested and flogged for the sixteenth time in 1920, and taken to Solovky in 1927, where he died ten years later. At the time of his act of union Father Potapy had never either met a Catholic or read a specifically Catholic book.

After 1919 a number of the Orthodox in eastern Poland returned to unity; most of them were descendants of the Byelo-russians "reconverted" to Orthodoxy by the Russian government in the nineteenth century (cf. p. 76). Pope Pius XI wanted to give them a bishop-in-ordinary, but the chauvinistic policy of the Polish government made this difficult, so a resident episcopal visitor was appointed in 1931.

Working among these people were the Jesuits,[45] who had their headquarters at Albertyn, near Vilna, on which depended a score of Slav-Byzantine priests. It was a completely Eastern establishment, and over forty students were being trained there

---

[45] Father Vladimir Ledochowski began to prepare an Eastern branch of the Society of Jesus in 1920, at the wish of Pope Benedict XV. There are now many priests of the Society who are Byzantines (and a few of other rites), and in Rome there are Eastern chapels at the general house (St Vladimir's) and the Gregorianum (Our Lady of Kazan's).

for work among all or any of the Slavonic peoples. Similar work was being carried on by the Redemptorists, who have had a Slav-Byzantine branch since 1905, originating among the Ukrainians in Canada. Their principal house in eastern Poland, outside Galicia, was at Kovel. Capuchin friars minor of Slavonic rite also conducted a fruitful ministry, and in 1927 the Missionary Sisters of the Sacred Heart were founded in Warsaw specifically for work amongst the Byelorussians.

The provinces concerned, Volhynia etc., are now once again part of Russia. The institutions referred to, and others, were ruined by war after 1939, and under the Soviet regime there is no hope of building them up again for so long ahead as human eye can see. The apostolic visitor mentioned above, Bishop Nicholas Czarnecky, a Redemptorist, was deported to the U.S.S.R. with the Ukrainian bishops in 1945, and died in a Siberian labour camp in 1959. Another victim was Father Niemunsevich, of Albertyn, who was shot by the Nazis.

Present State

Western Europe. The Catholics among the expatriate Russians in Paris, Lyons, Brussels, The Hague, Berlin and elsewhere number about 2,500, with churches at those and other places. Their episcopal visitor resides at Louvain, and there is a Russian ordaining bishop of Byzantine rite in Rome.[46]

A centre for Russian studies, "Istina", was opened at Lille by Dominican friars (in association with the college of St Basil, founded in 1923 to train Russian clergy but now closed). Archimandrite C. J. Dumont, o.p., became director of the house of studies and in 1936 it was transferred to Paris. Since 1947 "Istina" has been centred at Boulogne-sur-Seine. Byzantine Jesuits founded an important Russian establishment, including a boarding-school for boys, at Namur. This, too, was transferred to Paris (Meudon), in 1941, where it survived the war years; very favourable relations are maintained with the Orthodox. At Gelrode, near Louvain, there is a house of studies and centre for young Russians and Byelorussians, conducted by Olivetan Benedictine monks.

[46] The present bishop, Andrew Katkov, is a member of the congregation of Marian clerks regular of the Immaculate Conception, founded in Poland in 1673, which has an active Byzantine branch. Bishop Sipovich, named on next page, is another member of the same congregation.

There is a number of Byelorussians amongst the displaced persons scattered over the world. They have a centre at Finchley in London, which was established in 1947 by Father Cheslav Sipovich, of the Marian congregation, who was ordained bishop in 1960 and appointed visitor of the Byelorussians in western Europe.[47]

America. The first Catholic Russian chapel in North America was St Michael's in down-town New York, opened by Archpriest Andrew Rogosh in 1935. The second was in Los Angeles. The year after the Institute of Contemporary Russian Studies was begun at Fordham University in 1950, Byzantine-rite Jesuit fathers opened a Russian Centre, with its own chapel, in the grounds of the university; from thence another centre has been established, in San Francisco. A Russian church has been provided for Boston by the generosity of Cardinal Cushing. There is also a chapel in Montreal, and one for Byelorussian monks at the Benedictine abbey at Lisle, Illinois.

In South America the Society of Jesus is responsible for Russian churches and schools for boys and girls at São Paulo and Santos in Brazil and Buenos Aires in Argentine. The centre at the last-named was built up by a remarkable priest, Father Philip de Régis, s.j. (d. 1955), who had been rector of the Russian college in Rome.

The Far East. The aftermath of the second world war brought ruin and dispersion to the Catholic Russian institutions in Manchuria and China, whose centres were at Harbin, under Archimandrite Nicholas, and Shanghai; churches, schools, colleges, orphanages, all came forcibly to an end. In co-operation with the International Relief Organization, Father F. Wilcock and his fellow Jesuits were able to organize the evacuation of nearly all non-Soviet Russians from Shanghai.

A great work in the training of priests to minister amongst Russians and Byelorussians has already been done by the *Russicum* college in Rome, founded for that purpose in 1929. This college is directed by members of the Society of Jesus; the adjoining church of St Antony the Abbot is, as well as the college chapel, the public church for Russian Catholics in the

---

[47] The little chapel at Marian House, Finchley, is noted for its eikons, its choir and its friendly atmosphere.

124

City. There is also in Rome a convent of Russian nuns and an institute for young women.

Russian and Byelorussian Catholics have the Byzantine liturgy, in Church Slavonic, in strict accordance with the Russian so-called synodal books, and their religious customs and outlook are completely Eastern. Russians attach much importance to liturgical purity and "hybridization" is carefully avoided. Married men are, of course, entitled to be ordained deacon and priest, but voluntary celibacy is encouraged.

BIBLIOGRAPHY

A. Palmieri, *La Chiesa russa* (Florence, 1908).

J. N. Danzas, *The Russian Church* (London, 1936).

P. Pierling, *Rome et Moscou* (Paris, 1883).

A. Berg, *Die römisch-katholische Kirche und die orthodoxen Russen* (Berlin, 1926).

ed. G. Bennigsen, *Religion in Russia* (London, 1940).

P. Volkonsky, "Aperçu sur l'origine de l'Église catholique byzantine-slave en Russie" in *L'Unité de l'Église*, no. 42 (Paris, 1930).

D. Attwater, *Leonid Feodorov* (Fordham, N.Y., 1954).

H. Iswolsky, *Soul of Russia* (London, 1944).

ed. G. P. Fedotov, *A Treasury of Russian Spirituality* (London, 1950).

11. OTHER BYZANTINE ELEMENTS

Albania. Two-thirds of the Albanians are Moslem; the rest are dissident Orthodox and Latin Catholics in the proportion of about two to one. From 1628 there was a body of Catholics of the Byzantine rite in the coastal region of Chimarra, served for a time by Basilian monks from Sicily, but the mission collapsed in 1765.

Before 1939 there was a handful of Byzantine Catholics in Albania, with four priests, chiefly at Elbasani, Korytsa and Vlora; and Italo-Albanian nursing sisters were in charge of the public hospital at Argyrokastro. These last were expelled by the government in 1946, during the persecution directed against both Catholics and Orthodox.

Georgia, or Iberia, lies between Armenia and Russia, south of the Caucasus, and was evangelized during the fourth century. probably from Armenia and Syria. Later, it came under the influence of Constantinople and drifted into schism in the earlier years of the thirteenth century. From then on Western missionaries worked in Georgia, and at least one king and one katholikos were formally Catholic. In 1801 the Emperor Alexander I annexed Georgia to his dominions, and its Orthodox church became an exarchate of the Church of Russia; it was released from this at the revolution, only to fall into the hands of a Soviet socialist republic.

In 1917 there were $2\frac{1}{2}$ million Orthodox Georgians and about 40,000 Catholics, of whom 32,000 were of the Latin rite and the rest of the Armenian (Byzantine Catholics were not allowed in imperial Russia). After the revolution of 1917 some of them wished to return to their own tradition, the Byzantine rite in their own language, and they were cared for by priests of a congregation founded at Constantinople by Father Peter Karishiaranti in 1861 to minister to his countrymen of whatever rite. These four priests died in Soviet prisons, and the position

126

in Georgia is very uncertain. In 1955 a chapel for Georgian residents was opened in Paris, in the crypt of the church of our Lady of Comfort.

Estonia. Estonia is predominantly a Lutheran country, but there were 200,000 Orthodox (a third of them Russians) and a few Latin Catholics. For some years Catholic priests of the Byzantine rite (Capuchins and Jesuits) ministered in two centres, Narva and Esna. Progress was slow but promising; but the Soviet annexation of Estonia put an end to the work indefinitely. The celebration of the Liturgy in Estonian was accorded to this group in 1929.

Finland. Finland is a Protestant country with a small Orthodox minority, including some Russians. The beginning of a Byzantine Catholic centre was made at Terrioki in 1938, but it was broken up by the Russo-Finnish war in the following year. A priest was sent from the *Russicum* in 1949, and he opened a chapel at the village of Rekola, near Helsinki. There the Liturgy is celebrated alternately in Finnish and Slavonic.

Latvia. There were the beginnings of a Catholic Byzantine group in this country, thanks to a Russian priest, Father Vasilyev, and Professor Valpitro of Riga University. Soviet domination brought this work to an end.

BIBLIOGRAPHY

M. Tamarati, *L'Église géorgienne* (Rome, 1910).
D. M. Lang, *Lives and Legends of the Georgian Saints* (London, 1956).
C. Bourgeois, *A Priest in Russia and the Baltic* (London, 1953).

CHAPTER V

THE ALEXANDRIAN RITE

1. THE COPTS

FROM its beginnings the heresy of Monophysism (see p. 4) had its stronghold in Egypt, where the patriarch of Alexandria, Dioscoros, was its spokesman and leader. After six years of controversy and violence he was deposed and his teaching condemned by the Council of Chalcedon in 451. Practically all the clergy and people of Egypt (and many in Syria) refused to accept the decisions of the council, not altogether on account of religious enthusiasm but because political passions also were involved: it was bad enough to be subject to a foreign emperor without having "Byzantine theology" as well. The century that followed was an outrageous period of ecclesiastical quarrelling, minor schisms, persecution, political chicanery and physical violence. The see of Alexandria was bandied between hierarchs who were sometimes orthodox but more often monophysite, till in 567 two lines of patriarchs were definitively established: one for the mostly foreign minority of orthodox Catholics, the other for the solid mass of Egyptian monophysites, today called the Coptic Church.[1] With the modification that the orthodox line is now separated from Rome, that is still the position.

The monophysite Egyptians continued to be troubled by domestic quarrels, by the Catholics, and in 616-628, by Persian invaders who bitterly persecuted them. Eleven years later the Arab conquest was begun, and the anti-imperialist Copts are said to have given aid to the khalifa against the Byzantines. They had their reward, and for century after century were oppressed by Arabs, Mameluks and Turks; massacres were

[1] A Copt is simply an Egyptian (Arabic *Kibti*= Gk. [Aἰ] *gúpt* [ιος]), in actual use a Christian Egyptian.

frequent and apostasies so numerous that today 93 per cent of the Egyptians are Moslem. But there were also many martyrs. The Copts did not get on well with the Crusaders, and though two legates of the Coptic patriarch John II signed an act of union at the Council of Florence it never became effective.

Early in the seventeenth century Capuchin missions were established in the Levant by Father Joseph of Paris (Joseph Leclerc du Tremblay, "Grey Eminence"), and a foundation was made at Cairo in 1630. For a time it prospered, under the direction of Father Agathangelo of Vendôme. The patriarch opened all his churches to the friars, and Father Agathangelo gave spiritual conferences in the dissident monasteries of the Lower Thebaid.[2] Unhappily, and not for the only time in history, the great obstacle to reunion was the European Catholics resident in the country. Father Agathangelo referred to the household of the French consul as a "synagogue of Satan", and the general behaviour of the Europeans was such that when the Coptic patriarch complained bitterly that "the Roman Church in this country is a brothel" Father Agathangelo could not deny his reasons for saying so. He appealed to the cardinal prefect of Propaganda to have the worst offenders excommunicated. But nothing was done, and Father Agathangelo went off in despair to Ethiopia and to martyrdom.

THE CATHOLIC COPTS

In 1697 the Friars Minor of the Observance were given charge of a prefecture apostolic in Upper Egypt and the Jesuits came to Cairo, but the Coptic mission languished until about 1740, when a dissident bishop, Amba Athanasius, became a Catholic and was put in charge of those of his rite. At this time the learned Raphael Tukhi was editing and publishing the Coptic liturgical books in Rome and was made ordaining bishop for Coptic seminarists in the city. Unfortunately Athanasius, "by nature a good man, who loved truth", had not the strength of character that the difficulties of his position called for, and he lapsed into schism. His first two successors as vicars apostolic, John Faragi (1781) and Matthew Righet

---

[2] One of the two books he used for this purpose was *On the Holy Will of God*, by Father Benedict of Canfield (William Fitch), the first Capuchin missionary in England in penal times.

(1788), could not receive episcopal consecration, apparently because there was no Catholic bishop in Egypt and a voyage to Europe was too difficult. The third, Maximos Joed, was nominated in 1824 and consecrated by Ignatius V Kattan, Melkite patriarch of Antioch. Meanwhile, the Catholic Copts had no churches of their rite and had to use those of the Franciscans; this and the overlapping of jurisdictions caused numerous difficulties. It was believed that the Khedive Mohammed Ali wished the Catholics to have a patriarchate of their own, and accordingly it was erected by Pope Leo XII in 1824. But it was not made operative, and there was a further succession of three vicars apostolic, of whom the learned Aghapios Bishai represented his church at the Vatican Council.

In 1893 the Franciscans made over ten churches to the sole use of the Copts, and two years later Pope Leo XIII divided the 5,000 faithful into three dioceses and appointed Cyril Makarios as administrator; in 1899 he was advanced to the rank of patriarch. Amba Makarios held a synod of his church at Cairo in 1898, and continued to govern it for ten years, when certain difficulties made it necessary for him to resign. The patriarchal throne then remained vacant until 1947, when Amba Mark II Khuzam was appointed. This hierarch governed the church for over thirty years (1926-1958), first as administrator and then as patriarch, and it was a time of steady increase in numbers and effectiveness. Khuzam was a hierarch of unbounded energy, whose life was a succession of good works; he was succeeded by Amba Stephen Sidaruss.

PRESENT STATE

Patriarch. The title of the head of the Catholic Copts is Patriarch of Alexandria and of All the Preaching of St Mark. He has the common-law rights and duties of all patriarchs, but hitherto he has been nominated by the Holy See instead of being elected by the bishops. He resides at Cairo, and the patriarchal diocese covers the whole of Lower Egypt. The civil power recognizes him as the competent judge in the matrimonial and testamentary causes of his people.

Bishops. The episcopal sees are Assiut, Minya and Thebes (residence at Sohag). Normally the bishops are chosen by the patriarch and synod, but they too have hitherto been nominated by the Holy See.

Parochial clergy. The senior seminary, founded at Tahta in 1899, and the junior seminary, formerly conducted by Jesuits at Cairo, are now both directed by the Coptic secular clergy at Meadi. Other aspirants go to the Jesuit seminary for Easterners at Bairut. The clergy have been bound to celibacy since the synod of 1898, but dispensations are accorded to married priests reconciled from the dissidents. *Kummus,* "abbot", is a title of honour sometimes conferred on clergy of distinction.

Religious institutes. The *Friars Minor* have a long history of missionary work in Egypt (going back to St Francis himself), and they now train priests of the Coptic rite in their seminary at Giza; some members of the *Society of Jesus* have passed to the rite. The *African Missionaries of Lyons* work in the Nile delta; outstanding among them was Kummus Jacob Muyser (d. 1956), a Dutchman, who for thirty years was priest at Faqus and a Coptic scholar of the front rank. There are at present no Catholic Coptic monks. An indigenous congregation of *Sisters of the Sacred Heart* was founded in 1912, by Bishop Maximos Sedfawi of Minya and Bishop Ignatius Berzi of Thebes; the eighty members teach in schools.

The Faithful. Catholics of Coptic rite numbered 80,500 in 1960. With few exceptions they are of the poorest class of Egyptian *fellahin*, especially in Upper Egypt, and those in the cities are mostly of the same origin. Socially, they are the weakest of the many Catholic communities in Egypt, but they are also by far the most deeply rooted in the country and its Christian tradition. Much educational and other work has been done for them by foreign religious, who are now commendably concerned to enable these people to stand on their own feet. The dissident Coptic Christians number over 1¼ million.

LITURGY AND CUSTOMS

Church buildings. A church of the Coptic rite is divided for the whole of its width into sanctuary, choir, nave and narthex. The northern side of the nave is reserved for women, at the southern side the sexes may be together. Between the sanctuary and the narrow choir there is a screen like a Byzantine *eikono-stasis* (formerly of carved and inlaid wood, often lattice work); as the central door is not closed during the Liturgy the altar is not entirely hidden. Within the triple-domed sanctuary (*haikal*) are three altars in a line, each in an apse, standing clear of the wall; they are of brick or stone with a flat wooden top, covered by linen or silk cloths; on each are two or four candles, one at each corner, and a sort of box in which the chalice stands during the Liturgy. On the *haikal*-screen are a few pictures, and others, with mosaics and wall-paintings, around the church. Actually many Catholic Coptic churches at the present day are tiny poor buildings with no screens and having a "Western" altar with gradines and flowerpots, but preserving the wooden *mensa*; the Blessed Sacrament is reserved in a tabernacle. Such churches as that of St Pachomius at Faqus and the cathedral at Assiut are a very different matter, and a general all-round improvement has begun.

Vestments. These correspond to those of the Byzantine rite. The chasuble (*burnus*) is open all down the front, rather like a cope. Bishops wear the *omophorion* but not always the *sakkos*. The *tailasan* is a broad strip of material ending in a hood, which dissident priests wear over the head all through the Liturgy. The celebrant's feet should be bare. Out of church the clerical hat (the dissidents wear a turban) is a black cylinder about six inches high, growing wider to the top—a thoroughly Egyptian-looking headdress (bishops cover it with a veil). All wear the wide-sleeved *gibbah* over the cassock, of any dark colour.

Liturgical books. These were arranged and printed in Rome by Raphael Tukhi between 1736 and 1764. Patriarch Makarios published the missal, ritual and office-book at Cairo (1898-1906), and some of them have been reprinted there since, the Divine Office in 1930, revised by Patriarch Khuzam.

Altar-vessels and bread. The vessels are very similar to those of the Byzantine rite, with several large and small veils to cover the offerings, but the paten is larger and deeper. The bread (*kurbana*) is leavened, round and thick. *Ripidia* are carried in processions, and a hand-cross is used to give some blessings.

Music. The Coptic lay people have a remarkable knowledge of the text of their liturgy and they take an active part in it, singing the traditional chant by heart, with copious variations. Some of this music was first written down by the Jesuit fathers Blin and Badet at the end of the past century. Cymbals, triangles, and occasionally the flute (*mizmar*) are the only instruments.

Liturgical language. This is Coptic, (i.e. the last stage of Egyptian, a tongue otherwise dead for three centuries), with many Greek words and some phrases. Arabic is the vernacular of Egypt and more and more tends unofficially to displace Coptic in the Liturgy: it is used officially for the Divine Office and certain occasional rites. The Bohaïric dialect of Lower Egypt is used throughout the country.

THE EUCHARISTIC LITURGY

The Coptic Liturgy is a form of the original Greek Liturgy of Alexandria which has undergone strong monastic and Syrian influences, and later been further modified. It has three alternative anaphoras: "St Basil" for use on ordinary days and Sundays; "of St Mark", or "St Cyril", rarely used; and "of St Gregory Nazianzen", for great feasts (this last is addressed throughout to our Lord). The Catholics have a form of "low Mass", which is often celebrated in a low voice. The Coptic Liturgy (*Prosfora*) may be concelebrated with any number of celebrants on specific occasions; there is no Liturgy of the Presanctified.

THE DIVINE OFFICE

There are seven "hours", collectively called *al-Agbieh*, namely Prayer of Sunset (*al-Ghurub*), of Repose (*an-Naum*), of Midnight (*Nusf al-Lail*), of the Dawn (*al-Bakar*), and of the Third, Sixth, and Ninth Hours; bishops and religious have an extra evening office, "of the Veil of Darkness" (*as-Satar*). The night-office has three nocturns of twelve psalms and a gospel each, with *troparia* and prayers, and the Creed after each nocturn; the other hours each consists of twelve psalms (some "at choice"), a gospel and *troparia* (*al-Bakar* has nineteen psalms); all the hours have several short prayers, the *Trisagion*, Lord's Prayer, and *Kyrie eleison* (41 times). Nearly all the Office is in Arabic since 1906.

133

THE SACRAMENTS

Baptism is a very long rite. After prayers and blessing of the oil of catechumens the priest anoints the forehead, breast, hands and back of the child. Then there are exorcisms, renunciations and profession of faith by the godparent, and the anointings of the breast, back and hands are repeated. The water is blessed at great length: there are three lessons and a gospel, prayers for the sick, dead and others not immediately concerned, a little oil of catechumens is poured into the water three times and it is breathed upon crosswise thrice; there is a marvellous panegyrical exorcism and benediction of the water, modelled on the prayer of the eucharistic anaphora, and a little chrism is added. Then the deacon brings the child "from the west to the east over against Jordan" (the font), and the priest immerses it three times saying, "N., I baptize you in the name of the Father . . .", etc. Baptism is ministered by pouring water in cases of necessity, of adults and of conditional baptism.[3] The rite ends with a characteristic "prayer at the pouring away of the water".

Confirmation follows immediately. The child is anointed with chrism on the forehead, mouth, breast, etc., in such a way as to make 36 anointings, with varying formulas; then the priest imposes his right hand and breathes on the child, saying, "Receive the Holy Spirit and be a cleansed vessel. . . ." The child is dressed in a white robe, with a girdle and fillet ("crown") and final prayers are said.

Penance. Absolution is given in a long form of which the first part is deprecatory, asking Christ's forgiveness in virtue of his promises to the Apostles; the second part is an invocation of forgiveness from the Blessed Trinity through the Church; it ends with the penitent saying "I have sinned; absolve me", to which the priest replies "God absolves you".

Eucharist. Communion in both kinds was never abolished amongst the Catholic Copts, but for some time it was usual to give it in one kind only, the communicant kneeling. Now it is more usual to receive it standing and in both kinds, separately or by intinction. The words of ministration are,

---

[3] This is often necessary for converts from the dissidents, owing to the careless and fanciful ways in which some of their priests are said to administer the sacrament.

134

"This is in truth the body and the blood of Emmanuel our God." The receiver answers, "Amen."

Anointing. Again a very long rite, in which seven priests one by one light seven lamps or candles, with an epistle, psalm, gospel and prayer at each lighting. Finally the gospel-book is laid on his head and the sick man is anointed once on the forehead, throat and wrists, with a prayer that he may be healed in body and soul, and further prayers (including "Glory to God in the highest") said. In practice one priest only is present and he lights all seven lamps, with the prayers appropriate thereto; an abridged version of this office was published for Catholic use in 1933. This rite is called the Office of the Lamp.

Orders. Readers are ordained by a prayer and a blessing, subdeacons by imposition of hands on the temples; deacons and priests receive imposition of the right hand on the head and a sign of the cross on the forehead, and are invested with the stole and chasuble respectively. The formula for ordaining a bishop names the powers which he is to exercise, and all bishops present lay their hands twice on his shoulders and forearms, the consecrator's right hand on his head. The formula for a priest is: "Fill him with the Holy Spirit and the grace and wisdom . . .", etc. "We call you, N., to be a priest for the ministry of the altar which was first given to right-believers, in the name of the Father. . . . Amen."

Marriage. The wedding service consists of two parts, the betrothal (epistle and gospel, three long prayers, the Creed, a thanksgiving, and a blessing of the wedding garments) and the crowning. After an epistle (Ephes. 5:22-6:3), gospel (Matt. 19:1-6), litany and prayers, the priest blesses oil and anoints both parties on the head and wrists; then he crowns them while "Worthy the bridegroom and his bride" is sung thrice. The rite is concluded by exhortations, broken up by antiphons sung by the choir.

Calendar. The Copts date their years according to the "era of the Martyrs", i.e., beginning from 284, the date of the accession of Diocletian. Their year has twelve months of thirty days each, and a "little month", ordinarily of five days; but the Catholics of Lower Egypt fix Easter by the Gregorian computation and those of Upper Egypt by the Julian. The Church's annual cycle of seasons is strongly marked, each great feast having its own period; so, too, is the life of the earth—the rising of the Nile, seed-time, harvest.

Feasts are divided into three classes, and there are numerous saints' days, most of them Egyptian. A number of festivals are common to the Coptic and Roman calendars, but most of them fall on different dates; they commemorate the Primacy of St Peter the Apostle on Mesore 7 (July 31), together with the High-Priesthood of Aaron. Peculiar festivals are those of the Four Incorporeal Living Creatures (Ezech. 1:5-14), referring them to the four evangelists, and of the Four and Twenty Elders (Apoc. 4:4). These are also commemorated in the eucharistic liturgy. Of more recent Western feasts, Corpus Christi and the Sacred Heart are the principal ones. Sundays and nine other days are holy days of obligation.

Penitential seasons. According to the old Coptic discipline, half the days of the year are fasting days of varying degrees of severity. This has been considerably modified amongst Catholics. A fortnight before Lent begins there are three days of penitence called the "fast of Nineveh". This observance is known in all Eastern churches except the Byzantine: it commemorates the penance of the Ninevites at the preaching of Jonas.

General observations. Copts make the sign of the cross from left to right, and the Catholic lay people show respect by genuflecting instead of the customary prostration on both knees, which is confined to the Liturgy. Water is solemnly blessed at the Epiphany (a common Eastern custom, referring to our Lord's baptism), at the Supper of the New Covenant, i.e., Maundy Thursday, and on SS. Peter and Paul's day; on the last two days there is a washing of feet in every church. The usual Western devotions, Benediction with the Blessed Sacrament, rosary, stations of the cross, etc., are practised, but the effects of Western influence are far less noticeable in Upper than in Lower Egypt, as might be expected. In the bigger cities, as Bishop Skandar of Assiut has remarked, the Coptic liturgy is regarded as "beneath contempt in some churches, and only fit for uneducated and boorish rustics", and this has helped to

COPTIC CATHEDRAL AT ASYUT

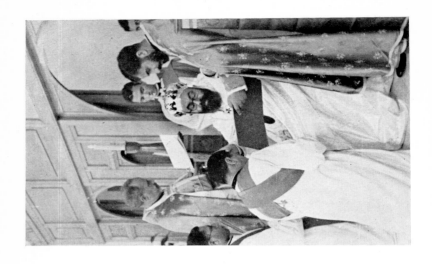

ORDINATION OF A COPTIC SUBDEACON

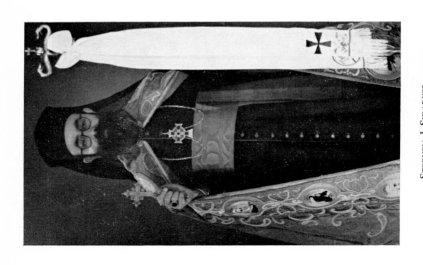

STEPHEN I SIDARUSS
Patriarch of Alexandria of the Copts

COPTIC CHURCH AT FAGUS

SYRIAN PATRIARCHAL CHURCH, BAIRUT

Fr N. Liesel

THE ETHIOPIC LITURGY

The eucharistic bread is brought to the altar in a vessel of wickerwork or metal

produce "a skeleton of a rite which is a gross scandal". However, things are getting better, and in 1958 the bishops appointed a commission to revise and reform public worship in all its aspects.

BIBLIOGRAPHY

C. Macaire, *Histoire de l'Église d'Alexandrie* (Cairo, 1894).
E. R. Hardy, *Christian Egypt* (Oxford, 1952).
A. Colombo, *Le origini della gerarchia della chiesa Copta cattolica nel secolo xviii* (Rome, 1953).
Bute, *The Coptic Morning Service* (London, 1908).
Notre Messe selon la liturgie Copte (Cairo, 1952).
R. M. Woolley, *Coptic Offices* (London, 1930).
M. de Fenoyl, *Coutumes religieuses coptes* (Cairo, 1953).
Eastern Churches Quarterly. In 13 issues between vii, no. 6 (1948) vol. and xi, 7 (1956) there is a series of detailed articles on Coptic rites and ceremonies by O. H. E. Hadji-Burmester.

2. THE ETHIOPIANS

The Ethiopians[4] proper are partly of Semitic stock, and their
ancestors before the Christian era probably emigrated to Africa
from southern Arabia. They now occupy the mountainous
country between the Sudan, Kenya and the Red Sea. They are
homogeneous neither in race nor religion, but the nucleus is
Ethiopic and Christian.

The first authentic evangelization of the Ethiopians of which
there is record was towards the middle of the fourth century,
when two youths from Tyre, Frumentius and Aedesius, spared
from a massacre of their fellow voyagers, attained influence at
the Ethiopian court at Aksum and preached the Gospel there.
St Frumentius was eventually consecrated bishop for his
converts by the then archbishop of Alexandria, the great St
Athanasius himself. A more extensive evangelization was
carried on some hundred and fifty years later by the "Nine
Saints", who were monks and probably monophysites from
Syria. In the time of Justinian there was lively competition
between the Catholics and monophysites of Egypt for control
of the Ethiopic mission; the last-named won, and the Ethiopian
church became hierarchically dependent on the Coptic patriarch
of Alexandria, and accordingly monophysite. Until the sixteenth century little is known of the history of Christianity in
Ethiopia: especially after the Arab conquest of Egypt communication even with the oppressed mother-church was difficult
and often interrupted. There was a religious and intellectual
revival in the thirteenth century, followed by the arrival of
Dominican missionaries, who for a time had some success;
persecution began and the mission was broken up. The relics
of the martyrs are still venerated, by the dissidents around
Neebi. The Ethiopian Church was represented at the Council
of Florence, and an embassy was sent to Rome; but the only

[4] "Ethiopia" and "Ethiopians" are to be preferred because those are their own names for their
country and themselves, and there is nothing against them. The more usual "Abyssinia" and
"Abyssinians" originated as an offensive nickname, "the mongrels".

result was the establishment by Pope Sixtus IV of a church, monastery, and hospice for Ethiopian pilgrims behind St Peter's, San Stefano dei Mori, "of the Blacks".[5]

At the beginning of the sixteenth century Ethiopia was engaged in a struggle with Moslem invaders, and the negus Labna Danghel (1508-1540), who had come into contact with Catholicity through the Portugese military expeditions in the Red Sea, asked the king of Portugal to get the pope to send a prelate who would take the place of their primate from Egypt, hoping thereby to get Portuguese military aid as well. After a curious incident in which a Portuguese adventurer, a physician named Bermudez, became abuna[6] for a short time, St Ignatius Loyola organized a mission, and in 1555 Pope Julius III appointed a Portuguese Jesuit, John Nuñez Barreto, as "patriarch of Ethiopia", with two other bishops and ten priests. Barreto never reached his destination and, though his fellow bishop Andrew Oviedo was able to, the mission had not much success: Labna Danghel's successors were not favourable to Catholicity, the danger of invasion was less pressing, and moreover, the Portuguese had asked for one-third of the kingdom, as well as the religious submission of the people, as the price of their assistance.

The mission had practically died out when a new development took place with the arrival, in 1603, of Father Peter Paez, a Jesuit of outstanding ability, of whom "the learned men of Gondar, even the most anti-Roman of them, still speak with admiration" (incidentally, he rediscovered the sources of the Blue Nile). He gained great influence over the negus Susneyos (Malak Sagad III, 1607-1632), who undertook a number of religious reforms and after some years was reconciled with the Holy See. At once Abuna Simeon excommunicated him, stirred up the people, and civil war broke out; it lasted for five years. Susneyos was victorious and proclaimed union with Rome for his whole kingdom.

[5] A monk who lived here, Tasfa Sion, published in 1548-1549 a translation of the New Testament into Ge'ez, which included the "common parts" and one anaphora of the Ethiopian Liturgy with a Latin version—the first published text of it. The monastery was unoccupied by 1700 and came for a time into the hands of the Copts, when it sheltered their great liturgical scholar, Raphael Tukhi (d. 1787). It is now the Pontifical Ethiopian College. A manuscript (Brit. Mus. Harl. MS. 5512) written here for the Ethiopian bishop Sahyun in 1549 contains a reference to "the cardinal of England", i.e., Reginald Pole.

[6] *Abuna*, "our father", was the title of the metropolitan of Ethiopia after the name given to St Frumentius, who was called *Abuna* or *Abba Salama*, "father of peace".

About this time Paez died (he was buried close by Lake Tana), and Pope Gregory XV sent Father Alfonso Mendez to take his place. Many of the Ethiopians were again in revolt: they had been badly upset by decrees against concubinage, divorce and so forth, and now the mistaken zeal of Mendez began to alter their rites and ceremonies to conform with Roman usages, and to impose celibacy on a pastoral clergy of whom practically every one was legitimately married. On the other hand, many of them welcomed the union; and all might have been well had not Susneyos and his officials sought to impose the reforms, necessary and unnecessary alike, by methods of the grossest cruelty and persecution: documents published by St Bonaventure's College at Florence in 1928 disclose a state of affairs that is almost unbelievable. The upshot was that when Fasilidas succeeded his father as negus in 1632 he let loose a counter-persecution and banished all Catholic priests from his country. The successor of Mendez, Apollinario de Almeida, who for eight years faced every suffering and danger, was put to death with two companions, as were the Capuchin friars Agathangelo of Vendôme and Cassian of Nantes, who were beatified as martyrs by Pope St Pius X in 1905. Pope Urban VIII had entrusted a new Ethiopian mission to the Franciscans, but it was fruitless, except in persecution for the missioners: the cause of unity had been ruined in Ethiopia for many generations to come.

This is one of the two outstanding examples of large bodies of Christians being lost to Catholic unity primarily through European arrogance and insufficiency; both were in the seventeenth century, and in both the Portuguese were the Europeans at fault: the other one was Malabar (see p. 200). Cardinal Hinsley, writing about Ethiopia in the *Dublin Review* of October 1935 said justly: "The coercive measures against the schismatics, enforced by Susneyos and more or less countenanced by the Jesuits, even though in accord with Abyssinian mentality and the customs of the age, were inexcusable in the eyes of the Church and before the court of Christian civilization. But indiscreet zeal soon brought its own punishment, and the zealots were the pitiable victims."

140

THE CATHOLIC ETHIOPIANS

Ethiopia was closed to Catholic priests for two hundred years: a native bishop, George Gabra Egzeabahar, sent there from Rome at the end of the eighteenth century was simply murdered, and several Capuchins had suffered before him. An attempt to establish relations, in accordance with tradition, between the Ethiopians and the Catholic Copts through Theodore abu-Karim, vicar apostolic in Egypt, came to nothing. The ordinary fate of any Catholic priest in Ethiopia was violent death. But in 1839 the famous Irish-French traveller A. T. d'Abbadie d'Arrast used his influence to get a prefecture apostolic established at Adua; it was confided to the Lazarists, with Bd Justin de Jacobis at their head, who did a wonderful work until he was banished in 1855. In 1846 the Capuchins established a vicariate in the Galla country under Mgr (afterwards Cardinal) Massaia, and another vicariate was organized from Alitiena by the Lazarists.

Mgr de Jacobis opened a seminary which he put in charge of a distinguished ex-monophysite monk, Gabra Michael, who eventually reconciled the reigning negus with Rome. But in 1854 this ruler was deposed by the vigorous soldier Kassa (Theodore II), and abandoned his faith in the face of persecution. The dissident primate, Salama, was recalled, and he seized and tortured Abba Michael in a vain attempt to make him apostatize. Having been reprieved from death upon the intervention of the British consul Walter Chichele Plowden (who had supported Theodore's usurpation), he was sentenced to perpetual imprisonment and died from hardship and exposure three months later. Gabra Michael was beatified as a martyr in 1926, thirteen years before the beatification as a confessor of his master, Justin de Jacobis ("Abuna Jacob"). In such ways did the Catholic Church in Ethiopia begin slowly to recover the people who were thrown away by European aggressiveness in the seventeenth century. The accession of Menelik II in 1889 brought peace to the missionaries and their flocks.

PRESENT STATE

Organization. The Catholics of the Galla and Kaffa districts and elsewhere, converts from heathenism, are all of the Latin rite and therefore are no concern of ours here. It was some time before there were any facilities for enabling Catholic Ethiopians to continue in the usages to which they were accustomed. But this was remedied in the north by the time the Capuchins were given a separate prefecture in Eritrea in 1894, and in 1930 an ordinariate of Eastern rite was formed in that Italian colony, Abuna Khidane Mariam Kassa being appointed its first bishop. In 1951 this became an exarchate, with its centre at Asmara, and at the same time another exarchate was set up at Addis Ababa for the rest of Ethiopia. The bishop of the latter has delegated jurisdiction over the Latin-rite Catholics of certain districts.

Parochial clergy. In 1919 Pope Benedict XV restored the church behind St Peter's, the old St Stephen's of the Abyssinians ("Blacks"), to serve as the chapel for a college of their rite which he founded close by. This seminary is under the charge of the Capuchins, who now have some friars of Ethiopic rite, and they conduct another seminary at Gaggiret, near Asmara. There is an Ethiopian seminary at Kheren, for Eritrea. The clergy are bound to celibacy, but married priests reconciled from the dissidents receive dispensation. The Catholic Ethiopian clergy are a most devoted body of men, with a very strong sense of their pastoral responsibilities.

Religious institutes. Monasticism (often of a very loose kind) has always been widespread in Ethiopia, and there are today hundreds of monks among the dissidents. Twenty-three young Ethiopians and two priests were in 1931 accepted at the Cistercian abbey of Casamari, in Italy, to be trained to form a nucleus of Catholic monks in their own country. Sixteen of these young men were professed in 1933, and a monastery has now been opened near Asmara. There are a number of Ethiopian as well as European sisters, who teach in school.

The Faithful number 35,000 in Eritrea, and some thousands elsewhere, with a number of Latin-rite Catholics as well; these make up a tiny minority amid millions of dissident Christians, Moslems and heathen. They are an intelligent people, devoted to their religion, but for the most part rather ignorant and poor.

In 1935 the Italian dictator Mussolini invaded Ethiopia and on 8 May 1936 announced the annexation of the whole country to the Italian crown. In the years that followed there was some outside criticism of the Holy See for its alleged alacrity and thoroughness in trying to use for ecclesiastical ends the political situation, brought about by barefaced aggression. But, quite apart from the fact that Rome did little more than reorganize already existing mission territory in view of new conditions, the Italian civil authorities actually favoured the Moslems at the expense of Christians. Even in Eritrea, Ethiopian Catholics (especially those who had some education) strongly opposed the invaders (not always for strictly patriotic reasons); and on the whole it would seem that the Italian invasion did less harm to the cause of unity than might have been expected. In any case the Ethiopians had shown themselves little disposed to give up their religious isolation. Eritrea was an Italian colony for over fifty years, but in 1939 there were still only about 14,000 Ethiopian Catholics there in a population of over 600,000: this does not suggest the likelihood of any great change in the country at large. The future of the Church in Ethiopia is evidently with the national rite and the indigenous clergy.

LITURGY AND CUSTOMS

The Ethiopic liturgical rite is substantially that of the Copts, translated into Ge'ez, but owing to need of revision of the books the Catholics for some time used the Roman rite in that tongue. Pope Pius XI ordered that this revision should be carried out in strict accordance with the best Ethiopic liturgical tradition and this has been done so far as the text is concerned; European influence had led to some regrettable modifications in accessories: a glaring example was the church of the Ethiopian College itself at Rome, which was completely Western, even to the Latin text upon the altar cloth.

Church buildings. The normal plan of an Ethiopian church is now circular, divided into three concentric circles with the altar in the middle, but there are many old churches of basilican shape in Ethiopia and those of the Catholics are rectangular. The dissidents treat with great reverence the *tabot*, a box on the altar that rests on the wooden altar-board (there are national legends about the Queen of Sheba and the Ark of the

Covenant concerning this piece of furniture); Catholics replace it by a tabernacle containing the Blessed Sacrament, and the altar top is of stone.

Vestments. These are of the usual Eastern type, with a very full chasuble having a sort of embroidered shoulder-cape (*lanka*), with five short pendants; bishops wear a "crown" of rather exotic pattern. Clerical dress consists of a round black cap with a wide-sleeved gown over a cassock.

Liturgical books. The book of the Liturgy was published at Asmara in 1890 and 1913, but in an unsatisfactory form; an entirely new edition was undertaken at Rome, and it appeared, excellently printed by the Vatican Press, in 1945. Some years earlier the Ethiopic rite of ordination was printed for the first time. An edition of the Divine Office was published in Rome in 1952. The Ge'ez version of the Roman *Rituale* was last printed, at Asmara, in 1924; the proper Ethiopic rites will soon become available.

Altar-vessels and bread. The altar-vessels are as in the Latin rite. The bread is an extraordinary example of hybridization: in Eritrea, unleavened is practically universally used by Catholics; elsewhere, unleavened at a "low Mass" but leavened at a solemn celebration. Blessings are given with a hand-cross.

Music. The Ethiopian chant, enharmonic, of course, has received little study. To Western ears it is wailing and barbaric, and is accompanied *ad libitum* by drums, cymbals and rattles or bells. Some of the chants bear a resemblance to those of the Jewish synagogue, and other influences can be detected.

Liturgical language. This is Ge'ez,[7] the classical Ethiopian tongue, a semitic language allied to Arabic, dead since before the thirteenth century. The present vernacular dialects, Amharic, Tigrinya and Tigré, are descended from Ge'ez.

THE EUCHARISTIC LITURGY

As has been said above, the Liturgy (*Keddase*) is "according to the order of our fathers the Egyptians", translated into Ge'ez and modified by time and other influences. There are seventeen anaphoras, that "of the Apostles" being most commonly used;

[7] Meaning "free", i.e., the language of the ruling people.

this one is independent of the present Coptic rite, being derived from the famous *Apostolic Tradition* of Hippolytus. The "common" parts of the Liturgy are a form of the Alexandrian "St Mark". There is no concelebration or Liturgy of the Presanctified; the Catholics have a form of "low" celebration for ordinary days.

THE DIVINE OFFICE

The Ethiopic office (Matins, Cock-crow and other usual hours) consists of psalms, with biblical lessons and many short poetical compositions interspersed.

THE SACRAMENTS

These rites resemble those of the Copts more or less closely, but it is difficult to get reliable particulars of them. At an *ordination* the new priest does not concelebrate the Liturgy with the bishop.

Eucharist. Among Catholics there is diversity and a good deal of freedom in the manner of receiving communion. At a solemn Liturgy it is always in both kinds, by intinction or separately, standing; at a "low Mass" generally in one only, but sometimes in both. At the Ethiopian College in Rome communion in one kind is altogether forbidden; the Body and Blood are ministered separately (the Blood in a spoon); the words used are, respectively, "The bread of life which came down from Heaven, the body of Christ," and "The cup of life which came down from Heaven, the precious blood of Christ." The recipient replies "Amen" to the first, and "Amen, Amen" to the second.

Calendar. According to Ethiopian chronology we are now (1960) in the year A.D. 1952, but their annual calendar is similar to that of the Copts. Their new year's day is August 29 according to the Julian reckoning, September 11 according to the Gregorian which the Catholics follow (at the cost of much complication).

Feasts. The calandar of feasts is that of the Copts, with local saints added or substituted, *e.g.*, Takla Haymanot, on December 24. It has had to undergo a good deal of modification for Catholic use, for the dissidents celebrate, e.g., Pontius Pilate—

145

according to Fortescue, because he said he was innocent! But no later Western feasts have yet been adopted.

Penitential seasons. There are forty fasting days in Lent, which includes Sundays; fifteen days before the Assumption; three days "of Nineveh" before Lent; the eves of Christmas and the Epiphany; and in a modified form every Wednesday and Friday. Strict fasting includes abstinence from eggs and milk as well as meat, but there is no fasting at all during the fifty days of paschal-time. These severe rules may be lightened in practice, but, as in other parts of the East, many of the faithful attach great importance to the traditional fasts.

BIBLIOGRAPHY

J. B. Colbeaux, *Histoire politique et religieuse de l'Abyssinie*, 3 vols. (Paris, 1929).

A. H. Jones and E. Monroe, *Abyssinia* (Oxford, 1935).

D. Mathew, *Ethiopia* (London, 1947).

J. Duresse, *Ethiopia* (London, 1949).

T. Somigli, *Etiopia francescana nei documenti dei secoli xvii e xviii*, 2 vols. (Quarrachi, 1928).

T. M. Semharay, *La messe éthiopienne* (Rome, 1937).

———— *De indumentis sacris ritus aethiopici* (Rome, 1930).

A. R. Hailu, *Messa Etiopica detta degli Apostoli* (Rome, 1946).

D. Attwater, *Eastern Catholic Worship* (New York, 1945), pp. 94-113.

C. Korolevsky, *Living Languages in Catholic Worship* (London, 1957), pp. 141-163.

CHAPTER VI

THE ANTIOCHENE RITE

1. THE SYRIANS

THE position in the patriarchate of Antioch after the Council of Chalcedon was much the same as in that of Alexandria, except that even western Syria was never solidly monophysite like Egypt. Those who refused to accept the Council's decrees were to a considerable extent moved by political, anti-imperial passions, and were egged on by Egyptian monks. The patriarchal throne of Antioch, like that of Egypt, was bandied between orthodox Catholic and monophysite occupants until the Emperor Justinian I imprisoned all bishops professing or suspect of Monophysism. The sect would then probably have died out in Syria had it not been for the action of the Empress Theodora, who favoured the dissidents. At the request of the chief of the Ghassanid Arabs, Harath ibn-Jaballah, she procured the clandestine consecration of two monks in the year 543, one of whom, Jacob Baradai, spent the rest of his life secretly organizing the monophysites in Syria. He gave them a patriarch (called "of Antioch" but residing in eastern Syria) and is said to have ordained twenty-seven bishops and over two thousand priests. From this time on there are two churches in Syria, that of the orthodox Catholics (Melkites) and that of the monophysites, commonly called the Jacobite Church, after its tireless organizer.

The Jacobites welcomed the Arab invasion in 636, and were alternately patronized and persecuted by their conquerors; large numbers of them turned Moslem. They had fairly amiable relations with the Crusaders, and in the twelfth and thirteenth centuries, as in the West and in Ethiopia, there was a revival

147

of religious and intellectual life. Its great ornament was Barhe-braeus (Gregory Abu-l-Faraj), who was as good as he was learned. At the instance of Dominican and Franciscan missionaries there were several movements for union with Rome, notably in 1237 and 1247, but this promising phase was followed by a long period of internal disorder. After the Council of Florence there was a further prospect of union, but it came to nothing.

In consequence of the encouraging attitude of the Jacobite patriarch, Naamat-Allah, Pope Gregory XIII sent a legate to Aleppo in 1583, who paved the way for the establishment of the Capuchins and Jesuits there in 1626. Jacobites at once began to come into communion with the Holy See and in such numbers that by 1656 they were strong enough to elect a Catholic, Andrew Akijian, to the vacant Jacobite see of Aleppo. He was consecrated by the Maronite patriarch, and five years later became Syrian patriarch. The dissident Jacobites resorted to violence, and the persecution went on for a hundred years. Andrew's successor was Peter, ex-Jacobite bishop of Jerusalem, to whom the Jacobites opposed a patriarch of their own; Peter was thrown into prison at Adana in 1701, together with an archbishop and ten priests. The two prelates died in chains, leaving the Catholic Syrians without a leader, and during the succeeding eighty years they were all but destroyed by the severity of the repressive measures taken against them.

In 1691 their bishop at Mardin, Athanasius Safar, went to South America to collect funds for the establishment of a seminary—surely one of the first to cross the Atlantic on such an errand, and probably the first Syrian to set foot in the New World. Like so many who have followed him, Safar found the Americans to be generous people, and in 1696 he was able to buy a property in Rome. But the enterprise did not prosper, and in 1753 the college was closed and the buildings sold.

In Syria, as elsewhere in the Levant, the activities of the civil representatives of France were often pernicious at this time. Their consul at Aleppo obtained Turkish support for Andrew Akijian by bribery; and in 1704 the ambassador at Constantinople (Ferréol; cf. p. 175) wrote, "It will be easy for me to make (Isaac bin-Jobair) patriarch of the Syrians at Aleppo".

But it was not. Isaac refused the office and retired to Rome, where he translated *The Imitation of Christ* into Syriac.

THE CATHOLIC SYRIANS[1]

Before he died in 1783 the then Jacobite patriarch of Antioch nominated as his successor the archbishop of Aleppo, Mar[2] Michael Jarweh. He had recently become a Catholic and, hastening to take possession of the patriarchal residence at Mardin, he gained the support of four bishops and sent to Rome for confirmation of what he had done. The anti-Catholic party meantime elected another patriarch, who succeeded in getting a *berat* of recognition from the Turkish government before Jarweh, who was put in prison. Jarweh escaped, first to Baghdad and then to the Lebanon, that secular refuge of persecuted Catholics. He established himself in a Maronite monastery, then a school, at Sharfeh, and governed his followers from there till his death in 1801. Michael Jarweh is accounted the first patriarch of Antioch of the Catholic Syrians.

In 1830 the patriarchal residence was moved to Aleppo and the Turks recognized the Catholics as a separate body from the Jacobites, their patriarch becoming civil head of the "nation" (*milleh*) in 1843. Between 1820 and 1850 five Jacobite bishops became Catholics,[3] and in the latter year the patriarch Gregory Jarweh moved his residence to the centre of Jacobite influence, Mardin, persecution both by dissidents and Moslems having made Aleppo untenable. This led to more reconciliations, again including several bishops,[4] but the progress of the Catholic Syrians was abruptly checked by World War I.[5] In 1915 Mar Flavian Michael Malkeh, bishop of Gazira, was murdered in prison by the Turks, with four of his clergy. The patriarch Ephrem II Rahmani (1898-1929), left Mardin and

---

[1] Sometimes called, with their dissident counterpart the Jacobites, *West* Syrians, or *Pure* Syrians, to distinguish them clearly from the Chaldeans and Nestorians, though a good half of them in fact live in Iraq and the eastern parts of Syria.

[2] *Mar* (Syriac, "lord"; fem. *mart*) is used in all Syriac rites as a title for saints and bishops.

[3] For an account of one of them, see Attwater, *Eastern Saints*, s.v. A Syrian Saul.

[4] And an ex-patriarch, Mar Abdul-Massih, in 1913, but he returned to schism soon after. The only other noteworthy case of schism in later years was that of Mar Gregory Sattuf, bishop of Homs, who went back to the Jacobites in 1905 and later became patriarch. Their original abjurations of Jacobitism were chiefly due to quarrels and grievances—that is so often the case in these "submissions"; the reconciliation of Mar Ivanios in India was a most happy example of better things.

[5] The patriarch Philip Ankus assisted at the Vatican Council.

went to live at Bairut, where the patriarchal residence is now fixed. Rahmani worthily maintained the fame of the Syrian Church for learning, and his reputation as a scholar extended to the West.[6]

PRESENT STATE

Patriarch. The Syrian Patriarch of Antioch is elected by the bishops of his church, in the conditions and with the rights and duties set out by the common law (cf. p. 58).[7] He always takes the name of Ignatius (in memory of the great bishop of his see martyred at Rome *c*. 107) in addition to another name. He has jurisdiction over the faithful of his rite in the old Turkish empire and Egypt, and lives at Bairut. The patriarch Mar Ignatius Gabriel Tappuni was made a cardinal in 1936.

Bishops. Although this Syrian church is distinguished as West, half its faithful are in fact in Iraq. The sees accordingly are Mardin and Amida, the patriarchal diocese, administered by a titular archbishop as vicar; Aleppo, Baghdad, Damascus, Homs, Mosul, which are archiepiscopal, and Hassakeh, which is episcopal; but all the bishops are subject directly to the patriarch. Lebanon, Palestine and Egypt are patriarchal vicariates. A vacant see is filled by the patriarch and bishops in synod, the clergy of the diocese having an advisory voice. The choice must be approved by the Holy See.

Parochial clergy. Since the second synod of Sharfeh in 1888 priests have been bound to celibacy, but dispensations are accorded to converts from the Jacobites. In 1930 the patriarchal seminary at Sharfeh (founded in 1801) was put under the direction of the Subiaco Benedictines of the French province, who since 1901 had conducted a seminary of the Syrian rite at Jerusalem; this continued to be maintained by them as a junior house. After half a century's devoted work of the utmost value, done in closest contact with the Syrian clergy, the monks withdrew. Thereupon, in 1951, these establishments were entrusted to Augustinians of the Assumption from the Dutch province, under whom the junior seminary also was moved to Sharfeh. Other aspirants to the priesthood go to the Syro-

---

[6] He published the first full text, with Latin translation and introduction, of the Syriac *Testamentum Domini* (Mainz, 1899).
[7] The code of Eastern canon law provides for the observance of any particular patriarchal rights and duties that may be customary in a given church.

Chaldean college at Baghdad, the Jesuit's interritual seminary at Bairut, and elsewhere.

The vicar general of each diocese is called *chorepiskopos*, and this title is sometimes accorded to priests occupying responsible posts outside the dioceses. It is conferred by the bishop with an imposition of hands. Bishops-elect always receive the chorepiscopal blessing eight days before their consecration, if they have not already received it. The *periodeut* ("visitor") is a diocesan prelate who has charge of the discipline of the clergy. There is no permanent office of archdeacon.

Religious institutes. The few monks and nuns of this rite were dispersed during World War I. There had been at Sharfeh from 1785 a congregation of priests whose existence was very precarious; an attempt was made to revive them at Mardin in 1882 as the *Missionaries of St Ephrem*, but they still numbered only a few priests. There was a wealthy and ancient monastery at Mar Behnam, near Mosul, with a few student brethren in charge of a secular priest. The bishops therefore asked the Benedictines at Sharfeh to undertake the formation of a monastic foundation, under the Rule of St Benedict but adapted in all respects to Syrian requirements. The object of the foundation was to combine monastic with active life, but excluding the care of parishes. The first Syrian monk of this enterprise was simply professed in 1935, but its progress was brought to a standstill by the war which so soon followed.

The Faithful of the Syrian rite number some 80,000 in the patriarchal territory, chiefly in Syria and Iraq. Many of them were originally refugees from the Turks. The Jacobites, who suffered from the same massacres and deportations, are not many more. The Syrians are mostly very poor and simple, and have insufficient good schools of their own; they are helped so far as possible by Western congregations working in the Levant, particularly the Jesuits, and by the Maryamat sisters.

OTHER JURISDICTIONS

There are some 5,000 Catholic Syrians (not to be confused with the Catholic Melkites or the Maronites, also Syrians) in the United States. They have no priests of their rite, and those of the faithful who still practise their religion mostly frequent the churches of the Melkites or Maronites. The results of World War II seem so far to have prevented anything new being done to improve their religious condition. There are some thousands in various other parts of the world, almost entirely without clergy. There are two priests in the Argentine, and one each in Chili and Paris,[8] for the colonies in those places. Brisbane apparently has a church for its 700 faithful, but no priest. This defect, lack of clergy, is a matter of great anxiety to the patriarch and bishops. The Syrians have a church in Rome, St Ephrem "in Campo Marzio".

LITURGY AND CUSTOMS

Church buildings. In a Syrian Catholic church there are generally three altars in a row, the middle one, under a *ciborium,* having a tabernacle, crucifix and an indeterminate number of candles. The two side altars are sometimes only used as credence-tables. The altar top (*tablitho*) is of wood or stone, and always portable, covered by a "corporal" with a silk or linen cloth beneath. There is sometimes an open screen with three doors, but without pictures or lights on it. It should have a large curtain, with a smaller one for the altar alone, to be drawn across at certain times. *Ripidia* stand behind the altar for use in processions. In front of the sanctuary and separated from it by wooden railings is the choir, raised one step above the nave. Normally there are no seats, and men are accommodated in front, women behind. Round statues now take the place of pictures in some town churches, and confessional boxes have been adopted. The Catholics have some ancient churches around Mosul and the cathedral of Aleppo; others look like bad Latin churches.

Vestments. The eucharistic dress consists of a white alb (*kuthino*), stole rather of the Byzantine pattern (*uroro*), embroidered belt (*zunnoro*), cuffs (*zendo*), and a chasuble (*phaino*) like a cope without hood or orphreys. The deacon wears an

[8] Their church of St Ephrem in the rue des Carmes was formerly the chapel of the Irish College. Its priest, Chorepiscopus Gabriel Khuri-Sarkis, is founder and editor of the important review *L'Orient Syrien.*

CARDINAL IGNATIUS GABRIEL TAPPUNI
Patriarch of Antioch of the Syrians

BENEDICT MAR GREGORY THANGALITHIL
Archbishop of Trivandrum of the Syro-Malankarese

BEGINNING OF THE MALANKARESE SYRIAN LITURGY

THE MARONITE RITE

The kiss of peace is passed from hand to hand

ungirdled *kuthino* of any colour, with his stole falling back and front over the left shoulder.

A bishop adds to the sacerdotal garments an embroidered hood (*masnaphto*) and the *omophorion*, which is like a large scapular embroidered with crosses falling back and front over the *phaino*. Catholic bishops affect the Roman mitre (the Jacobites have none) and crozier, but the patriarch carries a pastoral staff of the Byzantine pattern. The ordinary dress of the clergy is a black gown or cassock (violet for prelates), with a wide-sleeved open gown (*jubba*) and *kalemaukion*. Catholic bishops have adopted that headdress (over a small black hood, *eskhimo*) in place of their traditional turban; they carry a hand-cross, wrapped in a silk veil, to bless with. Out of doors they carry an ebony staff (the Byzantine *khazranion*).

Altar-vessels and bread. Both chalice and large deep paten are either fitted with metal lids or covered with linen cloths; there is also a larger veil to go over both vessels. The "purificator" is now in use, but it is still called a sponge. A spoon is needed for the priest's communion. The altar-bread is round, thick and leavened, with a little salt added; it is stamped with twelve crosses. Syrian prescriptions about altar-bread are very exacting; e.g., it is supposed to be baked fresh for each Liturgy, and it must not be used if it has fallen to the ground. The reserved host, on which a few drops of the consecrated Wine are sprinkled, must be renewed every day. Cymbals, or similar things, are used during the Liturgy as the altar-bell is in the Latin rite.

Liturgical books. These have been printed from time to time at Rome, Bairut and elsewhere. That of 1922, of Sharfeh, was a reformed and improved edition. A new edition of the *Pontifical*, prepared at Rome and Sharfeh and in every way worthy of Syrian tradition, was published, in two volumes, in 1950-52.

Music. The Syrian chant has been the subject of a good deal of study, encouraged by the patriarch Rahmani; the Benedictines at the Jerusalem seminary set it down in Western notation. As the native singers know it by tradition alone, it not having been written, its variations are endless. It is strictly rhythmical and richer and more varied than the chant of the Maronites and Chaldeans.

Liturgical language. This is Syriac, i.e., the "Edessene" dialect of Aramaic (the language of Jesus Christ),[9] with the "western" pronunciation and characters. The people speak Arabic (except a few who still have a corrupt Syriac), and the scriptural lessons and certain pre-anaphoral prayers of the Liturgy are sung or read in that tongue. The rubrics in the older books are Arabic printed in Syrian characters (i.e., "Karshuni"). Syrians call the Liturgy *Kurobho*, "sacrifice", literally "approach".

THE EUCHARISTIC LITURGY

From the fourth century the fundamental rite of Antioch was the Liturgy of St James, imported with other usages from Jerusalem. The rite underwent other influences, and from its developed form the present West Syrian and Maronite rites are in part derived. It was originally in Greek, but was soon translated into Syriac in various places, and after the monophysite schism the orthodox Catholics maintained its use in the first language, the Jacobites in the second; it was one of the sources of the Byzantine, the Armenian and perhaps the Chaldean Liturgies.[10] There are now considerable discrepancies between the Greek and Syriac versions of the anaphora "of St James the Brother of the Lord". Other anaphoras in use are "of St John the Evangelist", "of the Twelve Apostles", "of St Mark the Evangelist", "of St Eustace of Antioch", "of St Basil of Caesarea", and "of St Cyril of Jerusalem". There are sixty-four known Syrian anaphoras, but only these seven are printed in the Catholic books. The Liturgy is celebrated in the evening on the eve of Easter and of Christmas, and then entirely in Syriac (as also on the feast of St Ephrem).

The Syrians may use their Liturgy of the Presanctified on ferias in Lent as well as on Good Friday. They never concelebrate; but on Maundy Thursday and a few other occasions the Liturgy may be celebrated simultaneously by several priests, at one or at several altars improvised in the sanctuary; each consecrates separate *oblata*, the senior alone celebrating aloud

---

[9] Such phrases of Scripture as *Ethpatakh* (Mark 7:34), *Eli, eli, lamana shbktani* (Matt. 27:46), *Telitha kumi* (Mark 5:41) and *Maran-atha* (1 Cor. 16:22), and the words *korban, mammona, rabuni,* etc., are in this tongue.

[10] The local Orthodox, in later times, abandoned the Antiochene rite for its Byzantine daughter, as we have seen above. They have revived the use of the Greek St James twice a year, at Zakynthos and Jerusalem.

and facing the people, the others on either side of him facing one another. There is now an approximation to "low Mass".

DIVINE OFFICE

The Syrian canonical prayers have seven "hours", which are recited in two parts: office of the Ninth hour, Vespers (*Ramsho*) and prayer of Protection (*Suttoro*) in the evening; Night Office (*Lilyo*) with three nocturns, Lauds (*Teshebhotho*), Morning Prayer (*Saphro*) and offices of the Third and Sixth hours before the Liturgy. The office is peculiarly rich in hymns and poetical compositions,[11] and there are few psalms, in some hours none at all. Each hour begins with the *Trisagion* thrice and the Lord's Prayer, and always includes prayer for the dead; the *Te Deum* is sung at Lauds. What psalms there are are mostly invariable, according to whether it be a weekday or Sunday or great feast. The version of the holy Scriptures used for liturgical purposes in all the Syrian rites is the Peshitto. Daily recitation of the Office was made obligatory on the clergy by the synod of Sharfeh in 1888. Wherever there are two or more priests together they are directed to sing all of it in church, but this is rarely observed except on the eve of a Sunday or of a feast.

THE SACRAMENTS

Baptism. The water is blessed for the occasion before each baptism. After certain prayers the priest pronounces the exorcisms and anoints the child with oil three times on the forehead. Then he seats it in the font and pours water on its head three times, saying, "N. is baptized in the name of the Father, and of the Son, and of the Holy Spirit, unto everlasting life." He at once proceeds to

Confirmation, which consists essentially of anointing with chrism the forehead, eyelids, nostrils, lips, ears, hands, chest, back and feet, with the words: "N. is sealed unto everlasting life in the name of the Father . . . , with holy chrism, the sweet perfume of the Anointed of God, sign and seal of true faith and of the accomplishment of the gifts of the Holy Spirit."

Penance is ministered with the Western formula, translated into Syriac or Arabic.

---

11 Many by, and still more attributed to, St Ephrem the Deacon, doctor of the Church, whose feast both Latins and Syrians observe on June 18.

Eucharist. The communicant stands, and the celebrant puts a particle into his mouth; as each particle has at the breaking of the Bread been anointed with the precious Blood, he receives under both kinds. The words of administration are: "The cleansing coal of the body and blood of Christ our God is given to his faithful servant for the forgiveness of sins and everlasting life." The receiver replies, "Amen". "Coal", i.e., burning ember, is a common name for the Blessed Sacrament in the East; also called "the pearl" (cf. Isa. 6:6). Deacons and subdeacons are communicated with the spoon from the chalice.

Anointing is now ministered according to a rite that is partly Western and partly Syrian, the sacramental form being adapted from an ancient Syrian form of absolution. The oil of the sick is blessed by the bishop on Maundy Thursday. The proper Syrian Office of the Lamp is very long.

Orders. The orders of the Syrian rite are singer, reader, subdeacon; deacon, priest, bishop. All orders are conferred during the Liturgy by laying on of hands and delivery of instruments of office, without anointing. The formula resembles that of the eucharistic invocation of the Holy Ghost. The subdeacon is given a lighted candle, as his particular business is to care for the lights. Before ordination to the diaconate and upwards a profession of faith must be signed. There is no concelebration at the ordaining of bishops and priests.

Marriage. The wedding rite consists of two parts, the blessing of the rings and the crowning. A ring is given to each party and each is crowned with a wreath. The priest commits them to the care of one another, but there is no explicit contract, which is, however, implicit in the assurance that they have to give, that they are freely entering into matrimony.

Calendar. The Gregorian reckoning is in use and the ecclesiastical year begins on the Sunday nearest to October 31. The calendar is substantially the ancient one of the Church of Antioch; many of the feasts that we have in common are observed on different days. The seasons are Advent, Christmas, preparation for Lent, Lent, paschal-time, time after Pentecost, time after Holy Cross.

Feasts. Corpus Christi, the Sacred Heart and Trinity Sunday are adopted from the West, and the Immaculate Conception,

All Saints and St Joseph transferred to our dates. In addition to Sundays there are twenty general holy days (not all of obligation) as well as local ones; they include the Praises of our Lady (Dec. 26), St Ephrem (June 18), the Praises of St John the Forerunner (Jan. 7), and St George (April 23).

Penitential season. During Lent (seven weeks) a complete fast from food and drink lasts till noon, with abstinence from certain foods for the rest of the day, except on Saturdays and Sundays. The fast of Nineveh and other days are marked by abstinence.

General observations. Catholic Syrians make the sign of the cross as in the West. Western devotions are in use, as is Benediction with the Blessed Sacrament in a Syrian form. Holy Cross day (Sept. 14) is a great occasion, marked by the lighting of bonfires, and on the Assumption the Aleppines eat blessed grapes in memory of their dead. In the country parts the people are much attached to their own ways and customs; but in the towns they often try to approximate themselves to Western ways, in the words of a Benedictine monk working in Syria, "out of snobbery".

BIBLIOGRAPHY

H. Lammens, *La Syrie*, 2 vols. (Bairut, 1921).

A. H. Hourani, *Syria and Lebanon* (London, 1946).

G. Khuri-Sarkis, *La liturgie syrienne* (Paris, 1950).

H. W. Codrington, *Studies of the Syrian Liturgies* (Ramsgate, 1952).

J. Jeannin, *Mélodies liturgiques syriennes et chaldéenes*, 2 vols. (Bairut, 1925-28).

C. K. von Euw, *The Union of the Syro-Jacobites with Rome in the Mid-seventeenth Century* (in the press).

2. THE MARONITES

The Maronites are Syrians, living chiefly in Lebanon, and fundamentally of the same people as the Catholic Syrians (described previously), Jacobites and local Melkites of both obediences. Their existence as a separate "nation" is apparently entirely due to their ecclesiastical origins. There are no non-Catholic Maronites,[12] but the tradition (not found in writings previous to the sixteenth century) of their perpetual orthodoxy has now been abandoned by all except a few die-hards.

The origins and early history of the Maronite Church have aroused controversy, not always conducted with urbanity. It would seem that after the Council of Chalcedon the monks of Bait-Marun, a monastery built around the shrine of St Maro,[13] a fifth-century hermit, on the right bank of the river Orontes between Emesa (Homs) and Apamea, distinguished themselves by their opposition to the monophysites. This conduct was naturally approved by the emperors, who favoured the monastery in consequence, so that its influence spread throughout Syria Secunda.

But in the first half of the seventh century Emperor Heraclius, seeking to unite his Syrian subjects against the invading Arabs, concocted with the patriarchs of Constantinople and Antioch a theological formula which they hoped would conciliate the monophysites. Unfortunately it was heretical, and was promptly condemned by three successive popes and the patriarch of Jerusalem.[14] But Heraclius and his successor stuck to it, and the monks of Bait-Marun faithfully followed their patrons the

---

[12] Yet if you ask a Maronite if he is a Catholic he may say, "No. I am a Maronite." To him "Catholic" means Catholic Melkite. Nevertheless, he does not object to frequenting Latin churches: some Catholic Orientals do, as much as the average Westerner would dislike having to frequent an Eastern church.

[13] He must not be confused with the seventh-century "St John Maro, Patriarch of Antioch", who is known only from Maronite tradition. Grave doubts have been thrown on the latter's existence.

[14] And finally by the sixth oecumenical council (III Constantinople) in 680. The heresy was Monothelism, i.e., the denial that our Lord had a human as well as a divine will; it struck at his real manhood.

emperors. After the Arab conquest and the third general council of Constantinople they and the people under their influence did not, for some unknown reason, return to orthodoxy, and it seems they continued to profess Monothelism long after it had died out everywhere else.[15] It is surmised that, while the patriarchs of Antioch were in exile at Constantinople during the first half of the eighth century, the monks decided to elect a primate for themselves and so began the separate line of Maronite patriarchs of Antioch. After the destruction of Bait-Marun at the end of the ninth century the monks and their dependents withdrew themselves entirely into the Lebanon mountains.

In the year 1182 almost the whole nation of the Maronites, 40,000 in number, moved, as the chronicler William of Tyre says, "by an inspiration from Heaven", submitted to the Holy See through Amaury, the third of the Latin patriarchs whom the Crusaders had set up at Antioch. The Maronite patriarch Jeremias II al-Amshiti was present at the Lateran Council in 1215, and Rome had no doubt of their previous Monothelism then, for when Jeremias went home, with a papal legate, Pope Innocent III wrote insisting that he should make a solemn profession of faith in the two wills in Jesus Christ.

The Maronites who had emigrated to Cyprus were apparently separated till after the Council of Florence, for they were reconciled in 1445, with their bishop at their head, and there seem to have been others disaffected here and there even during the late middle ages. But by the beginning of the sixteenth century the Maronites were stabilized, and since the fifth Lateran Council (1512-1517) they have been in close and uninterrupted contact with the Holy See. In 1584 Pope Gregory XIII founded the Maronite College in Rome. An outstanding figure was Germanos Farhat, archbishop of Aleppo (1670-1732), founder at Ehden of the Aleppine Antonian monks. He was a great scholar, widely travelled in Europe, and of surpassing holiness of life.

By the eighteenth century ecclesiastical discipline had become

---

[15] The traditional Maronite explanation is that they denied the two wills (if they did) in error and in ignorance of the decisions of the oecumenical council. When they first heard of its teaching —from the Crusaders!—they at once embraced it. Their unorthodoxy may well have been simply verbal.

very lax among the Maronites and the existence of abusive customs made reform difficult. The Holy See accordingly insisted on a plenary synod, which was eventually convened in 1736 at the monastery of Saidat al-Luwayzeh, "our Lady of the Almond Trees". The famous scholar Joseph Assemani, himself a Maronite, was the papal delegate; and decrees were enacted aiming at the abolition of an excessive number or bishops, the sale of dispensations, the failure to reserve the Blessed Sacrament in rural churches, the neglect of the poor and of church buildings, the remarriage of widowed priests, and other abuses. To these were added certain liturgical prescriptions, some of which were necessary and some were not: e.g., the enforcing of the already customary usages of unleavened bread in the Eucharist and communion in one kind only for the laity. The acts of this synod were formally approved by Pope Benedict XIV but it took a century for them to be generally accepted and enforced. Their troubles were further aggravated by disputed patriarchal elections and by the activities of a nun of Aleppo named Anna Aggami. In spite of the errors into which she fell (which culminated in her claiming to be hypostatically united to the Second Person of the Holy Trinity!) her reputation for holiness gained her the support of the patriarch, Joseph Stephani, and of a Lazarist father, Godez. The Holy See had to interfere in 1779, condemning her, censuring her partizans, and dissolving the sisterhood she had founded. But there were those who maintained her sanctity fifty years afterwards. The great Maronite figure of the nineteenth century was the patriarch Paul Massad, who ruled for thirty-five difficult years. Four of his bishops assisted at the Vatican Council, but Massad himself did not attend—it is said because he feared that pressure would be brought to bear on him to abate some of his privileges.

After the Turkish conquest the people of the Lebanon, Maronites and Druzes,[16] were never governed directly by the Turks but came under the control of the native amirs.[17] The resulting semi-independence caused the Lebanon to be the

---

[16] A sect that broke away from Islam in the eleventh century; secular rivals of the Maronites.

[17] In 1730 a Maronite "prince" (*shaykh*?) from Kasrawan was travelling in the extreme southwest of England; he is referred to in the town records of Penzance and St Ives, where his name is given as "Abu Gemblat Hassar Abaisci, of Mount Libanus".

refuge of oppressed Catholics of Eastern rites, Melkites, Syrians, Armenians, until they were emancipated from the civil control of the dissident patriarchs after 1829. But by the beginning of the nineteenth century the feudal organization of the Lebanon was cracking; after the abdication of the vigorous old amir Bashir II Shabab and the evacuation of Syria by Mohammed Ali (1840), the political policies of the great powers precipitated a deadly struggle between Maronites and Druzes, aggravated by the internal reforms imposed on Turkey by the Congress of Paris after the Crimean war. The situation went out of control on 30 May 1860, the occasion being a quarrel between a Druze and a Maronite at Bait-Mari. The Druzes were armed and ready, but the Christians had allowed themselves to be disarmed by the Turkish authorities on the pretence of maintaining order. In three weeks every Maronite village of the main and southern Lebanon was pillaged and burned, and six thousand Maronites were murdered, maimed or outraged; the abbot of Dair al-Kamar was flayed alive and his twenty monks pole-axed. Khursud Pasha marched into the district with a battalion of soldiers, fired a single gun, and then left his troops to join in the massacre. On July 9 it broke out at Damascus, where in three days the adult males alone numbered three thousand victims. Of these, eight Friars Minor and three Maronite laymen were shown by the circumstances of their death to have been martyrs of the faith, and were beatified by Pope Pius XI in 1926. The Maronites were brothers, Francis, Muti and Raphael Masabki. In all, 16,000 Maronites were slain and 100,000 rendered homeless.

France sent a military expedition to restore order, and the Lebanon was given a constitution drawn up by a commission of the European powers; it became an autonomous province of the Turkish empire with a governor general, who was a Christian not belonging to any of the chief local communions. In 1926 the country was reorganized as the Republic of Lebanon (then under French mandate). The district of Kasrawan, north-east of Bairut, is almost exclusively Maronite.

The Maronites are properly proud of their devotion to the Holy See; but they are an independent people and tenacious of their rights and privileges, the more so that in the past Western influence has sometimes tended to be coercive. The help they gave to other oppressed Catholics in the seventeenth and eighteenth centuries, and the persecution they suffered themselves from time to time, must not be forgotten.

PRESENT STATE

Patriarch. The Maronite patriarch of Antioch[18] is elected by the bishops gathered in synod, in the conditions and with the rights and duties provided by the common law (cf. p. 58). His jurisdiction is over all the faithful of his rite in the old Turkish empire in Asia and Egypt. The patriarchal residence has been fixed in many places; it is now at Bkerkeh in the winter and Dimaneh in the summer, both in Lebanon.

At the time of the death of Patriarch Antony Arida at the age of ninety-two in 1955, the affairs of the Maronite church were in the hands of an apostolic commission. The general situation was delicate and somewhat disturbed, and Pope Pius XII judged it desirable that he himself should appoint a successor; he chose Mar Paul Meuchi, at that time archbishop of Tyre. In his letter of appointment, the pope emphasized that this was an exceptional measure, in no way intended to derogate from the right of the Maronite bishops to elect their patriarch. The bishops accepted the papal nomination unanimously.

Bishops. The Maronite dioceses have been clearly delimited and their bishops permanently resident only since the synods of 1736 and 1818. The sees, except Bairut, are all episcopal and dependent directly on the patriarch (but each holder is called archbishop); they are Gibail and Batrun (the patriarchal diocese), Bairut, Aleppo, Baalbek, Cairo, Cyprus (practically all its subjects and their bishop live in Lebanon), Damascus, Sarba, Sidon, Tyre and Tripoli. There is a patriarchal vicar for Palestine. Vacant sees are filled by the patriarch and bishops in synod, the lower clergy having an advisory voice; the choice must be confirmed by the Holy See. Among the bishops' means of support is a poll-tax on every adult in his diocese.

Parochial clergy. Parish priests in the rural parts are nearly all married and often the support of their families is a very

18 The concession of this title can only be looked on as an act of grace. It was first acknowledged by Pope Alexander IV in 1254.

onerous burden, as it usually is for the country clergy else-where. This class among the clergy was but poorly instructed, for though there were several diocesan seminaries only two were of any size. However, a general central seminary for the whole patriarchate was established in 1934. It is situated at Ghazir and is directed by Jesuit fathers, the rector being of Maronite nationality. The Maronite College at Rome, first founded in 1584, was refounded in 1891, and is now also under the direction of the Jesuits,[19] but it can accommodate only twenty-four students. A considerable number of Maronite priests are trained in the Oriental seminary of the Society of Jesus at Bairut. The college at Ain Warka, originally established in 1660 but long closed, was reopened as a junior seminary in 1949.

The offices of *chorepiskopos* and *bardut* ($\pi\epsilon\rho\iota o\delta\epsilon\upsilon\tau\acute{\eta}s$, visitor), carry with them variable duties, e.g., to confirm and to confer minor orders for the bishop; archpriests and archdeacons are practically titular only.

Religious institutes. As is appropriate to a church that had its origins in a monastery, monasticism has always had many followers among the Maronites. Their monks of the middle ages led a rather go-as-you-please and unorganized life, and in 1695 the learned patriarch Stephen ad-Duwayhi started a congregation modelled on Western lines, under the so-called Rule of St Antony, the traditional patriarch of the solitary life. The enterprise prospered and spread, absorbing existing monasteries; but, as in the case of the Melkite Basilians, the particularism of Aleppo caused trouble and in 1770 two distinct congregations were formed, the *Baladite* ("rural") *Antonians* and the *Aleppine Antonians*. During the same time a bishop, afterwards patriarch, Gabriel Blauzawi, united other monasteries into a congregation, which received the name of *Antonians of St Isaias*, from its mother house.

The life and constitutions of all three congregations of Maronite Antonians closely resemble one another. They are now canonically what are called "non-monastic religious orders", and some of the hieromonks serve parishes;[20] they

[19] Its most famous alumnus is the Syriac scholar Joseph Assemani (al Sam'ani), 1687-1768.

[20] The Baladites also do missionary work among the half-Moslem, half-pagan Nuzayris around Biadieh in the Alauite country.

are bound to perpetual abstinence from flesh-meat and tobacco. A few of them are hermits, living alone in the neighbourhood of their monasteries; these do not normally receive visitors, keep almost perpetual silence, fast daily and are bound to certain hours of manual work every day.[21] A notable proportion of the Baladites are monks who are not ordained. The habit is a black gown with a small round hood, leather belt, and sandals. All together there are about 700 of these monks, 500 of whom are priests. Each congregation has an abbot general at the head. There are numerous monasteries and residences, some of which have only one or two monks, who are engaged in looking after landed estates. Much land in Lebanon belongs to the Antonians, and excessive territorial wealth has been the cause of certain irregularities among them;[22] the synod of 1818 and others had to take strong measures against monastic abuses.

The Aleppine congregation has a small college for its students in Rome. The causes of beatification of three nineteenth-century Antonians, two monks and a nun, are before the Congregation of Rites.[23]

The *Missionaries of Kraim* form an active congregation, preaching, giving retreats, and running a printing press. They were founded by Father John Habib in 1865.

The *Antonian nuns* were originally enclosed and contemplative, with solemn office in choir, but are now chiefly engaged in conducting schools, orphanages, etc. There are also *Visitation* nuns, *Sisters of the Holy Family* (founded by Patriarch Elias Huwayek in 1895), and Franciscan tertiary *Sisters of the Cross* (founded 1930), engaged in teaching and other charitable works. The Sisters of the Sacred Hearts of Jesus and Mary (*Maryamat*), an inter-ritual congregation originated by two Jesuit fathers in 1853 which does splendid educational work in Syria, has a large proportion of Maronite members.

The Faithful. Religious statistics for Lebanon have been subjected to considerable criticism from various quarters, but there is no doubt that, in spite of much emigration, the number

---

[21] The cause of beatification of one of these hermits has been begun: Father Sharbel Makhluf (1828-1898). Cf. P. Daher, *A Cedar of Lebanon* (Dublin, 1956).

[22] For example, recognized "irregular monasteries" wherein observance was relaxed and the superior (*reis*) sometimes to be found surrounded by his relatives or other lay people, who were supposed to assist him in the administration of the property of the monks.

[23] For an interesting account of a Maronite monastery, see Doughty's *Arabia Deserta*, Vol. II, chap. xiii, criticized in the *Dublin Review*, Jan., 1934.

of Maronites in the patriarchate is large. The diocesan figures given in the *Annuario Pontificio* for 1960 total over 630,000 people (14,000 in Egypt, 2,500 in Cyprus, 2,500 in Palestine). The greater part of them are peasants and mountaineers, faithful to their religion and anxious to improve themselves— schools are eagerly sought. But the commercial and professional middle-class has grown rapidly of recent years, especially in Bairut itself; and, as Abbé Labourt wrote fifty years ago, some influences from the West are "outrageously bad". The Maronites owe an incalculable debt to the Jesuits, who have worked in Syria from 1625 till 1773 and from 1831 on; their university and its Oriental seminary at Bairut have been the door to intellectual and professional activities for many Maronites and others. The Lebanese today are faced with new and difficult problems, and Catholic higher education no longer expresses itself almost exclusively in the French language and according to the French genius.

OTHER JURISDICTIONS

United States. Maronites are to be found in every large city of the United States and their number is difficult to estimate: but it seems to be over 50,000. They are subject to the American bishops but there are *chorepiskopoi* empowered to confirm, consecrate churches and altars, etc. They have some fifty parishes. Their first permanent priest was Father Peter Korka-mas, who established a church in New York city and started a mission in Boston, about 1895; the first Maronite arrived in the latter city so long ago as 1854.

South America. There are considerable Maronite colonies in Uruguay and Argentine, and the 60,000 in Brazil are in charge of a ritual vicar of the archbishop of Rio de Janeiro.

Elsewhere there are 6,000 or so, with churches at Leghorn, Paris, Sydney, in Canada and other places; and 3,000 in South Africa, where their centre is Johannesburg.

LITURGY AND CUSTOMS

The Antiochene usages of the Maronites began to be modified at the end of the sixteenth century, to a large extent by borrowed externals that now obscure the fundamentally real Eastern character of the surviving rite. The later *church buildings* tend to look exactly like those of the West; but there are ancient Maronite churches in Lebanon retaining a screen before the sanctuary, and having the altar set in an apse, with the episcopal chair and seats for the other clergy behind it. The appointments of their churches and their *altar-vessels, etc.*, are entirely Western, though blessings are given with a hand-cross and *ripidia* are carried in processions. Altar-breads are unleavened and just the same as ours. Their *music* is in origin that of the Syrians, with cymbals to mark the rhythm, but very different in detail.

Vestments. The eucharistic dress of a priest is purely modern Roman,[24] except that he generally wears embroidered cuffs instead of a maniple. The lower clergy have Syrian vestments (all with stoles worn in varying ways), and generally the bishops do too (with Roman mitre and crozier). Servers have cassock and cotta. A hieromonk celebrates with his hood (*schema*) drawn over his head.

The ordinary dress of the clergy is a black cassock (violet for prelates, red for the patriarch) with a round flat cap; wide-sleeved gown and low turban are for formal occasions. Bishops wear their turban over the Syrian *eskhimo* (hood).

Liturgical books. These were printed in Rome from 1594, and a definitive edition was drawn up and issued after the 1736 synod, reprinted at Rome, Kosayya and Bairut. They include a "missal" and "breviary" arranged in the Roman way. A new and better edition of the *Ritual* was printed at the Jesuits' press in Bairut in 1942. The *Pontifical* has never been printed; but the new Syrian edition is now available for the use of Maronite bishops.

The *liturgical language* is Syriac, but the lessons and some other prayers are in Arabic, and the use of this vernacular tends to increase. Rubrics are in Karshuni.

THE EUCHARISTIC LITURGY

This is simply the common parts of the Syrian Liturgy of

---

[24] When they borrow from the West, Orientals always choose the worst patterns. The first Maronite priest I ever saw, in a church at Cairo, had a chasuble of staring green, stiff as a board, with pink roses sprawling all over it. A very curious observance of some bishops is to change their *phaino* for a chasuble before the consecration.

St James into which one or other of the *anaphoras* is inserted, a version of the Antiochene rite, with features of its own and subjected to "adaptation, often useless and servile, to Roman usages" (Labourt). Though in principle every Liturgy is sung, there is a uniform way of celebrating "low Mass", but at this the use of incense and some singing is normal. The people kneel throughout, women normally separate from men. Concelebration often takes place in monasteries and big churches, and sometimes in smaller ones on certain occasions. The Liturgy of the Presanctified is confined to Good Friday.

Of twenty-five known anaphoras, eight are printed for use. The most recent and commonly used is called "of the holy Roman Church", because some of its texts are modelled on those of the Roman canon; but it also includes a good many responses by the people, choir or server. The gospel is read in Syriac and other languages, as well as the usual Arabic, at Christmas. The priest's private prayer before leaving the sanctuary is a manifestation of devotion to the altar of sacrifice, as in the pure Syrian rite.

THE DIVINE OFFICE

This has been obligatory on the clergy since 1736. It is a recasting of the Syrian Office, with the same hours, except that it lacks Lauds.

THE SACRAMENTS

The Ritual published in 1942 was the first step in a radical reform of the Maronite liturgical books. It cleansed the rites from hybridism and is a judiciously abridged recension of West Syrian usages, with the traditional variants due to the particular history of the Maronite church. But the baptismal form is active, "I baptize you, N., lamb of Christ's flock, in the name etc., unto everlasting life"; the form of absolution is also indicative. Confirmation, in the Syrian form, is reserved to the bishop.

Since before 1736 the *Eucharist* is given to lay people, kneeling, under the species of bread only, with the words: "The body of our Lord Jesus Christ is given to you for the pardon of faults, for the forgiveness of sins, and for life ever-lasting. Amen." When the Liturgy is sung solemnly the deacon receives communion in both kinds.

Calendar and feasts. These closely resemble those of the Syrians, with the same Western importations, and others, e.g., Rosary Sunday and the Name of Mary. There are twenty-three holy days, of which St Maro (Feb. 9) is naturally one of the most important. Feasts of Old Testament saints are numerous. The Gregorian reckoning was first adopted in 1606 at Tripoli and elsewhere.

Penitential periods. Lent lasts seven weeks (no fasting on Saturdays and Sundays); Wednesdays and Fridays outside Easter and Christmas time are days of abstinence, as well as some other days, including the Nineveh fast.

General observations. In addition to all the principal Western "popular devotions" (especially those in honour of the Blessed Sacrament) the Maronites have adopted and adapted certain Roman liturgical observances, e.g., the blessing and imposition of ashes (first Monday in Lent), the covering of pictures and statues during Passiontide, blessing of palms, and the washing of feet on Maundy Thursday, on which day, also, the patriarch must consecrate chrism. These are all carried out with con-siderable dramatic effect and popular excitement, which are further displayed in their own special customs, such as the "Raising of Lazarus" (eve of Palm Sunday), and the "Burial" and "Resurrection of Christ". The Liturgy is celebrated at midnight on Christmas, the Epiphany and Easter.

BIBLIOGRAPHY

H. Lammens, *La Syrie*, 2 vols. (Bairut, 1921).

A. H. Hourani, *Syria and Lebanon* (London, 1946).

P. Dib, *L'Église maronite jusqu'à la fin du moyen âge* (Paris, 1930).

P. Raphael, *Le rôle des Maronites dans le retour des Églises orientales* (Bairut, 1935).

P. Dib, *Étude sur la liturgie maronite* (Paris, 1919).

J. P. Gorayeb, *The Maronite Liturgy* (Buffalo, N.Y., 1915).

La Messa siro-maronita (Rome, 1943).

H. W. Codrington, *Studies of the Syrian Liturgies* (Ramsgate, 1952).

3. THE MALANKARESE

On pages 199-202 will be found a brief account of the Christians of Malabar in India and the events which led to their schism in 1653. Within ten years a majority of them had returned to unity, but the rest remained obdurate under their leader the archdeacon Thomas Palakomatta (Parambil). He had received as commission only a sort of investiture by the imposition of hands of twelve priests, and he tried in vain to get episcopal orders from the Nestorians of Mesopotamia. Then he approached the Jacobite patriarch in the same country, who sent a bishop, Mar Gregory, to visit Malabar. He does not seem to have consecrated Thomas nor apparently, in spite of Jacobite episcopal visitations from time to time, were any of his first four successors (all called Thomas) consecrated. However, the schismatics certainly obtained a valid hierarchy in 1772, when the sixth Thomas was made bishop (as Dionysius I) by the episcopal delegates of the Jacobite patriarch. The Malabar Jacobites claim that they never formally accepted monophysite errors, and Dionysius himself was ready to acknowledge the pope, but nothing lasting came of long negotiations. It is not clear when the dissidents began to abandon their Chaldean or East Syrian liturgy for that of the Jacobites, the West Syrian or Antiochene; but it is said that this substitution was not complete until well into the nineteenth century.

Throughout the eighteenth and nineteenth centuries the story of the Malabar Jacobites is a wearisome succession of squabbles, lawsuits and sub-schisms, complicated since 1816 by Protestant missionary efforts. Some attempts were made at reunion with Rome during the eighteenth century and they were all abortive, partly through the policy of the local Western authorities; though there were a number of individual reconciliations to the Chaldeo-Malabarese, there was no important

169 M

reunion till our own day. In 1909 the Jacobite patriarch of Antioch, Abdullah Sattuf, came to Malabar, quarrelled with the metropolitan Dionysius VI about church property and administration, and excommunicated him; for fifty years the "orthodox" Jacobites were split into two litigious parties, those who wanted to depend on the patriarch of Antioch and those who wanted to be independent.

Nevertheless, side by side with this deplorable state of affairs, there has been a quickening of religious consciousness among some of the Malabar Jacobites; an example was when in 1919 Father Givergis (George) Panikkerveetil, rector of the principal Jacobite seminary, founded at a place he called Bethany a religious brotherhood, "of the Imitation of Christ", for missionary and educational work, followed by a similar institute for nuns (for whom there was no provision among the Jacobites). In 1925 Father Givergis was consecrated bishop, taking the name of Ivanios (John).

At a synod of Jacobite bishops of the anti-patriarchal party held in the same year to consider measures for the spiritual regeneration of their church, Mar Ivanios was commissioned "to open correspondence with the Church of Rome with a view to explore the avenues for ending schisms so far as Malabar was concerned". In response to his overtures, the Holy See replied that if the bishops abjured their errors and schism their Antiochene liturgy and customs would be maintained and, upon verification of the validity of their baptism and ordination, the bishops would be confirmed in their offices and jurisdiction.

Of the five bishops concerned only two, Mar Ivanios and his suffragan Mar Theophilos, accepted the invitation. They were received into the visible communion of the Catholic Church on 20 September 1930, followed at once by two *rambans* (solitaries, who were also bishops designate) and other clergy, religious of the Imitation, and a thousand lay people (including the octogenarian parents of Mar Ivanios); there have been many more since then, including two more bishops. To distinguish them from their fellows of the Chaldean and Latin rites in Malabar, they are called the Malankara Catholics.

Unlike so many reunions with Rome in the course of history this movement was distinguished as an entirely religious one,

170

without any element of political, social or other temporal consideration in it. On the contrary, the new Catholics had to suffer a good deal of petty persecution sometimes, and they lost all their ecclesiastical property, churches, cemeteries, etc., upon leaving the Jacobite body. The Brothers of the Imitation set the admirable example of not going to law in order to try and retain their possessions; they were literally penniless and homeless till a generous and sympathetic Hindu came to the rescue with a small piece of land. The reunion has had far-reaching effects among the Jacobites, who can now become Catholics without having to abandon their familiar rites and customs, and, in the case of married priests, without giving up either their wives or their sacerdotal functions, as was their case in joining the Chaldeo-Malabar or the Latin rites.

PRESENT STATE

The Malankara province of Malabar consists of the arch-diocese of Trivandrum and the diocese of Tiruvalla in Kerala. The faithful number over 100,000 (including new converts from Hinduism), and there are nearly 200 priests, some of them married.

Religious institutes. The members of the *Brotherhood of the Imitation of Christ* are missionaries to India, primarily by prayer and contemplation; they wear the yellow gown of the Hindu holy man (*sannyasi*), they avoid all flesh-meat, and their monastery is called an *ashram*. In drawing up their rule the founder Mar Ivanios sought a synthesis of the prescriptions of St Basil, St Benedict and St Francis of Assisi. Their superior is called the *reesh*, "governor". The *Sisters of the Imitation* conduct schools, and the *Daughters of Mary* do social work.

Sannyasi is the name given to a Hindu ascetic who has wholly renounced the world in order to seek God in a life of contemplation and complete poverty. Beginning with the famous Jesuit Robert de Nobili three hundred years ago, there have been European missionaries who sought to bring this life before Indian eyes in Christian terms. In our own day two French priests, the late Father Monchanin and a Benedictine, Dom Le Saux, started an ashram ("hermitage") not far from Trichinopoly in Madras. More recently still, two monks, a Belgian Cistercian and an English Benedictine, set up another ashram, in the heart of the Indian church at Kurisumala in Kerala. Their experiment is of relevant interest in that its life of worship is based on the West Syrian liturgy, as used by so many Malabar Christians, Jacobite and Catholic.

LITURGY AND CUSTOMS

These are simply those of the West Syrian rite, without most of the few modifications which the Catholics of that rite have introduced. The *church appointments* are florid, and statues in churches have had to be forbidden; pictures must be "used with moderation" and not be placed on the altar.

At least all the audible parts of the *eucharistic Liturgy* are in the people's tongue, Malayalam. Incense is used at "low Mass", and blessings are given with a hand-cross. Communion is in both kinds, by intinction. Blessed bread is distributed after every celebration. The *sacraments* are all ministered according to West Syrian tradition.

The clergy wear the wide-sleeved gown, black or white, with a round flat cap, and bishops the turban over the small hood. Priests who fill certain responsible offices, e.g., vicar general, rank as prelates and have the title *prodott*, "visitor".

Devotions in honour of the Blessed Sacrament have been introduced in the form of exposition and benediction. The last-named consists of an excerpt from the last part of the Liturgy, with a hymn and a blessing with the Holy Things (covered) added.

BIBLIOGRAPHY

F. X. Vattathara, *Le mouvement de Bethanie* (Louvain, 1931).
Mar Ivanios, "The Malabar Reunion" in *Pax*, no. 114 (Prinknash, 1931).
————— *A Handbook of the Holy Mass* (Trivandrum, *c.* 1948). Malankara use.
See also the bibliography on page 208.

CHAPTER VII

THE ARMENIAN RITE

THE scattered people whom we call Armenians were formerly localized in the country which is bounded, roughly, by the Caucasus and Taurus Mountains, the Black Sea and the Caspian Sea: Greater Armenia was to the east of the river Euphrates and Lesser Armenia to the west, later covering Cilicia to the Mediterranean. The Armenians are an Indo-European people, who call themselves Haikh and their country Hayastan, on account of a mythical descent from Haik, great-grandson of Noah. They have always been a very distinct people, with what we should now call a strong national sentiment, but their geographical situation was against their enjoying sovereignty for very long consecutive periods and they have been controlled and exploited in turn by the Medes, Romans, Persians, Byzantines, Arabs, Turks and Russians.

The conversion of the Armenians to Christianity was in part the work of St Gregory the Enlightener,[1] a Parthian, who was made bishop by the metropolitan of Caesarea in Cappadocia in 294. He baptized the king, Tiridates, and Armenia had the distinction of being the first nation to embrace Christianity officially and as a body. In time the new church repudiated its canonical dependence on the church of Caesarea, and became an isolated body under its own primate (the *katholikos*). During the first half of the fifth century St Isaac (Sahak)[2] the Great reformed the Armenian Church on Byzantine lines, and St Mesrop and others translated the Bible and the liturgy into their vernacular. Owing to war with their Persian overlords

---

[1] The non-Catholic Armenians are often distinguished as "Gregorians", they having evolved the theory that St Gregory established a completely independent national church under his own rule.

[2] The Armenian language has two pronunciations and spellings, eastern and western. Where the first has the sounds g, d, b, the second has k, t, p, and so on. The common termination -ian in proper names means "son of": e.g. Lazarian, son of Lazarus.

173

the Armenians took no part in the monophysite troubles which culminated in the Council of Chalcedon (451); but some fifty years later, moved largely by political motives, a national synod at Dvin repudiated that council. The Armenian Church thus cut itself off from the communion of the Catholic Church, and has ever since been reputed monophysite.[3]

For the next seven hundred years the story of Christian Armenia was one of oppression, persecution and warfare, the land being bandied about between Persians, Arabs and Turks, with periods of partial and contested independence under Armenian rulers and of uneasy association with the Byzantine Greeks. The people welcomed and helped the Crusaders against their Moslem oppressors, and at the end of the twelfth century those who had fled westward and formed the kingdom of Little Armenia in Cilicia were reunited to Rome. Outside Cilicia the union was weak or non-existent, but the Western ritual and disciplinary practices adopted from the Crusaders affected the whole Armenian Church and have persisted to this day. The union was maintained till the Saracens took Akka in 1291, and in a weak and decayed form till the end of the kingdom of Little Armenia in 1375. After that, though individual katholikoi were in communion with Rome, the church as a whole was in schism again.

During the following centuries Western missionaries were very active among the Armenians and about 1320 there appeared that curious phenomenon, the Friars of Unity of St Gregory the Enlightener. These were under the direction of the Dominican Order on the one hand and of an Armenian abbot on the other, and they tried to combine Eastern monasticism with the Rule of the Friars Preachers. As often happens with such experiments the West crowded the East out, and it became to all intents and purposes a Western order with an Armenian exterior, using the Dominican rite translated into Armenian. But these friars did a tremendous amount of work and are said at one time to have numbered 600 members. The congregation survived till the eighteenth century, when the remnant was absorbed in the ordinary Dominican Order. Another

[3] It is sometimes argued that Chalcedon was rejected under a misapprehension and that the Armenians are not and never were monophysite. Henri Grégoire calls them "anti-Nestorians", Nestorianism being the "second national religion" of their Persian enemies.

Dominican-Armenian congregation existed from 1307 to 1650, the Brothers of St Basil. Their nucleus was some monks who fled oversea from Moslem oppression in Asia Minor and established themselves at St Bartholomew's church in Genoa. In time they became a purely Italian body.

Armenia sent four representatives to the Council of Florence and a decree of reunion was published, but nothing of importance came of it, except the famous instruction *pro Armenis*, on the sacraments, in the bull *Exsultate Deo*. The dogmatic parts of this document were strictly binding, but its disciplinary and liturgical particulars were simply descriptive of Roman customs; nevertheless they have had an unfortunate effect on Catholic Armenian usage.

THE CATHOLIC ARMENIANS

Owing to the efforts of the Friars of Unity and others there were always groups of Catholics of the Armenian rite (for instance, in the Nakshevan province of Persia), and in the middle of the seventeenth century a Catholic was made patriarch of his nation in Constantinople. But an already troubled position was made worse by the startling religio-political activity of the French ambassador, Marquis de Ferréol, who abducted a subsequent dissident patriarch, Avedik of Tokat, and sent him to be tried by the Inquisition in France. During the ensuing persecution there suffered, in 1707, Ter[4] Gomidas Keumurgian, who was beatified as a martyr in 1929.

The number of Armenian Catholics in the Near East continued to increase in spite of persecution,[5] and in 1742 Pope Benedict XIV established a patriarchal see in Asia Minor, at Kraim in the Lebanon, with the title of Cilicia. Its headquarters were moved to Bzommar, near Bairut, a century later. The first patriarch was Abraham Artzivian. In 1830 French influence obtained the recognition by Turkey of the Catholic Armenians as a separate "nation" (*millah*), with a civil head and an archbishop as religious head at Constantinople. This dual authority caused grave difficulties till, in 1846, the two offices were united

---

[4] *Ter*, short for *terter*, the title of a married Armenian priest.

[5] So numerous were they in Constantinople that the word "Catholic" in that city popularly meant one of the Armenian rite.

175

in the person of Archbishop Antony Hassun, and in 1867 his elevation to the patriarchal throne also unified the two ecclesiastical primacies of Constantinople and Cilicia.

In the same year Pope Pius IX issued the bull *Reversurus*, which regulated the election and powers of the Armenian patriarch and bishops and restrained the participation of the laity in ecclesiastical affairs. Many took this bull as an infringement of secular rights, and the commotion lasted for ten years, entailing the schism of several bishops, all the so-called Antonian monks, and a number of lay people. When peace was restored, the great Antony Hassun resigned his office and died, a cardinal, in Rome four years later (1884). He assisted at the Vatican Council.

But internal trouble continued, especially at Constantinople, a section of the lay people standing out for their old influence. The plenary synod of 1911 produced good results, but interested parties used the latent discontent for their own ends, and it became active again in 1927. A compromise was effected two years later.

During the massacres by Turks and Kurds in the war of 1914-1918 the Catholic Armenians lost seven bishops, over one hundred priests, forty-five nuns, and thirty thousand lay folk; over eight hundred ecclesiastical buildings and schools were pillaged and destroyed, and a dozen dioceses laid waste. Moreover, the formation of a soviet socialist republic in Russian Armenia cut off an indeterminate number of Catholics from their fellows. A conference of the Armenian bishops at Rome in 1928 reorganized their church in view of these events and of the new conditions obtaining.

PRESENT STATE

Patriarch. The "Patriarch of the Catholic Armenians and Katholikos of Cilicia" is the head of all the faithful of his rite except those referred to below. His see is now at Bairut (it was at Constantinople from 1867 to 1928); a new residence has been built in the suburb of Ashrafieh as a gift from Pope Pius XI. He is elected by the bishops in synod under the usual conditions, and has the usual rights and duties of a patriarch (cf. p. 58). He always takes the name of Peter. Gregory Peter XV Agagianian, elected in 1937, was made a cardinal in 1945; in the discharge of the many special duties entrusted to him he became one of the best known and most respected prelates of the Catholic Church.

Bishops are chosen by the patriarch and bishops in synod, the clergy of the vacant diocese having the right to advise; the election must be confirmed by the Holy See. The present sees are the patriarchal diocese of Bairut, the archdioceses of Constaninople, Aleppo and Baghdad, and the dioceses of Kamichlieh in Syria, Alexandria in Egypt and Isfahan in Persia. The other fourteen dioceses were utterly disrupted in 1914-1918. The few faithful of Palestine are in charge of a patriarchal vicar. The patriarch has a titular archbishop as auxiliary, and a bishop as vicar for Bairut.

Parochial clergy. These are formed principally in the national college at Rome, founded 1883 and conducted by Armenian secular priests, in the patriarchal seminary at Junieh, in the seminary at Bairut, and others abroad; the bishops aim at a more unified arrangement. Married men may be ordained to the priesthood, but the custom of voluntary celibacy is practically universal. The patriarchal clergy form a sort of religious congregation at Bzommar, an establishment now over two hundred years old and a great spiritual centre of exiled Armenians.

The office of *vartapet* is a rank peculiar to the Armenian hierarchy, conferred by a kind of ordination rite. They are celibate secular priests of superior learning and ability who are put in charge of responsible posts; they are in origin the only authorized preachers under the bishops. The *archpriest* is a sort of rural dean.

Religious institutes. Since the defection of the "Antonians" under Father Malachy Ormanian in 1871, monasticism has been represented, and most worthily, only by the *Mekhitarists.* These monks were founded by the Venerable Mekhitar of Sivas in 1701, with the Rule of St Benedict as the basis of their constitutions. War drove them to Venice, where they settled on the island of San Lazzaro in 1717; later, a separate branch was established at Vienna. The good they have done for their countrymen by missionary and educational work and the printing and diffusion of books is incalculable. The catalogue of their publications is amazing. It ranges from the Bible to the pagan classics and from Buffon's *Birds* to *Uncle Tom's Cabin*. And in other languages besides Armenian—over twenty books in English are listed. Byron was a frequent (and welcome) visitor at San Lazzaro, and he even projected making a new translation of the Bible from the Armenian version. These monks have done more than anybody else for the religious and cultural welfare of their people during the disasters of the past two hundred years, and they are greatly respected by the dissidents. The Venice abbey has small houses and colleges at Rome, Paris, Bikfaya, Alexandria and Sèvres, and the Vienna abbey others at Constantinople, Cairo and Piraeus. The order has over one hundred monks, of whom about eighty are priests.

The *Sisters of the Immaculate Conception*, founded by Cardinal Hassun in 1852, conduct schools and orphanages in various places. Their mother house and novitiate is at Rome. A recent superioress, Mother Elbis, was a woman of remarkable intellectual and literary attainments.

The Faithful. The Catholic Armenians under patriarchal jurisdiction number some 53,000, of whom many are refugees in Syria and Lebanon. When in those countries Soviet representatives, in 1946, offered them a home in the Armenian S.S.R., only about a thousand accepted the invitation; it was later reported that the Soviet authorities did not honour their promises and put pressure on those who returned to repudiate their church. It is curious that, while a non-Catholic Armenian is generally an adherent of his national church or of nothing, the Catholics are often quite ready to abandon their own rite; there is accordingly an unknown number of them who belong to the Western church, sometimes by a tradition dating back several generations.

OTHER JURISDICTIONS

U.S.S.R. Of the number and state of Catholic Armenians in Russian territory little certain information is available; they were estimated at 50,000 or less in 1917. An apostolic administrator, with residence at Tiflis, was appointed for them in

1921; he was Father James Bagaratian who died, a confessor of the faith, in the penal camp at Solovky in 1936. By 1940 all their clergy were dead, deported, in hiding or in exile, and every church closed.

Since 1939 the Catholics of Armenian rite in former Poland have been within the U.S.S.R. There were Armenians living in Galicia in the fourteenth century, and after great difficulties the majority of them, with their bishop, were reconciled with Rome between 1630 and 1681. It is not surprising that, hemmed in by Poles and Ruthenians, they became very "hybridized" and many joined the Latin rite. In 1939 there were about 5,000 still faithful to the local version of their own, with an archbishop at Lvov (he was immediately subject to and appointed by the Holy See). In 1946, after the usual charges of "collaboration" and public trials, the administrator of the see was sent to Siberia and the whole church "liquidated".

Greece. There are 3,000 or more Catholic Armenians settled in Greece. They are in charge of an ordinary, who is immediately subject to the Holy See.

Poland. A number of the Polish Armenians, including a few clergy, escaped from Galicia to the neighbourhood of Wroclaw (Breslau). Remembering their work for Armenians in the past, the Dominicans there have organized a centre of pastoral ministry for these refugees.

Rumania. Two-thirds (some 35,000) of the old Armenian colony in Transylvania have been Catholics since the later part of the seventeenth century, and in a measure retained their rite. These too have now been "liquidated". They had an ordinary at Gherla (Armenierstadt).

France and Belgium. The Catholic Armenians in these countries number about 13,000, with a few clergy. Those in France are in charge of an episcopal exarch. The chief centres are Paris, Lyons, Marseilles, Valence and Brussels.

United States. There was an Armenian in the colony of Jamestown, Virginia, so long ago as the earlier years of the seventeenth century, and others in New York when it was still New Amsterdam. The first Catholic priest was Vartapet Madiros Mighirian, who arrived in 1899 and ministered in Boston and New York. Catholics of Armenian rite in the

United States now number 5,000, more or less, and are subject to the local bishops. Some of their few clergy are Mekhitarist monks. Owing to the poverty of the faithful the Liturgy has had to be celebrated in Latin churches, but they now have churches of their own in Paterson, N.J., Philadelphia and Watertown, Mass.

There are also small Catholic Armenian communities in Argentine, Brazil and other lands.

LITURGY AND CUSTOMS

Church buildings. An Armenian church is usually rectangular in plan, and its typical characteristic is a central dome which outside forms a low round tower with a cone-shaped roof. Inside it rather resembles a Latin church; sometimes they are almost indistinguishable. The sanctuary is open, considerably raised from the nave, and should be approached by two lateral flights of four or five steps; the altar may stand in the middle, beneath a *ciborium*, but is usually nearer the east wall in the midst of a sort of open screen. The altar table (of stone) is narrow and has at the back several gradines; on it is a crucifix, an indeterminate (but large) number of candlesticks, a small hand-cross with which blessings are given, and a tabernacle containing the reserved Sacrament. On the north side is a credence table or niche in the wall. Numerous lamps burn before this and other altars, of which there are generally two simpler ones, one on either side.

In front of the sanctuary is a raised and enclosed space for the choir. The singers stand here in a semicircle, dressed in a long, wide-sleeved ungirdled garment with a short shoulder cape, varied in colour: I have seen them apple-green and heliotrope.

The nave now often has seats; properly, women are separated from men, sometimes in galleries, but this is passing out of use. There are a few pictures, e.g., behind the altars, and round statues and stations of the cross are now often found in Catholic churches.

Vestments. The vestments are the white *shapik* (equivalent to the alb, and sometimes replaced thereby), embroidered cuffs

(*pazpan*), stole (*porurar*) in one piece hanging down in front
with a loop for the head, over it an embroidered cincture (*koti*);
then a tall, stiff, embroidered collar (*varkas*) which stands up
around the neck—this is nothing but an adaptation of the
medieval apparelled amice of the west, and a handsome ornament; and over all the *shurtshar* (chasuble) which is like a full
cope, without hood or orphreys; finally the priest wears on his
head the *sakhavart*, which is simply the episcopal crown of the
Byzantine rite, adopted by Armenian priests when their bishops
took to wearing Latin mitres in the twelfth century. Bishops
add the *emiporon*, a big *pallium* worn over the shoulders, and
the patriarch and archbishops have the *konker* (the Byzantine
epigonation), a lozenge-shaped ornament hanging at the right
side. The deacon wears a coloured *shapik*, ungirdled, with wide
sleeves, of silk or velvet and embroidered at wrists and shoulders
and a long stole (*urar*) over his left shoulder with the back end
drawn round to come under his right arm and across his chest.
When a bishop celebrates with six deacons, the protodeacon
wears the sacerdotal crown. There are no liturgical colours;
I have seen chasubles of golden-brown silk with small black
arabesques and another of plain saffron silk; black may be
worn for funeral services.

Bishops for choir dress put on the *pilon*, a garment like a long
very full cope, violet in colour, and a flat-topped cap covered
with a veil. Vartapets have the right to a staff-of-office (*gavazan*)
resembling a Byzantine pastoral staff, as well as to a veil over
their caps and sometimes a pectoral cross. In processions the
patriarch and archbishops carry a staff surmounted by a sort
of heraldic emblem of their diocese and are preceded by ministers carrying the archiepiscopal cross, the crozier and the
vartapet's staff.

The ordinary dress of the Catholic Armenian clergy is the
cassock, to which a full-sleeved black gown, open down the
front, is added on formal occasions. The traditional conical
cap is no longer in use by Catholics.

Liturgical books. The nine Armenian liturgical books are
analogous to those of the Byzantine rite and are well and clearly
arranged, the best of all Eastern church-books. Four of them
are required for the celebration of a solemn Liturgy, namely

the *Donatzuitz*, a sort of perpetual *Ordo*; the *Badarakamaduitz*, containing the celebrant's part; the *Giashotz*, containing the epistles and gospels and other parts for the ministers; and the *Sharakan*, which contains the hymns and chants of the choir. But "low Mass" is common among the Catholics, and in 1879 the patriarch Hassun provided for this by publishing an edition of the *Badarakamaduitz* arranged on the lines of the Roman Missal. The principal other book is the *Mashdotz*, equivalent to our *Rituale*, a compilation of the twelfth century. The books have been printed at Rome, Venice and Vienna (by the Mekhitarists at the last two places).

Altar-vessels and bread. The chalice and paten are similar to those used in the West, covered with a veil; the linen purificator is now used instead of the sponge. The bread is unleavened (even for the non-Catholics, who are the only Oriental dissidents to use *azyme*) and resembles Western altar-breads, but the discs are thicker and less crisp. A drop of water is added to the wine, but not by the dissidents, who, alone of all ancient Christians, have an "unmixed chalice".

Music. The very ancient Armenian ecclesiastical chant is of the usual Eastern enharmonic type: most beautiful really, but barbarous to those ears unable to listen with patience to anything outside the diatonic and chromatic scales. The singing is properly unaccompanied, except for the shaking of *ripidia* (*keshotz*) with little bells attached, cymbals being clashed to mark the rhythm; but organs are now sometimes found in the churches, and polyphony is sometimes heard or the chant harmonized.

THE EUCHARISTIC LITURGY

The eucharistic Liturgy (*Patarak*) is essentially a combination of Syrian and Cappadocian elements, within a framework derived from Jerusalem, and is quite distinctive.[6] Its language is Classical Armenian, and the deacon's admonitions *Orthi* (ὀρθοί) and *Proskhume* (πρόσχωμεν) and *Amen* and *Alleluia* alone remain untranslated. It is remarkable among the Eastern liturgies in that, like the Roman Mass, it has one fixed anaphora.

[6] On 29 March, 1787, William Mawhood recorded in his diary that he and his wife and daughter "heard the Armenian Mass" in London at Lincoln's Inn Fields.

The general pattern of the service is that the choir or people sing while the celebrant prays in a low voice, ending his prayers aloud, often at the invitation of the deacon ("Sir, bless!"). Solemn celebrations are carried out with great magnificence. The Armenian Liturgy is never concelebrated by a number of celebrants nor is there a Liturgy of the Presanctified (according to the ancient canons, the Liturgy should be celebrated only on Saturdays and Sundays during Lent).

A curtain is drawn across the sanctuary, or before the altar, at certain points in the service; during Lent the larger curtain cuts off the sanctuary throughout the Liturgy. In some Catholic churches elevations and genuflexions (instead of prostrations) have been introduced at the consecration; and many priests at "low Mass" say even the words of consecration, as well as other parts, inaudibly. In certain places the tendency to hybridize Armenian usages is very strong. Blessed bread (*neshkar*) is distributed in Catholic churches only on Easter day.

THE DIVINE OFFICE

The canonical prayer of the Armenian Church is divided into nine offices, namely, Midnight (in honour of God the Father), Matins (the risen Christ), Sunrise (the Holy Spirit), prayers of the Third, Sixth and Ninth Hours (the descent of the Holy Spirit, the passion, and the death of our Lord respectively), Vespers (the entombment), Nightfall (invoking the peace of Christ) and Bedtime (for undisturbed repose). Sunrise and Nightfall are omitted on Saturdays and the eves of certain feasts, while "first Vespers" is supposed to be always celebrated in church. These offices consist principally of psalms, variable hymns (many attributed to St Nerses Klaietsi, who died in 1173) and prayers (several attributed to St John Mantakuni, d. 490). The psalms are divided into seven groups, one for each day of the week.

The Song of the Three Children, the gospel canticles and a form of *Gloria in excelsis* are sung at Matins, and there are readings from the Gospels on Sundays and great feasts. The so-called Prayer of Manasses (which is printed at the end of the Vulgate) is recited on weekdays in Lent at Matins and Vespers.

183

Since 1911 the daily recitation of the Divine Office has been obligatory upon all Catholic priests of this rite.

THE SACRAMENTS

Baptism is a long ceremony, which is begun outside the baptistery. The godfather renounces Satan and makes a profession of faith for the child. The priest reads Matthew 28:16-20, recites the Nicene creed with the godparent, and all go into the baptistery, saying psalm 117. After four lessons and a litany, the priest blesses the water, pouring three drops of chrism into it. The actual baptism is by the priest sitting the child in the font, facing east, and pouring water three times on its head, saying: "The servant of God N., coming by his own will to the state of a catechumen and thence to baptism, is baptized in the name of the Father . . . ," etc. Then the child is immersed thrice and the priest adds: "Being ransomed by Christ's blood from the slavery of sin and set free by the heavenly Father's power, he becomes a joint heir with Christ and a temple of the Holy Spirit."

Confirmation is ministered by the priest immediately. He anoints the child with chrism on nine parts of the body, saying: "Sweet oil is poured out on you in Christ's name, as the seal of gifts from Heaven." Then he ties round its head a string of twisted red and white threads with a small cross attached; this has been blessed before the baptism, and is removed ceremonially after eight days. He also clothes the child in a white garment and offers it to God before the altar.

Penance. Confessional-boxes are in increasing use, and absolution is given by an indicative formula very similar to the Roman one.

Eucharist. The custom of communion in both kinds has not been abrogated, but for the past hundred years or more it has not obtained in Catholic churches of this rite. Instead, the people receive a small particle, kneeling. The faithful are expected to go to confession and to communion at least at Christmas (or Epiphany), Easter, the Assumption, the Transfiguration and the Exaltation of the Cross; Easter only is obligatory.

CARDINAL GREGORY PETER XV AGAGIANIAN
Patriarch of Cilicia of the Armenians

Bishop   Vartapet

Protodeacon   Subdeacon

ARMENIAN CLERGY

ARMENIAN CHURCH AT BZOMMAR

By courtesy of   La Bonne Presse

CHALDEAN CHURCH AT MOSUL

CHALDEAN MONASTERY, DAIR AS-SAIDA

COURTYARD OF A MELKITE MONASTERY

Anointing. The proper Armenian form for the administration of this sacrament requires the presence of seven priests and is very long. It has been disused by the dissidents since the fourteenth century, while the Catholics have substituted a much modified version.

Orders. With the exception of the romanized Malabarese, the Armenians, Catholic and dissident, are the only Christians of the East who have four minor and three major, or sacred, orders. Minor orders are conferred by the handing-over of the instruments of office; vesting in the distinctive vestments and laying-on of hands are added for the subdiaconate and diaconate, and anointing with chrism as well for the priesthood and episcopate.

Marriage is entered into by a long and admirable rite which, when carried out in its entirety, begins at the bride's home, includes a crowning of both parties with wreaths of flowers and celebration of the Liturgy in church, and ends with a blessed loving-cup at the house of the groom. The contract is effected by explicit declarations by the parties, unlike most Eastern wedding-services, in which they remain implicit.

Calendar. The ecclesiastical calendar of the Armenian rite is constructed on different principles from that of any other church. Strictly, there are only seven fixed feasts, all others falling on the Sunday after a fixed date or on a day of the week following a certain Sunday which depends on the date of Easter; feasts may only be celebrated on Saturdays during penitential times and not at all in some others, e.g., Easter to Pentecost. These rules have been somewhat modified by the Catholics, who, moreover, gradually and unwillingly accepted the Gregorian reckoning between 1892 and 1912. Their national reckoning of years is from their eponymous ancestor Haik, who is put at 2492 B.C.

Feasts. The restrictions on the celebration of these reduces the number of saints' days to some 130 in the year, many of them of Armenian saints and several observed in groups, e.g., the Fathers of Nicaea, the Armenian Doctors, the Universal Doctors, the Egyptian Fathers, All Apostles. The chief fixed feasts observed by Catholics (and on the same dates as in the West) are Christmas, Circumcision, Epiphany, Presentation of our Lord, Annunciation, Birthday of our Lady, her Presentation and Immaculate Conception. Among the specifically Western feasts generally adopted are Corpus Christi, Christ the King and Trinity Sunday; feasts special to the rite include that of the Ark of God (i.e., the Church). There are ten holy days, in addition to Sundays.

Penitential seasons. These are traditionally many and long, and have been modified for Catholics, among whom details vary from place to place. There is no abstinence on Saturdays in Lent or on Wednesdays and Fridays in paschaltime.

General observations. Some of the Western traits referred to above date from the time of the Crusades and are shared equally by Catholics and dissidents. Others are due largely to the fact that so many of the faithful have for so long looked to France for protection and help, which has been generously forthcoming, especially at the hands of certain religious congregations. In spite of the fact that Armenians tend to regard their religious rites as a concrete manifestation of their nationality these same congregations have found many vocations to themselves among the Armenians, which, whatever it may be for the individuals concerned, is not a good thing for the Catholics of the Armenian rite as a whole, often depriving them of the direct services of very capable men.

Such observances as the rosary, way of the cross, benediction with the Blessed Sacrament, scapulars, etc., are popular, and the blessing of candles, of ashes and of palms have been adopted quasi-liturgically. On the other hand, there has been for some time a movement, in which the Mekhitarist monks are prominent, for maintaining Armenian habits, both of ritual and mind, in greater purity. Canon 612 of the plenary Armenian council held at Rome in 1911 declared that "devotions" are a supplementary cult in Eastern worship and should conform to the liturgy both in spirit and form. All Armenians, whether Catholic or not, make the sign of the cross from left to right.

BIBLIOGRAPHY

F. Tournebize, *Histoire politique et religieuse de l'Arménie* (Paris, 1910).
S. Weber, *Die katholische Kirche in Arménien* (Freiburg i.B., 1903).

M. Nurikhan, *The Life and Times of . . . Abbot Mekhitar* (Venice, 1915).
V. Langlois, *Notice sur le Couvent arménien . . . de Venise* (Venice, 1931).
L. Arakelian, *Armenian Liturgy* (Watertown, Mass., 1951).
L. S. Kogy, *Armenian Sunday Missal* (Vienna, 1947).
J. Issaverdens, *The Sacred Rites . . . of the Armenian Church* (Venice, 1888).
P. Bianchini, *The Music of the Armenian Liturgy* (Venice, 1877). The melodies are made chromatic.
J. Muyldermans, *Le costume liturgique arménien* (Louvain, 1926).
Breviarium Armenium . . . , in Latinam linguam translatum (Venice, 1908).

CHAPTER VIII

THE CHALDEAN RITE

1. THE CHALDEANS

WHATEVER may have been the beginnings of Christianity in Mesopotamia and Persia there was a church in Edessa at the end of the second century; from that city the faith spread eastward and another great centre was formed at Nisibis. At the beginning of the fourth century the Church in Persia was organized under his own direction by Papa bar Aggai, bishop of Seleukia-Ctesiphon; and in 424 the synod of Markabta proclaimed the Persian church under its katholikos independent of the patriarch of Antioch and the "Western fathers" generally (the hierarchical bond with Antioch through Edessa had always been tenuous). During this early period the church of East Syria and Persia produced a doctor of the Universal Church, St Ephrem (d. 373), and it was made illustrious by the theological schools of Nisibis and Edessa and by hosts of martyrs at the hands of the Persians.

In 431 the Council of Ephesus condemned the teaching of Nestorius, patriarch of Constantinople (see p. 4). Many of the Persian Christians and a party of the East Syrians, considerably influenced by anti-imperialist political considerations, were unfriendly to the council, and at a synod at Beth Lapat in 484 formulated their faith in terms not acceptable to the bishops of the rest of Christendom. They probably aimed at no more than a local autonomy like that of the recognized patriarchates, under the protection of the sovereigns of Persia, and were moved towards Nestorianism by their strong antagonism to its opposite, Monophysism; but by the seventh century the schism had hardened and the Moslem conquest of Syria and Persia confirmed their severance from the Catholic Church and their profession of the condemned teaching.

For eight hundred years the Nestorian Church was, with fluctuations of prosperity, a mighty organization, one whose missionary enterprise is unsurpassed in the history of Christianity. It had twenty metropolitan sees with many bishoprics and monasteries, extending to China and India. But the time of its greatest extension was soon succeeded by utter ruin. At the end of the fourteenth century the Mongol hordes of Timur Leng devasted Asia, sweeping away the Nestorian Church in a cataclysm of blood and apostasy. The remnants of the western part of his church gathered round their katholikos in northern Mesopotamia; of the eastern part, nothing remained (except in Malabar).

During the thirteenth century Dominican and Franciscan friars were active among the Nestorians, and the katholikos Yaballaha III had amiable relations with the Holy See,[1] several individual bishops became Catholics, and in the following century a number of Latin sees were set up, but they did not last long.

By the middle of the fifteenth century the office of Nestorian katholikos had become hereditary in a family, passing from uncle to nephew (it still does), and on the succession of Simon VIII Denha in 1551 a disaffected party elected a rival, John Sulaka. Sulaka at once turned to the Franciscans for help; they sent him to Rome, where he made a profession of Catholic faith and was appointed by Pope Julius III to be patriarch of those of his rite who should follow his example.[2] It was at this time that the name "Chaldean" began to be used to distinguish such people, as to call them "Catholic Nestorians" was obviously impossible. From now on there were two lines of patriarchs (or katholikoi), one Catholic, the other Nestorian. Sulaka himself was murdered by Moslems at Amida (Diarbekr) in 1555, allegedly at the instigation of his rival; he was succeeded

---

[1] He was a Sino-Turk, born in Pekin. He sent another Mongol, the monk Barsauma, on an embassy to Rome and the West. Barsauma received holy communion from the hands of Pope Nicholas IV, and himself gave it to King Edward I of England in Gascony. For all that, the profession of faith he carried was only doubtfully orthodox.

[2] On this occasion Cardinal Maffei declared to the assembly that, "The Chaldeans seem to have had the name of Nestorians without holding any Nestorian errors". Whether or not this was true at that time, it displays a striking difference of spirit from that of the Portuguese in Malabar a few years later (see pp. 200-201).

by Abdisho, who appointed two bishops for the Christians of Malabar.

THE CHALDEAN CATHOLICS

The successors of Sulaka all took the name of Simon (Shimun), and at times during the sixteenth century they made attempts (with the approval of the Holy See) to exercise their traditional jurisdiction over the Christians of their rite in India. But in the year 1692 Simon XIII apostatized, and from him the present line of Nestorian katholikoi is descended. They went to live in Kurdistan.

Meanwhile the line of Simon Denha had not been continuously in schism, for several of his successors (all of whom took the name of Elias) had been reconciled with Rome. Diarbekr particularly had become a Catholic centre, and in 1672 the metropolitan of this city, Mar Joseph, made his profession of faith and the Holy See allowed him to have the title of patriarch (but without specifying of where or of whom). He was succeeded by other "patriarchs" there, so that for twenty years, from 1672 till 1692, when Simon XIII lapsed, there were two Catholic patriarchs among the Chaldeans, and from 1692 till 1804 two Nestorian ones.

In 1778 Elias XIII succeeded his uncle as Nestorian patriarch at the same time that his young cousin John Hormizd, the metropolitan of Mosul, turned Catholic. In 1781 there was no Catholic patriarch in office, Diarbekr having become vacant by the resignation of Joseph IV, and in 1802 the administration of the see was confided to his nephew, the priest Augustine Hindi. There ensued a long and rather bitter rivalry between Hormizd and Hindi, both of whom wanted to be Catholic patriarch; the Holy See was not keen on either of them, and was hoping for the submission of Elias XIII. When the last-named died in 1804, without leaving a nephew to succeed him, the rivalry became worse, and there was strong temptation for his cousin John Hormizd to apostatize (he was in fact under censure for a time). At length Hindi also died, and in 1834 Rome appointed Hormizd to be patriarch at last.

The upshot of all this complication is that there has been a succession of Catholic Chaldean patriarchs ever since, who are in continuity with the original historical line of Simon Denha of the house of Mama. To avoid any chance of the assertion of the hereditary principle in the succession, the Holy See gave Hormizd a coadjutor with right of succession, and the patriarchal family gracefully renounced its improper privilege.

The first successor of Hormizd, Nicholas Zaya, after eight years resigned his see, in 1846, and the next patriarch, Joseph VI Audo, had a long and stormy period of office. He was an energetic and competent prelate but ambitious, and very anxious to recover the ancient but abolished jurisdiction of his church over the Syrian Catholics of Malabar. Twice, in 1860 and 1874, he sent bishops (Mar Thomas Rokos and Mar Elias Mellus) thither at the request of Malabarese malcontents, and caused much trouble thereby. Meanwhile, in 1869, the Holy See decided to apply the bull *Reversurus*, governing the appointment of bishops,[3] to the Chaldeans. Audo asserted that this was an infringement of Eastern rights, and made a very temperate protest before the assembled Vatican Council. The advisers of Pope Pius IX, however, took a severe view of the patriarch's general policy, and he narrowly escaped excommunication. He was eventually reconciled with the Holy See and was highly spoken of by Pope Leo XIII; the troublesome bull was modified.

Such distressing events weakened the cause of Catholic unity among the Nestorians in the nineteenth century, but it nevertheless made good progress. A great cultural work was done for his countrymen by Paul Bejan (1838-1920), a Chaldean born in Persia who became a Lazarist priest. He came to Europe and published magistral editions of their liturgical and other ecclesiastical books, as well as translations into the spoken Syriac of East Syrian ascetical works, lives of the saints, etc. An English translation of his text of the mystical treatises of Isaac the Syrian (of Nineveh) by A. E. Wensinck was published at Amsterdam in 1923.

The patriarch Mar Emmanuel II Thomas (1909-1947) reconciled two Nestorian bishops with several priests and their congregations, numbering altogether some 20,000 persons.

During the war of 1914-1918 the Chaldeans suffered equally with their neighbours from massacre and deportation. Six

---

3 This was the bull that caused a schism among the Armenians (see p. 176).

191

bishops (including the two ex-Nestorians), a score of priests, and thousands of their people were murdered by the Turks and Kurds, and four dioceses were destroyed.

PRESENT STATE

Patriarch. The Patriarch-Katholikos of Babylon of the Chaldeans lives at Baghdad,[4] and he has jurisdiction over the faithful of his rite throughout the Near East. He is elected by a synod of all the bishops, and has the usual rights and duties of a patriarch (cf. p. 58). He is an *ex-officio* member of the senate of Iraq. Mar Paul II Cheikho was elected in 1958.

Bishops. The sees are, in Iraq, Baghdad, the patriarchal diocese, and Mosul (comprising nearly three-quarters of the faithful), Kerkuk, Basra, Akra, Amadiya, Al-Khosh, Zakho; in Persia, Urmya, Sena; in Syria, Aleppo; in Lebanon, Bairut. Kerkuk, Sena and Urmya are called metropolitan sees, and Basra archiepiscopal, but all the bishops depend directly on the patriarch. Four other dioceses no longer exist in fact. There is an auxiliary bishop for Mosul and patriarchal vicars in Constantinople and Egypt. A vacant see is filled by the patriarch and bishops in synod, the lower clergy having an advisory voice. The choice must be approved by the Holy See.

Parochial clergy. The principal seminary is the patriarchal college of St Peter at Baghdad, which has about forty students. The French Dominicans, who have worked among the Chaldeans without a break since 1750, established another seminary for them (and for the Antiochene Syrians) at Mosul in 1882, directed by the friars with the help of priests of the rites concerned. After seventy-five years of valuable work, it was amalgamated with the patriarchal college in 1959. A college for the Chaldeans of Persia was opened by French Lazarists at Khosrova in 1845; it was reconstituted in 1923 at Urmya (Rezaya). A few students go to the Jesuit Oriental seminary at Bairut or elsewhere. The clergy are not bound to celibacy, but few of them are married; they mostly live in very poor circumstances. The rank of *chorepiskopos*, conferred as a title of honour by

---

[4] The title "of Babylon" seems to have been first given to Joseph II, of the Diarbekr line, by Pope Clement XI in 1701, from the erroneous identification of modern Baghdad with ancient Babylon.

the patriarch, and that of *archdeacon* are given by a liturgical rite.

Religious institutes. The only Chaldean monks are a small congregation of *Antonians*, called "of St Hormisdas", founded in 1808 by Gabriel Danbo, who for years was engaged in commerce at Mardin; after directing his foundation for twenty-four years he was murdered during a Kurdish insurrection. In all respects except corporate wealth the Chaldean monks resemble their Maronite brethren. There are as many simple monks as priests (some of the latter serve parishes), in three monasteries, one of which is very small. The most interesting, though no longer the mother-house, is Rabban-Hormizd, near Alkosh. This was founded originally in the seventh century and was re-established by Father Danbo; some of its buildings are very old. It is a pity that these religious are not more numerous, for they lead an austere life of hard work, and are an excellent influence in their church. The habit is a black tunic and hood, though the ordinary clerical turban is commonly worn as well. In 1960, at the invitation of the Chaldean patriarch Paul II, the Syro-Malabar *Carmelites* (see p. 204) agreed to send some missionaries to Iraq.

Sisters affiliated to the Dominican third order conduct village schools, and a recently formed congregation of other Chaldean nuns has two schools in Baghdad.

The Faithful totalled about 196,000 in 1960, the great majority living in the plain of Mesopotamia, north and northwest of Mosul.[5] Here a good deal of debased Syriac ("Sureth") is spoken by them; elsewhere Persian, Kurdish or Turkish, according to the neighbourhood, and Arabic in the towns. So long ago as the middle of the last century a Protestant clergyman, G. P. Badger, commented on the superior civilization, intelligence, and order of the Chaldeans in Mesopotamia, in his book *The Nestorians and their Rituals* (London, 1852, Vol. i, p. 176). This praise is, of course, relative, the Chaldeans having for many centuries been part of a shamefully oppressed and exploited people. Their present encouraging state is due

---

[5] There were no Nestorians left in these regions until during World War I persecution drove them towards Mosul from the mountains of Kurdistan. They are precisely the people who, under the name of "Assyrians", had to appeal to Europe for protection against their Moslem governors and neighbours in Iraq. They are now greatly outnumbered by the Chaldeans.

not a little to the enlightened services of the Dominicans in Mesopotamia, of the Lazarists in Persia, and of other Western institutes both of men and women. In 1932 American Jesuits opened a college at Baghdad, now Al-Hikma University, whose students include Christians of several communions, Moslems and Jews.

There has been no considerable emigration of Chaldeans across the seas. There are about 1,500 of them in the United States, with churches in Chicago and Detroit.[6]

LITURGY AND CUSTOMS

Chaldean *church buildings* have their own plan. The sanctuary is raised above the nave and generally separated from it by a solid wall reaching to the roof. This wall is pierced by a door some six feet wide, covered by a curtain to be withdrawn during the Liturgy; before it is a space for the choir. Men and women are separated and there are usually no seats. In the more modern Catholic churches the altar is against the east wall of the sanctuary, and is now of western pattern, with gradines, numerous candlesticks and artificial flowers; but the altar "stone" (*tablitha*) is of wood. The Blessed Sacrament is reserved in a tabernacle. On the north side of the sanctuary there is an altarlike "credence-table", the *prothesis*, and in older churches the baptistery is on the south side of the sanctuary. Outside the church is a partly covered courtyard wherein the Divine Office is celebrated during the summer. There are pictures and sometimes even stations of the cross but no statues in these churches.

Vestments. These are similar to those of the Syrians: *kotina* (now generally an alb); *zande* ("cuffs"); *urara*, sometimes, but improperly, worn crossed like the Western stole; *zunara*, girdle; *paina* or *maapra*, a copelike chasuble; and embroidered shoes. Bishops have adopted the Western mitre, crozier and ring, and have no *omophorion*. Deacons wear an ungirdled alblike garment, with a long stole disposed as a Western deacon wears it. The ordinary ecclesiastical dress is a round turban, wide, low and flat, black cassock (violet for bishops), and overmantle with wide sleeves.

[6] Father Gabriel Oussani, professor in the seminary at Dunwoodie, N.Y., was a Chaldean.

Liturgical books. The Chaldean missal was printed at Rome in 1767. The most used books, especially the *Takhsa*, priest's Mass-book with the addition of the variable parts of the Liturgy, and a pastor's manual were in 1901 accurately edited and beautifully printed by the Dominican press at Mosul, from which an Arabic Bible, Syriac dictionary, and other valuable works have been issued. This edition of the missal was republished by the patriarchal press in Mosul in 1936. Other editions have been published by the Lazarists at Urmya. A definitive edition of the four books of the Divine Office was brought out by Father Bejan in Paris in 1888. This was reissued in Rome in 1938. The first printed edition of the *Pontifical*, printed at the Jesuits' press in Bairut, appeared in 1959.

Altar-vessels and bread. Catholics make use of the same altar-vessels and accessories as in the West, with the hand-cross for episcopal blessings and *ripidia* for processions. The altarbreads are similar to Western ones in appearance but they are leavened and have a little salt added. The custom of baking them afresh for each celebration is almost extinct.

Music. The Chaldean enharmonic chant is one of the earliest existing forms of church music. It has been studied by the Benedictines formerly at Jerusalem and Sharfeh. The only instruments permitted are cymbals, triangles and so forth to mark the rhythm, and it is rather monotonous.

Liturgical language. This is pure Syriac, i.e., the Edessene dialect of Aramaic, with the Eastern pronunciation and characters, and with only the scriptural lessons in the vernacular.

THE EUCHARISTIC LITURGY

The people of Mesopotamia were evangelized mainly from Antioch, but their liturgy seems to have taken shape at Edessa; the East Syrian or Chaldean rite is still very archaic in pattern and tone. The usual eucharistic Liturgy (*Kuddasha*, "Hallowing") is called "of the Holy Apostles" (i.e., Addai and Mari, reputed apostles of the East Syrians and Persians), and has two alternative anaphoras, "of Theodore the Interpreter" (of Mopsuestia) and "of Nestorius". The Catholics naturally do not use these last names but call them "the Second", used on

Sundays and feasts from Advent to Palm Sunday, and "the Third Hallowing", used only five times in the year.

The Liturgy is celebrated in the evening before Christmas, Epiphany and Easter, and there is a form of Liturgy of the Presanctified for "Friday of Suffering". The Liturgy is not concelebrated; in former times most of the pre-anaphoral part could be carried out by a number of priests, each doing a part, and the presiding bishop then designated one of them to complete the sacrifice.

THE DIVINE OFFICE

This consists of only three "hours", Vespers (*Ramsha*), Night Office (*Lilya*) and Matins (*Sapra*), to which the Antonian monks add the "little hours", whose text they have borrowed from their Maronite brethren. The office is made up of a considerable number of psalms (the psalter is spread over a week), with hymns (many, of course, of or attributed to St Ephrem), prayers and litanies. "Glory to God in the highest" is sung at Matins on Sundays and feasts. From the Ascension until the beginning of November choir-office is sung in the courtyard instead of in church. The Lord's Prayer has a very prominent place throughout the Chaldean rite.

THE SACRAMENTS

Baptism. The rite of baptism is very long, being modelled on the eucharistic Liturgy, with corresponding prayers, chants, litanies and scriptural lessons. There is a preface leading to an "anaphora", wherein oil and the water are blessed; the child is anointed twice, the second time all over. The baptism proper comes at the place of the communion. The child is set down in the water, which is poured thrice over its head with the words, "N. is baptized in the name of . . ., etc., unto everlasting life."

Confirmation follows at once. The proper rite passed out of use centuries ago, and the priest now uses the Roman form, in Syriac.

Penance. This sacrament is ministered as in the West. Confessional-boxes are now to be found in many churches.

Eucharist. Communion in both kinds for all is envisaged in the liturgical books. But nowadays the people receive it under the species of bread only, standing at the sanctuary door. The words are: "The body of our Lord is given to the devout believer for the forgiveness of sin." Priests not celebrating on Holy Thursday, and deacons on the anniversary of their ordination, are given communion in both kinds, separately.

Anointing. The use of this sacrament does not seem to have developed in the East Syrian Church. Accordingly the Chaldeans since the sixteenth century have used the Roman rite for it, in Syriac; but the oil is blessed by an old local formula.

Orders. The Chaldeans have the usual five orders of the East. They are conferred by the laying-on of hands, the following words being said, accompanied by an invocation of the Holy Spirit: "N. is set apart, dedicated and confirmed for the office of the diaconate (priesthood; episcopate) and the work of Levi and Stephen (of Aaron; of bishop of the city of M.), in the name, etc." Emphasis is put on the apostolic character of the episcopate and on the graces and duties of the various orders. Archdeacons, *chorepiskopoi* and archbishops are made in a similar way.

Marriage. The ceremony is called *Buraka*, "the Blessing", and includes the usual Eastern crowning of the couple (with a red, white and blue fillet). It is very long and includes drinking from a loving-cup of wine by bride and groom, not, as in some rites, at the end, but near the beginning.

Calendar. The Gregorian reckoning was adopted gradually during the nineteenth century. The ecclesiastical year begins on December 1 and is divided into the following periods: Dedication of the church and the Annunciation, Epiphany, Lent, Easter, The Apostles, Summer, Elias and the Cross, Moses.

Feasts. There are only some sixty feasts in the Chaldean calendar, of which about half are movable, many of them saints' days celebrated on certain Fridays. There are several collective feasts (e.g., the Four Evangelists, the Greek Doctors, the Syrian and Roman Doctors), and some less ancient celebrations from the West—Corpus Christi, the Sacred Heart, St Joseph. Chrism is consecrated by the patriarch and there is a *mandatum* on Holy Thursday.

Penitential seasons. The fast of Lent includes Sundays, food, drink and tobacco being eschewed till noon; all Wednesdays and Fridays are days of abstinence, except from Christmas to the Epiphany and in paschal-time. The Ninevite fast is observed with special rigour, and the whole of the psalter is recited in the office on each of its days; a Chaldean priest tells me he has known lay people to go the whole of those three days without any food at all.

General observations. Despite his intransigence toward certain Roman legislation, it was the patriarch Joseph Audo who introduced several Western observances, such as Benediction with the Blessed Sacrament. In general, foreign influence has modified only accessories of the Chaldean rite, and encouraged private devotion by means of the rosary, scapulars, etc. The sign of the cross is made from left to right.

BIBLIOGRAPHY

J. Tfinkji, *L'Église chaldéene* (Paris, 1913).

H. C. Luke, *Mosul and its Minorities* (London, 1925).

P. Hindo, *Primats d'Orient . . . et Maphriens syriens* (Rome, 1936).

S. Bello, *La Congrégation de S. Hormisdas et l'Église chaldéene* (Rome, 1939).

J. C. MacGillivray, "Nestorians and Chaldeans in Modern Times" in *Clergy Review* (London, July 1931).

R. Rabban, *La Messa caldea detta "degli Apostoli"* (Rome, 1935).

D. Dahane, *Liturgy of the Chaldean Mass* (Chicago, 1939).

H. W. Codrington, *Studies of the Syrian Liturgies* (Ramsgate, 1952).

J. Jeannin, *Mélodies liturgiques syriennes et chaldéenes*, 2 vols. (Bairut, 1925-28).

2. THE MALABARESE

The Malabar Coast is that part of the west coast of India that lies between Mangalore and Cape Comorin; it includes the former Malabar district and states of Cochin and Travancore, which since 1956 have been comprised in the new state of Kerala. Kerala has a large number of indigenous Christians (Catholics of three rites, Jacobites, and Protestants of several communions), who are outnumbered by their non-Christian neighbours (Hindus, Moslems and others) only by two to one. They are of Indo-European stock and speak a Dravidian language, Malayalam, very like Tamil.

These Malabar Christians call themselves as a whole "Christians of St Thomas" and are quite sure they were evangelized by that apostle, whose alleged first shrine they show on the opposite coast, at Mylapore.[7] Nevertheless, their origins are a matter of great uncertainty. It is certain that there were Malabarese Christians before the sixth century, and there is a probable reference to them in the middle of the fourth; if the St Thomas tradition be mistaken, it is likely that they were first due to Christian traders from around the Persian Gulf, and so more or less directly a fruit of the missionary activity of the East Syrian Church (it does not follow that they were always, or ever, formally Nestorian). There is no doubt that their geographical position brought them into touch with the metropolitans of Revardashir and that their continued existence was due to their connection with the Nestorian Church: from the earliest times their liturgy was Chaldean and its language Syriac, and their traditions are unanimous that their bishops were sent to them from "Babylon" (Baghdad).

There are incidental references to these people in the earlier middle ages and in the records of the later medieval travellers, and the Holy See was aware of their existence. In 1122 an

[7] The *Anglo-Saxon Chronicle* states that in 883 King Alfred the Great sent Sigehelm and Athelstan with gifts to Rome and "to St Thomas and St Bartholomew in India", in fulfilment of a vow.

"archbishop of India", one John, went to Rome *via* Constantinople; and in 1328 Pope John XXII consecrated a Dominican, Friar Jordan, bishop and sent him with a letter addressed to the head of the Christians at Quilon. Twenty years later a Franciscan bishop, John of Marignolli, visited Quilon; he was well received by the Christians there, who made him presents, in consideration, he says, "of my office as legate of the pope". They had early received a grant of privileges from the Hindu kings, and at this time even had a ruler of their own, to whom Pope Eugenius IV addressed a letter as "My beloved son in Christ, Thomas, the illustrious Emperor of the Indians".

During the second half of the fifteenth century they were for a long time without a bishop, apparently on account of persecution by the Moslems of southern India, which prevented communication with the East Syrian katholikos. In 1490 Joseph the Indian made his way to Gazerta Bait Zabdai in Mesopotamia, with the result that two bishops were sent to Malabar; later on Father Joseph went to Rome, where he declared that both the East Syrians and Malabarese professed the Catholic faith and looked on the pope as their supreme pontiff. Other bishops were sent about 1503.

But for practical purposes direct contact of the Malabarese with the West begins with the coming of the Portuguese in 1498. It seems clear that the Malabarese religious leaders regarded the Portuguese from the first as their brothers in religion, affirming their own communion with the Holy See and acknowledging its primacy. And at first the Portuguese do not seem to have questioned their Catholicity (as St Francis Xavier did not when he was at Cranganore in 1549), recognizing their bishop, Mar Jacob, and clearly holding religious communion with him. But almost at once they began to show anxiety to "latinize" the Indian Christians. In 1553 Pope Julius III recognized the Catholic Chaldean patriarch, John Sulaka, whose successor, Abdisho, in 1556 sent two Chaldean bishops for the Syro-Indians. But the Portuguese, who had a Latin archiepiscopal see at Goa, were not familiar with the phenomenon of non-Latin Catholics and hardly believed it possible for right living and orthodoxy to flourish apart from specifically Roman observances; without adequate reason, they

A MARONITE MONK

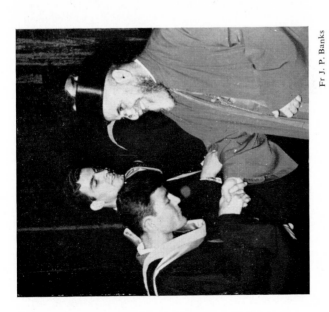

Fr J. P. Banks

THE CHALDEAN PATRIARCH AT
AL-HIKMA UNIVERSITY

MALABARESE CHURCH AT IRAPOLY

BISHOP, PRIEST AND LAY PEOPLE
OF THE MALABAR CHURCH

Fr E. Chalin

PAUL II CHEIKHO
Chaldean Patriarch

PETER PAUL MEUCHI
Maronite Patriarch

By courtesy of the

"Catholic Herald"

POPE JOHN XXIII AND BISHOP CHESLAV SIPOVICH
(See page 124)

scented the Nestorian heresy everywhere among these strange native Christians.[8] There followed a period of clash and intrigue between Europeans and Indians, in which the conduct of the ecclesiastics on either side was not uniformly edifying. For example, there is extant a letter from Pope Gregory XIII to the king of Portugal, dated 1578, asking him to see that the viceroy in India gave fair play to one of the Chaldean bishops, Mar Abraham, "whom we hear has been greatly vexed by some". The other, Mar Joseph, was also accused of Nestorianism, but the root of his offence seems to be that he refused to ordain Indians who had been trained in a Portuguese seminary without being taught their liturgical language. The jurisdiction of both these and other Chaldean bishops in India was recognized by the Holy See.[9]

When the last Chaldean bishop died, the archbishop of Goa, Alexis de Menezes, an Augustinian friar, made a visitation of the Syro-Indians and in 1599 convened a synod to deal with their affairs at Diamper (Udiamparur). The archbishop presided, assisted by Jesuit fathers, and at this assembly 153 sacerdotal and 660 lay deputies of the Syro-Indians made a profession of faith and anathematized the errors of Nestorius. Among the arbitary changes brought about by the Portuguese at this synod or later were: the abolition of the jurisdiction of the Catholic Chaldean patriarch in India and the substitution of Portuguese bishops for Syrians; a number of changes in the eucharistic Liturgy, and the introduction of communion in one kind, Roman vestments, and other innovations; the abolition of the Syrian Pontifical and Ritual; the imposition of clerical celibacy; and the setting up of the Inquisition.[10] As an example

[8] The Indians had the Nestorian characteristic of not using holy images in their churches. "We are Christians," they said. "We do not worship idols." That attitude may be a proof of religious ignorance but it is no proof of heresy. Mar Jacob was one of the bishops sent by the katholikos of the Nestorians about 1503. Things were apparently complicated by the word Nestorian being used as a racial or geographical appellation, without theological significance.

[9] Among the Jesuits at Goa at this time was an Englishman, Father Thomas Stevens. He it was who helped the merchant-adventurers John Newbery and Ralph Fitch to escape when they had been imprisoned by the Portuguese during their famous journey that began in 1583.

[10] "The Inquisition rarely succeeded in receiving hearty affection from its victims," observes Dr Fortescue dryly. J. S. Assemani says roundly in his *Bibliotheca orientalis* that most of the acts of the Synod of Diamper were an outcome of misguided zeal, ignorance of Eastern Catholic usages and undue attachment to those of the West. The synod has never been formally confirmed by Rome, nor could it be in its entirety for, as Mgr S. Giamil notes in his *Genuinae Relationes*, p. 610, some of its acts ran clean contrary to the decrees of the Holy See. The fact is that, in addition to his "imperialism", Menezes was obsessed by his suspicion of latent Nestorianism: but some of his actions have been unjustly exaggerated or misunderstood. In his *Histoire des conciles*, vol. xi, pp. 36-67 (Paris, 1949), Fr C. de Clercq declares that "The causes of all the subsequent dissensions... were provoked by Menezes' excessive reforms and by doing away with the Syro-Indian hierarchy".

of the scrupulosity of the European churchmen, it may be mentioned that frequent bathing was condemned twice in the synodical decrees, on the ground that in India washing often had a religious significance.

These measures caused grave discontent. There is no serious reason to suppose that the Indians secretly hankered after Nestorianism, and there is direct evidence that they respected the pope; but they disliked their Portuguese masters, with their domineering ways and innovations from Europe.[11] After several vain attempts to get redress of their grievances by lawful methods, almost the whole body of Syro-Indians went into schism in the year 1653. The occasion was the arrival of a monk, Ahathalla, at Mylapore, who may have been sent for by the Indian leader, the archdeacon Thomas, who declared himself to be a bishop for all the St Thomas Christians. He was seized by the Portuguese, and the Indians alleged that he was deliberately drowned in the sea off Cochin on the way to Goa. It is likely that he was an impostor, and there is some evidence that he was in fact deported to Lisbon by the Goan Inquisition.

Pope Alexander VII sent out Carmelite friars to deal with the trouble. One, Joseph Sebastiani, was made bishop, and by 1662 84 out of the 116 Indian "parishes" had returned to unity. The remainder very soon became that body now known as the Malabar Jacobites. In the following year the Dutch drove all other Europeans from Cochin. Before he went, Mgr Sebastiani consecrated bishop, as administrator for the Indians, a native priest who had led the faithful remnants of Catholics after 1653. This was Shandy Palliveetil (Alexander de Campo), and he ruled his church and consolidated the reunion for twenty-four years. Before he died he welcomed the Carmelites (Italian this time) back to Malabar; but his request for a Syro-Indian coadjutor and successor, granted by the Holy See, was not honoured by the papal commissioners: they chose an Eurasian of Western rite. It was a bad choice, and over twenty years of disturbance followed.

From 1701 there was a succession of Carmelite vicars

[11] That Portuguese ecclesiastical policy in India was not actuated solely by concern for the good estate of the Catholic Church is shown by the history of the *Padroado* troubles, which culminated in flat defiance of the Holy See in 1838.—When we consider the Westerners' phobia about Nestorianism, it is strange and instructive to reflect that those Malabarese who were not reconciled eventually allied themselves with a church of the opposite heresy, Monophysism.

apostolic, who ruled till 1887, not without difficulties.[12] The Syro-Indians never ceased trying to get indigenous bishops, either by petitioning Rome or by negotiating with Catholic Chaldean prelates in Mesopotamia. One of these, Mar Elias Mellus, sent to Malabar in 1874 by the Chaldean patriarch Joseph VI Audo (who was involved in trouble with Rome) stirred up a schism which still exists: the "Mellusians" are a tiny nominally Nestorian sect in Trichur.[13]

The way was paved to a more satisfactory situation by a French Jesuit, Bishop Charles Levigne, and an Englishman, Bishop A. E. Medlycott, during the later years of the nineteenth century. As vicars apostolic of the Syro-Indians they together endeared themselves to their flocks and carried through much-needed enterprises and reforms; and at last Pope Leo XIII, in the face of strong opposition from some quarters, appointed three Indian bishops. This was in 1896, when Malabar was divided anew into three vicariates apostolic; a fourth was made in 1911. Finally in 1923, Pope Pius XI restored to the Syro-Indians a regular hierarchy, of one archbishop and three suffragans. During their years of renewed home-rule the Malabarese have made considerable progress in every direction.

PRESENT STATE

Organization. The Malabar Catholics of East Syrian rite are now organized in two ecclesiastical provinces: the metropolitan see of Ernakulam, with the dioceses of Kothamangalam, Tellicherry and Trichur, and the metropolitan see of Changanacherry, with the dioceses of Kottayam and Palai. The bishops are appointed directly from Rome.

Parochial clergy. They are mostly formed at the seminary of Alwaye, an interritual establishment directed by Spanish Carmelites on almost exclusively European lines; others go to Latin seminaries at Kandy, Mangalore or Rome. All Malabarese priests are taught Latin, English and their liturgical

---

12 One of them, Miles Prendergast, was an Irishman. His career was unfortunate. He expected the secular clergy to live as strictly as mendicant friars, and he got himself so disliked that in 1831 he was recalled to Rome and asked to resign.

13 Both the Chaldeans and Indians wanted the restoration of the Chaldean patriarch's jurisdiction over the Syro-Malabarese, but the differences of race, culture and language were against it. Audo tried to bring the question before the Vatican Council. But as recently as 1831 the Holy See appears to have been less opposed to this arrangement; see Bello's *Congrégation de S. Hormisdas ... et l'Église chaldéene* (Rome, 1939), p. 85.

Syriac, and the sacerdotal standard is noticeably high. There were over 1,000 secular priests in 1960. Subdeacons and upwards are strictly bound to celibacy. Priests are called *kattanar* (the Lord's man) and the bishops *abuna* (our father); pastors are helped in their administrative duties by a council of lay people. Clerical dress is Western, including even the biretta, but a plain gown, black or white, is often worn for ordinary dress; the clergy are clean-shaven.

Religious institutes. Among the Syro-Indians there is a remarkable number of vocations to the religious life. The congregation of men, tertiaries of our Lady of Mount Carmel, had its remote origin in 1831 at Mannanam, and was definitively organized in 1855, under Father Cyriac Elias Chavara (the cause of whose beatification is being advanced). They were affiliated to the Order of Barefooted Carmelites, whose habit was adopted. They are now known as *Carmelites of Mary Immaculate*, and in 1960 numbered 768 priests and lay-brothers, organized in three provinces; their prior general resides at Ernakulam. The congregation's principal work is the giving of missions and retreats, both to Syrians and Latins, and by its pioneer efforts the Malabarese were the first modern Catholic Orientals to do missionary work among the heathen (they were till recently the only ones who had the opportunity). Among their works they conduct schools and have printing and publishing establishments. There is a small "Southist" congregation, called the *Oblates of the Sacred Heart*, and some members of the *Society of Jesus* are now of Malabar rite.

The principal congregations of women, chiefly engaged in teaching, are the *Carmelite Tertiary Sisters* and the *Franciscan Tertiary Sisters*. There are also *Sisters of Adoration*, some "Southist" convents of *Visitation* nuns, and the growing local congregation of *Sisters of the Destitute*, whose name sufficiently indicates their scope.

The Faithful. There are two social "castes" among Malabarese Syrians, called "Northists" and "Southists". The last-named are a small minority found in the diocese of Kottayam. There are various legends and theories to account for their origin (the social organization of this part of India is notably complex). The Northists claim to be the superior race, and even among the Catholics their mutual relations have not always been what they should be. The bishops discourage distinctions based on caste, especially with reference to low-caste converts from Hinduism.

The Malabarese have a strong taste for education; since the restoration of Indian bishops, schools of all grades have arisen on every hand and the people have made good use of them. Their religious temper is characterized by an addiction to elaborate observances and long prayers.[14] Except for the eucharistic Liturgy they are hardly distinguishable in their formal religious practices and outlook from Western Catholics, and their general edifyingness and the success of their institutions have been used as an argument for the latinization of Orientals—by those who forget that the price of latinization in Malabar is represented today by hundreds of thousands of Christians who are not in communion with the Apostolic See.

In addition to the 1,377,000 Syrians there are in Malabar many Catholics of the Latin rite, fruit of European missionary effort since the fifteenth century, and the smaller body of Malankara Catholics (see p. 169).

LITURGY AND CUSTOMS

Church-buildings. These are plain aisleless rectangles, with the roof of choir and sanctuary sometimes higher than that of the nave. The bigger and older churches have, especially on the western façade, a good deal of applied ornament and architectural features that are a curious mixture of Indian fashions with European baroque. They are furnished with stations of the cross, statues, confessional-boxes etc., just as in the West. The sexes are separated in church, men being in front.

Vestments. These are wholly Western, and generally of debased patterns; but the return to Syrian vestments has begun.

Liturgical books. The Missal was first printed in 1774 at Rome, and other editions have been published at Mannanam and Puthenpally. The translated Goan Ritual was also first printed in Rome, in 1775, and later re-issued in India, together with several liturgical manuals. Half a dozen editions of the Divine

---

[14] In some households evening prayers for the family last the greater part of an hour.

Office have appeared since 1871. The Chaldean Pontifical was adopted in 1959, and for some years a commission of the Sacred Eastern Congregation has been preparing a new edition of all the Malabar service books. Among its aims is to get rid of the many anomalies that at present disfigure Malabarese public worship, some of which are referred to in these pages.

Altar-vessels and bread. Chalice, paten etc. of the Western forms are used, and the bread is unleavened wafers.

Music. The liturgical chant of the Malabarese rite is Chaldean in origin but it, too, has undergone much Western influence, with surprising results. It has more recognizable resemblances to the plainsong of the West than the music of any other Eastern rite. A system of notation is being worked out for the chant in order that it may be printed.

Liturgical language. This is wholly the eastern Syriac, even in the biblical readings. But the desirability of some use of the vernacular Malayalam is now being felt, and some bishops have already given it a place in ordination services. The difficulty of imparting an adequate knowledge of Syriac to seminarians has been felt for a long time.

THE EUCHARISTIC LITURGY

This is simply the Chaldean Liturgy, with the sole anaphora "of the Holy Apostles" (SS. Addai and Mari), as modified in Malabar. It is called *Kurbana*, the Offering, and there is a fixed form of "low" celebration. The moving of the book from one end to the other of the altar and the ringing of a "sanctus-bell", introduced into this Liturgy and sometimes found in others as well, are quite meaningless ceremonies, at any rate at a solemn Liturgy, for they have arisen from the particular history of the Roman Mass. Before leaving the sanctuary the celebrant kisses the altar and says a prayer with reference to it similar to that in the Antiochene rite.

The most solemn form of celebration has a special name, *Raza*, "(holy) Mysteries"; incense is used at low Mass normally. The restored text of the Liturgy, though still unpublished, has already been used on a few special occasions. Concelebration is not used by the Malabarese; they have a Liturgy of the Presanctified on Good Friday only.

THE DIVINE OFFICE

This was the only rite of Malabarese worship left untouched by the Portuguese; it was abridged and rearranged, and the recitation of the new edition made obligatory, in 1876. There are three "hours", *Ramsha* (Vespers), *Lilya* (Night-office), and *Sapra* (Day-office), consisting almost entirely of psalms (the psalter is spread over a fortnight), with a few hymns and prayers. It is hoped that the new edition (Rome, 1938) of the Chaldean office will come into use in Malabar.

THE SACRAMENTS

The Synod of Diamper decreed that the Roman occasional offices should be translated into Syriac for the use of the Syro-Indians, and this was done from the *rituale* in use in the Portuguese archdiocese of Braga. These are the rites at present in use among the Malabarese for *Baptism*, *Penance*, *Marriage* and *Anointing*. In the wedding service the priest blesses, instead of a ring, a small gold cross, which the bridegroom then puts round the bride's neck. Funeral offices more or less follow the Chaldean forms. *Confirmation* is reserved to bishops.

Orders. These are now conferred in accordance with the Chaldean usages.

Eucharist. Communion is in one kind only: the people kneel leaning back on their heels in the Indian manner, and the words of administration are: "May the body of our Lord Jesus Christ be to this devout believer for forgiveness of sin and everlasting life. Amen."

Calendar and feasts. The Malabar calendar is practically the same as the general Western calendar; but by a curious anomaly the Divine Office is read according to a different calendar, more or less Chaldean and almost wholly ferial. Besides Sundays there are five holy days, Christmas, Ascension, Corpus Christi, Assumption and St Thomas the Apostle (on July 3).

Penitential seasons. Fasting and abstinence or abstinence only is observed in Lent (fifty days, excluding Sundays), Advent (twenty-four days), Nineveh (three days) and every Friday and Saturday.

General observations. All the Western "popular devotions" and observances, and in the same forms, are in great favour with the Malabarese. They even have "methods of hearing Mass": I have seen one taken from the works of St Leonard of Port Maurice. We have seen that, under the influence of the indigenous hierarchy and with Roman encouragement and co-operation, some of the more unhappy effects of foreign domination are being undone, in such undertakings as the reform of the Liturgy and other rites, the encouragement of Indian studies, and so on.

BIBLIOGRAPHY

A. Mingana, *The Early Spread of Christianity in India* (Manchester, 1926).
L. W. Brown, *The Indian Christians of St Thomas* (Cambridge, 1956).
E. Tisserant, *Eastern Christianity in India* (London, 1957).
G. Schurhammer, *The Malabar Church and Rome* (Trichinopoly, 1934).
The Carmelite Congregation of Malabar (Trichinopoly, 1932).
Fr Fabian, *The Liturgy . . ., of the Syro-Malabar Rite* (Mannanam, 1954).
C. Korolevsky, *Living Languages in Catholic Worship* (London, 1957), pp. 117-140.

CHAPTER IX

EASTERN MONASTICISM

IN the Catholic Church today the monastic order—to use the old term—is not homogeneous. There are great practical differences between life in a Benedictine monastery of the English or American congregations, with their educational and pastoral work, and in a monastery of the congregation of Solesmes, with its intense liturgical preoccupation and normal repudiation of activity outside the cloister walls; between the public prayer and organized agriculture of the Cistercians and the eremitical solitude of the Carthusians. Yet these are certainly all monks, engaged in the various legitimate developments which have taken place within monastic life in the West during fourteen hundred years.

This is strange and incomprehensible to the traditional monk of the East. Of the regular or technically religious life in its extended meaning he knows nothing; and within monasticism itself he knows of no distinctions equivalent to "Benedictine", "Cistercian", "Carthusian". He does not belong to any "order"; he is just a monk. There is only one "rule" (except for the few so-called Antonians), that of St Basil, drawn up in the form of question and answer for the use of his monastery in Pontus, and that does not meet the requirements of a rule as understood in the West. We call these monks Basilians, but the label is inaccurate, and meaningless to those of whom we use it. There was no such thing as an Eastern "Order of St Basil" until the Italo-Greek, Ruthenian and Melkite monks were reformed and reorganized during the past three hundred and fifty years. St Basil was not a legislator or maker of systematic foundations and "his" monks do not regard him as such. "They do not belong to St Basil's order but St Basil belonged to theirs," as it has been well put. Although St Pachomius made an experiment in federation sixteen hundred years ago in Egypt and there is an Orthodox monastic republic at Mount Athos today, with a governing council, a traditional Eastern monk still belongs to a certain monastery and to nothing else, and each monastery is independent of all the others.[1]

The life of the Eastern monk and nun is what we should call "purely contemplative". Their business is to flee "the world", to do penance, and to worship God. There are no lay-brothers in an Eastern monastery, and just as St Benedict legislated for independent, self-governing families of men not in holy orders, so it still is the exception for an Eastern monk to be a priest, and practically no distinction is made between the monk who is a priest (hieromonk) and the monk who is not. Normally these monks undertake no work outside their monasteries, and inside work is largely unorganized and at choice; their day is not precisely and minutely arranged, and there is an atmosphere of spontaneity and freedom about them. To Western eyes it looks a rather "go-as-you-please" life. And why not? For it is as emphatically religious in conception and execution as the more ordered and busy life of a Western monastery; as an English Benedictine abbot, Dom Cuthbert Butler, wrote: "The real use of a monastic house lies not in its activities and usefulnesses. It lies rather in things that cannot be counted by statistics or estimated by results." A monk of the East would consider that so obvious as hardly to be worth saying.

This kind of monachism is in its pure form now virtually extinct (except for individuals) among Eastern Catholics. There are happily still monks at Grottaferrata, leading a recognizably monastic life (see p. 68); and in the Rule of St Benedict the Armenian Mekhitarists have found inspiration for a form of that life admirably fitted to the needs of their church. But history and the necessities of the situation have compelled the Ruthenian and Melkite Basilians, and the Antonians in Syria, Lebanon and Iraq, to become in effect clerks regular or societies of clergy under vows.[2]

[1] It is worth remembering that a Benedictine monk is professed, not for the the whole "order", but for his own monastery, and the principle of individual self-governing monasteries still obtains to a considerable extent. There are some Benedictine monks who do not make use of the expression Order of St Benedict, but call themselves "monks of such and such an abbey".

[2] Some of these bodies are now officially called "non-monastic orders" (cf., e.g., p. 61).

But in the past strict monasticism has been even more influential in the East than in the West; it has left its imprint on every aspect of church life, from liturgical chant and the form of the Divine Office and the dress of bishops to the high ascetical standard of the faithful and the fasts imposed on them: monks have set the tone and fixed the background for whole churches (e.g., the Coptic Church). It therefore seems fitting to give a few paragraphs here to the revival of traditional Eastern monachism in one of its historic forms sponsored by the late Metropolitan Andrew Szepticky in Galicia from 1901 to 1945.

This revival was due radically to half a dozen Ukrainian peasants who wished to undertake a more perfect way of life but were considered unsuitable for acceptance by the Ruthenian Basilians. So about 1900 they began to live a common life of their own, under the direction of the parish priest of Olesko, a village near Zloszov. Here they were found by the Metropolitan Szepticky (himself a monk), who transferred them first to Vulka, near Lvov, and then to Skynliv. In 1906 he gave them constitutions (*typikon*), in 1908 ordained the first hieromonk, and later appointed an abbot (*hegumenos*) in the person of his own brother, Father Clement (Count Casimir Szepticky), who had been trained under the Benedictines of Beuron. In 1914 there were forty of these monks, but a Polish officer denounced them as Russian partisans; so they were conscripted, interned or deported to Hungary, and their monastery at Skynliv burned down in the Polish-Ukrainian war. After the war the metropolitan (who retained supreme authority over them as archimandrite) collected them together in his country-house at Univ and they began all over again.

These monks were called Studites, as emulating the life lived in the monastery of Studius at Constantinople in the ninth century. That observance simplified and systemized the customs of St Basil and, so far from being a particular code, was an attempt to gather up and express the spirit of all Eastern monastic legislation; it had a profound effect particularly on the early monasticism of Russia. The Ukrainian Studites aimed at no particular task, and accepted any vocation not at variance with Eastern ideas of monastic life. Most of the subjects were young peasants, used only to manual work, but even before 1914 Metropolitan Szepticky had made the nucleus of a foundation in Lvov itself, where those who were suitable could undertake intellectual pursuits. The morning office with the Eucharist lasted from five in the morning till after seven; but daily life was less precise and ordered than in a monastery of the West. Apart from divine worship, the principal business of the monks was manual work, to which those engaged in intellectual work also had to give some time daily. There was no ordinary limit to the quantity of food taken, but it was very plain and meat was served only on Sundays and feast days (not at all in Lent); the full Byzantine fasts were observed. No distinction, of course, was made in the way of life or otherwise between monks who were priests (hieromonks) and those who were not. The ideal set before the Studites was one in accordance with authentic traditions of Slav-Byzantine Christianity in every way, spiritual, ascetical, liturgical and monastic.

In 1939 the Studites had one principal *laura*, four lesser monasteries and several other small establishments, and foundations had been made outside Galicia. There were nearly two hundred monks. Twenty-six were priests and seven permanent deacons. There were also three Studite houses of women, with about forty nuns; they were strictly enclosed and bound to choral office, but conducted orphanages etc., within their precincts.

During and following 1939-1945 the Studite monasteries were all destroyed or confiscated and their members dispersed; some were killed, others imprisoned or sent to labour-camps, where many died. Among those who succumbed to brutalities and hardship was the venerable abbot of Univ, Clement Szepticky; he died in Siberia in 1948. About a dozen monks were able to escape to freedom and come together again. After temporary sojourns in various places in western Europe they found a home in Canada. Since 1951 they have constituted a small monastery at Woodstock, in the province of Ontario, where they seek to perpetuate the work that half a dozen peasants and Andrew Szepticky began so long ago and so far away.

Another aspect of this subject that cannot be passed over

unnoticed is the contribution made by monks of Western origin. At many places in this book indications have been given of work done in and for the Christian East in modern times by Western orders and congregations, sometimes leading to the formation of an Eastern-rite branch of the institute concerned. That of the Jesuits (going back to their earliest years) in many lands, and of the Augustinians of the Assumption in Bulgaria, Rumania and Turkey, stands in a class by itself both for extension and scope; and then there are the Dominicans in Iraq, the Carmelites in Malabar, the Redemptorists amongst the Ukrainians, Friars Minor, Capuchins, Lazarists (Vincentians) and others in various places. But in this chapter it is a question of monks, properly so called.

The idea common to Pope Leo XIII and Cardinal J. B. Pitra, to Bishop Gerard van Caloen and Metropolitan Szepticky, that the Benedictines are a sort of natural link between East and West, was shared by Pope Pius XI; and in 1924 he issued a letter, "Equidem verba", calling on the monks of St Benedict to take an active part in the Eastern field of apostleship. It can hardly be denied that the results of that letter have not been so considerable as was hoped; but even had it achieved nothing else it would be remembered for its first-fruits, the founding by Dom Lambert Beauduin in 1925 of the monastery of Amay-sur-Meuse in Belgium, moved in 1939 to Chevetogne.

This community consists wholly of choir-monks (not necessarily in holy orders), and in 1960 it numbered eight nationalities amongst its members. They are about equally divided between the Western and Byzantine rites: the Divine Office according to each and the eucharistic Liturgy in Latin and Greek or Slavonic are sung every day in the respective churches. Their special work has been summed up as, by prayer, learned study, writing and personal contacts of various kinds, "to prepare the ground for a restoration of unity between the separated Eastern churches, especially the Russian, and Rome, by bringing about in both West and East a favourable psychological atmosphere: a mutual knowledge, understanding and esteem based on appreciation of their rich common heritage from Christian antiquity—the teaching of the Fathers, monasticism, liturgical life" (Dom Roger Gazeau).

So carefully and objectively, in so friendly a spirit, is this programme carried out that Amay-Chevetogne has become recognized on all hands as a spiritual rallying-point of Christian reconciliation. One of its most effective means is its quarterly review, *Irénikon*, to which Orthodox writers are happy to contribute and from whose pages many a Catholic has first learned to appreciate the Christian East: and it is "the most important documentary source on the Eastern churches published in Europe". In 1949 an associated convent of Benedictine nuns using the Byzantine rite was opened at Cureglia, near Lugano in Switzerland. The nuns are of several nationalities, using Slavonic as their liturgical language. Among their good works is the provision of holidays for refugee Russian children, and lay visitors of both sexes are welcome to stay there.

An American monastery, of Czech (Bohemian) origin, was the next to act on Pius XI's wishes, the abbey of St Procopius at Lisle, Illinois, under the leadership of the venerable Abbot Prokop Neuzil, in 1926. Here two groups of Byzantine-rite monks, Ruthenian and Byelorussian, were formed within the monastery; and so well did the experiment succeed that it eventually became possible to plant out a daughter-house of Ruthenian monks, now Holy Trinity Priory at Butler in Pennsylvania. In 1956 the enterprise of Abbot Prokop's successor, Abbot Ambrose Ondrak, inaugurated the first of a series of reunion congresses at Lisle, which may be regarded as the continuation of the well-known congresses at Velehrad in Czechoslovakia which war and its results brought to an end; and in 1960 a small Byzantine church and centre for reunion work were opened in Chicago.

There has been some response from German-speaking lands, as at the abbeys of Coesfeld in Westphalia and Niederaltaich in Bavaria and the house of the Olivetan congregation at Tanzenberg in Carinthia; before the last war Dom Chrysostom Baur, monk of Weingarten, directed a training-college for Slav-Byzantine clergy in Munich. It has been recorded above (p. 150) that till recently Subiaco Benedictines from France were established amongst the West Syrians, whose clergy they trained.

There is a convent of nuns with Byzantine members at

Schootenhof, near Antwerp, which was directed by Abbot Constantine Bosschaerts, of the Olivetan Benedictines, up to his untimely death in 1950; and at Gelrode monks of the same congregation conduct a house of Eastern studies and have the care of Eastern-rite students in the University of Louvain.

From some points of view the undertaking of the Cistercians of Casamari Abbey in Italy is as interesting as any. As has been said above (p. 142), they have been instrumental in establishing a house of Ethiopian monks of their order near Asmara. Monks have so important a place in the Christian history and life of Ethiopia, and conditions of life in that country are such, that it may well be that this event will prove to be the seed of a new flowering of Eastern Catholic monasticism.

BIBLIOGRAPHY

H. Delehaye, "Byzantine Monasticism" in N. H. Baynes and H. Moss, *Byzantium* (Oxford, 1948), pp. 136-165.
B. Gariador, *Les anciens monastères bénédictins en Orient* (Lille, 1912).
Pax, no. 84 (Caldey Abbey, 1927). Catholic Byzantine monasticism.
Revue liturgique et monastique (Maredsous, 1925), pp. 202-209. Studites.
A volume of *Orientalia Christiana Analecta* (Rome, 1958) contains the papers, in French, German and Italian, given at a conference on Eastern Monasticism held at the Oriental Institute in that year.

APPENDIX

DISTRIBUTION OF THE
CATHOLIC EASTERN CHURCHES
IN 1960

	Number of faithful
Alexandrian Rite:	
i. Copts (Egypt)	80,500
ii. Ethiopians	50,000

Antiochene Rite:

i. Syrians in patriarchal territory	80,000	
in U.S.A.	5,000	
in other places	5,000?	
		90,000
ii. Maronites in patriarchal territory	630,000	
in North America	55,000	
in South America	75,000?	
in other places	10,000?	
		770,000
iii. Malankarese (India)		108,000

Armenian Rite:

In patriarchal territory	53,000	
In Europe	16,000	
In the Americas	6,000?	
		75,000

Byzantine Rite:

Byelorussians in western Europe and elsewhere		?
Greeks in Greece and elsewhere		3,000
Italo-Greek-Albanians in Italy and Sicily	64,000	
in U.S.A. and Brazil	20,000?	
		84,000

Number of
Byzantine Rite—cont.   faithful

Melkites in patriarchal territory	220,000
in North America	40,000
in South America	95,000?
elsewhere	2,500?

357,500

Rumanians in North America	6,000?
elsewhere	4,000?

10,000

Russians in western Europe and elsewhere	3,500?

Ruthenians:

in Hungary	195,000
in western Europe	78,000
in Canada	221,000
in South America	230,000?
in Australia	30,000
Ukrainians in U.S.A.	312,000
Carpatho-Ruthenians in U.S.A.	221,000

1,287,000

Yugoslavs	56,000

Chaldean Rite:

i. Chaldeans in Iraq etc.	196,000
in U.S.A.	1,500

197,500

ii. Malabarese (India)	1,377,000

The Eastern faithful are at present organized in 72 effective dioceses, of which six are patriarchal sees, and nine exarchates whose bishops are ordinaries. Immigrants not included in these circumscriptions are organized in various ways, according to local conditions.

DISRUPTED CHURCHES

In addition, since 1939, two metropolitan archbishoprics of the first importance and eight other dioceses, together with an exarchate and several lesser circumscriptions have been disrupted by communist governments. These comprise the following:

			Number of faithful
Armenians in U.S.S.R.	....	50,000	(in 1917)
in Poland		5,000	(1939)
in Rumania	....	35,000	(1939)
		90,000	
Bulgars		7,000	(1950)
Byelorussians		18,000	(1939)
Carpatho-Ruthenians		600,000	(1947)
Rumanians		1,563,000	(1948)
Ukrainians		4,000,000	(1945)

GLOSSARY

Most of the terms noted are used and explained in the text, but are repeated and briefly defined here for convenience of reference. Liturgical terms mostly apply to the Byzantine rite. *Ar.* = Arabic, *Gk.* = Greek, *Lat.* = Latin, *Sl.* = Slavonic, *Syr.* = Syriac.

ABA, ABBA (*Syr.*, father). The title of an Ethiopian priest.

ABUNA (*Ar.*, our father). Form of address of Ethiopian bishops and of all clergy in some Arabic-speaking lands; also formerly the official title of the head of the dissident Ethiopian Church.

AER (*Gk.*, air. *Sl.*, *vozdukh*). Large veil covering the chalice and paten.

AKOLOUTHIA (*Gk.*, sequence. *Sl.*, *slujba*). The daily divine office.

ALEPPINES. Maronite and Melkite congregations of monks, centred at Aleppo.

AMBA, ANBA (*Coptic*, father). The title of a Coptic bishop or saint.

AMBO (*Gk.*, a raised place). A sort of pulpit in front and to one side of the *eikonostasis* in some churches.

AMNOS (*Gk.*, lamb. *Sl.*, *agnetz*). The first and principal part cut from the *prosphora* for consecration.

ANALOGION (*Gk.*). A lectern or small table.

ANAPHORA (*Gk.*, offering). Equivalent term to "canon of the Mass", sometimes used for the whole Liturgy. Most Eastern Liturgies have several alternative anaphoras.

ANOINTING (*Gk.*, *eukhelaion. Sl.*, *eleosvyaschenie*). The sacrament called Extreme Unction in the West.

ANTIDORON (*Gk.*, a gift instead of [holy communion]). Blessed bread.

ANTIMENSION (*Gk.*, instead of a table). A cloth with relics laid on the altar for the Liturgy to be celebrated on.

ANTONIANS. Monks of the Maronite and Chaldean rites.

APOCRISIARIUS (*Lat.*, from *Gk.*, *apokrisis*, answer). A legate or nuncio.

APODEIPNON (*Gk.*, after-supper. *Sl.*, *povecherie*). Complin.

APOLYSIS (*Gk.*, dismissal. *Sl.*, *otpust*). The conclusion of a liturgical office.

APOSTOLOS (*Gk.*). The lesson from the Epistles or Acts; the book containing them.

ARCHBISHOP. In strict Byzantine usage the head of a series of metropolitan provinces. No longer so used.

ARCHIEREUS (*Gk.*, high priest). A bishop. The pope is *Ho tes Romes Archiereus*.

ARCHIMANDRITE (*Gk.*, guardian of a fold). The superior of a large monastery or of a congregation; also a titular dignitary.

ARTOKLASIA (*Gk.*, breaking of bread). Blessing of bread, wine and oil at Vespers on a vigil.

ARTOPHORION (*Gk.*, bread-carrier. *Sl.*, *kovcheg*). The tabernacle of an altar.

ASTERISKOS (*Gk.*, star). A metal frame to keep the veil off the host.

AZYME (*Gk.*, unleavened). Unleavened altar-bread.

BALADITES (*Ar.*, rustics). Maronite and Melkite congregations of monks.

BASILIANS. Improperly, Eastern monks in general; properly, certain Catholic congregations.

BEATITUDE, HIS, YOUR, or BLESSEDNESS. The style of address and reference given to an Eastern patriarch.

BEMA (*Gk.*, step). The sanctuary of a church.

BYZANTINE. Primarily, appertaining to Byzantium (Constantinople); by extension, appertaining to all those churches using the Liturgy, etc., of Constantinople.

"CANONS, THE." Canon law.

CHARTOPHYLAX (*Gk.*, keeper of records). A diocesan chancellor.

CHEROUBIKON (*Gk.*). The "hymn of the Cherubim", intoned just before the great entrance in the Byzantine Liturgy.

CHIROTONY (*Gk.*, stretching forth of hands). The sacrament of Holy Orders; ordination or consecration.

CHOREPISKOPOS (*Gk.*, rural overseer). A title of honour in several rites, sometimes with duties attached. It is occasionally rendered into the horrid word "chor-bishop".

CIBORIUM (*Lat.*, from *Gk.*, a cup). A canopy of wood or stone, supported by pillars, covering an altar.

CONCELEBRATION. The celebration of the Liturgy by several celebrants together at one altar, all consecrating the same bread and wine.

CREED. The creed of Nicaea-Constantinople is the only one used liturgically in any Eastern rite.

CROSS. The "Russian cross" has three bars, the top one representing the title and the bottom one (sloped down from left to right) representing the foot-rest. The "Greek cross" is equilateral.

CROWN. The Byzantine episcopal mitre, worn also by Armenian priests.

CROWNING. The marriage rite, from its chief observance.

DESPOTA (*Gk.*, ruler, master). The Greek form of address to a bishop.

DIAKONIKON (*Gk.*, of the deacon). The part of the sanctuary to the south of the altar; a liturgical book for the deacon's use.

DIKERION (*Gk.*). A two-branched candlestick.

DIPTYCHS (*Gk.*, twice-folded). The commemoration of the living and the dead in the Liturgy, whose names were formerly written on two conjoined tablets.

DISKOS (*Gk.*, quoit). The Byzantine paten.

DISSIDENT. Non-Catholic Christian, especially of an Eastern church.

DOORS. "Holy", the central doors of the *eikonostasis;* "royal", the central doors from the narthex into the nave. The "holy doors" are sometimes called "royal".

EIKON (*Gk.*, image). A flat painted sacred picture, often covered with embossed metal except over the faces and hands.

EIKONOSTASIS (*Gk.*, picture-stand). The screen separating the nave from the sanctuary, and adorned with pictures.

EILETON (*Gk.*). A linen corporal.

EKPHONESIS (*Gk.*). A "lifting of the voice" at the last words of an inaudible prayer.

ENKOLPION (*Gk.*, that worn on the breast). An oval medallion worn on a chain round the neck.

ENTRANCE, LITTLE, GREAT. Processions, with the gospel-book and the bread and wine respectively, in the Byzantine and Armenian Liturgies.

EPARCHY (*Gk.*, province). Any episcopal diocese.

EPIGONATION (*Gk.*, *epigounis*, thigh. *Sl.*, *palitsa*). A lozenge-shaped episcopal vestment, worn above the right knee. Peculiar to the pope in the West.

EPIKLESIS (*Gk.*, invocation). A prayer that the Holy Spirit may come down upon the bread and wine and turn it into Christ's body and blood, and imploring the grace of the sacrament for the recipients. It comes after the words of institution.

EPIMANIKIA (*Gk.*, upon the sleeves. *Sl.*, *poruchi*). Liturgical cuffs.

EPITRAKHELION (*Gk.*, upon the neck). The sacerdotal stole.

EUKHELAION. *See* Anointing.

EUKHOLOGION (*Gk.*, prayer-book. *Sl.*, *Sluzebnik*). A book containing the texts of the Liturgies and other offices.

EXARCH (*Gk.*, ruler). The primate of an independent church, between a patriarch and an archbishop; but more usually now a priest or bishop with a special charge. Also a title of honour.

FILIOQUE (*Lat.*, and from the Son. *Gk.*, *kai ek tou Huiou*). The phrase added to the Nicene Creed in the West which Photius in 863 declared to be a "corruption of the faith".

GE'EZ. Classical Ethiopic, the liturgical language of that rite.

GYNAECEUM (*Lat. Gk.*, *gynaikites*). The part of a church reserved for women.

HAGIA (*Gk.*, holy things). The sacred elements after consecration.

HAIKAL (*Ar.*, temple). The sanctuary of a Coptic church.

HEGUMENOS (*Gk.*, leader). An abbot.

HESPERINOS (*Gk. Sl.*, *Vechernya*). Vespers.

HEXAPTERYGON (*Gk.*, six-winged). Another name for the *ripidion*.

HIERARCH (*Gk.*, sacred ruler). Any high member of a hierarchy, but especially an archbishop or patriarch.

HIERATIKON (*Gk.*). A book containing the prayers most used by a priest, a variable compilation. Also called the *Leitourgikon* or Little Eukhologion.

HIERODEACON. A monk who is a deacon.

HIEROMONK. A monk who is a priest.

HOROLOGION (*Gk. Sl., Chasoslov*, book of the hours). A book containing the common prayers of the Divine Office, etc.

ICONOCLASM (*Gk.*, image-breaking). The campaign against the veneration of holy images and the accompanying persecution, centred at Constantinople, from *c.* 726 till 787 and from 814 till 842.

JULIAN CALENDAR. Issued by Julius Caesar in 45 B.C., corrected under Pope Gregory XIII in 1582. The Julian reckoning is now 13 days behind the Gregorian.

KAMELAUKION (*Gk., kamelos*, camel, *aukhen*, nape of the neck). The clerical hat of the Byzantine rite, at first made of camel-hair cloth.

KAMISION. The long ungirdled vestment proper to minor clerics.

KANON. A rhythmical hymn, sometimes very long.

KARSHUNI. Arabic written in Syriac characters.

KATHOLIKOS (*Gk.*, general delegate). The title of the heads of the Nestorian, Armenian and Georgian churches, now equivalent to patriarch.

KOIMESIS (*Gk.*, falling asleep. *Sl., Uspenie*). The feast of the Assumption of our Lady.

KONTAKION (*Gk.*). A hymn referring to the day's feast.

KUMMUS. A Coptic abbot; also a title of honour for any priest of that rite.

KYR (*Gk.*, lord, master). The title of a Byzantine bishop.

LANCE, THE HOLY (*Gk., lonkhe. Sl., kopye*). The Byzantine liturgical knife.

LAURA (*Gk.*, alley). Formerly a monastery consisting of rows of cells or huts; now any sizeable monastery.

LITURGY, THE (*Gk., leitourgia*, a public duty or work). The Eucharistic Sacrifice, i.e. Mass.

MANDYAS (*Gk.*). 1. A short cloak, part of the monastic habit. 2. A sort of cope, worn by bishops.

MAR (*Syr.*, lord). Title given to saints and bishops in the Syriac rites; fem., *mart*.

MELKITES (*Syr., malok*, king). Name given to the Byzantines of Syria, Palestine and Egypt, especially nowadays to the Catholics.

MENAION (*Gk., men*, month). A liturgical book in six or twelve volumes, containing the proper parts of the Divine Office for fixed feasts.

MESONYKTIKON (*Gk.*, midnight. *Sl., Polunoschnitsa*). The night-office.

METANY (*Gk.*, penitence). Great, a complete prostration; ordinary or little, a profound bow, taking the place of the Western genuflection.

METOKHION (*Gk.*). An estate or cell belonging to a monastery.

METROPOLITAN. In strict Byzantine usage, equivalent to a Western archbishop. Catholics now use the title almost indifferently with archbishop.

MOLEBEN (*Sl.*). An occasional service of thanksgiving or petition.

MYRON (*Gk.*, sweet oil). The Holy Chrism, which may be blessed only by patriarchs or other primates; Confirmation therewith.

MYSTERY (*Gk.*, something hidden. *Sl.*, *tain*). The ordinary word for a sacrament in the East.

NARTHEX. The western vestibule of a church.

NESTEIA (*Gk. Sl.*, *post*). Fasting and/or abstinence from certain foods.

OLD BELIEVERS OR OLD RITUALISTS. Russian sectaries who refused the reforms of the Patriarch Nikon of Moscow in the seventeenth century. Before the revolution they numbered, with other sects, over 20 millions, but are commonly reckoned by Westerners as members of the Orthodox Church.

OMOPHORION (*Gk.*, borne on the shoulders). The large Byzantine *pallium*, worn by all bishops when celebrating the Liturgy; a smaller one is used for convenience at certain parts.

ORARION (*Gk.*). The deacon's long stole.

ORTHODOX (*Gk.*, *orthodoxos*, *Sl.*, *pravoslav*, right-believer). The name for all those who accepted the Council of Chalcedon; now usually confined as a title to the Eastern Orthodox Church.

ORTHROS (*Gk.*, daybreak. *Sl.*, *Utrenya*). The office equivalent to Matins and Lauds.

PANAGIA (*Gk.*). "All-holy", used for the Mother of God as we say "our Lady". Also another name for the *enkolpion*.

PANNYKHIDIA (*Gk.*, all night). An office for the dead.

PANTOKRATOR (*Gk.*, all-mighty). An image of our Lord ruling from Heaven, Christ the King.

PAPPAS (*Gk.*, father, i.e., pope). All Greek-speaking priests are called *pappas*, and the equivalent (*pop*) is common among the Slavs but is considered wanting in respect; they say *batyushka* "little father". "Pope" is one of the official titles of the Orthodox patriarch of Alexandria.

PAREKKLESIA (*Gk.*, beside-church). A side chapel or addition to a church.

PATRIARCH (*Gk.*, ruler of a family). A bishop who holds the highest rank after the pope in the hierarchy of jurisdiction. A patriarch can be subject to no other prelate except the pope. In the West the title is honorary, except for the pope himself, who is "Patriarch of the West" or "of Rome".

PERIODEUTES (*Gk.*, visitor. *Syr.*, *bardut*, Malayalam, *prodott*). A title of honour given to priests holding positions of responsibility in the three churches of Antiochene rite.

PHENOLION (*Gk.*). The Byzantine chasuble.

PRAVOSLAV. *See* Orthodox.

PRESANCTIFIED, LITURGY OF THE. A Liturgy in which there is no consecration; a Host consecrated at a previous Liturgy is consumed at the communion.

PROSKOMIDE (*Gk.*, preparation). The preparatory part of the Liturgy, at which the ministers vest and the bread and wine are prepared.

PROSPHORA (*Gk.*, oblation). The Byzantine altar-bread, like a small loaf or cake.

PROTHESIS (*Gk.*, setting-out). The part of the sanctuary to the north of the altar, where the bread and wine are made ready.

PROTODEACON. Archdeacon or senior deacon. Archdeacons are generally deacons, not priests, in the East.

PROTOPOPE —PRESBYTER —PRIEST. An archpriest, "rural dean" (distinguish from *archiereus*).

PROTOPSALTES (*Gk. Sl., regent khora*). The chief cantor.

PROTOTHRONE. The first see of a patriarchate, after the patriarch's; e.g., Tyre is the protothrone of Antioch; or a primatial see, e.g., the see of Rome is the protothrone of the world, Constantinople of the East.

RABBAN (*Syr.*, our father). The Syrian term corresponding to hieromonk (*q.v.*).

RASON (*Gk.*). The wide-sleeved gown proper to the Eastern clergy.

RIPIDION (*Gk.*, fan). A metal liturgical fan affixed to a pole.

ROSARY (*Gk., konbologion. Sl., chotky*). The Eastern rosary usually consists of one hundred beads at each of which a metany is made and words equivalent to "Lord, have mercy on me, a sinner" said. It is a mainly monastic practice. Most Eastern Catholics use the Western rosary.

"SAINT SOPHIA." A barbarous name often given in English to the church of the Holy Wisdom at Constantinople.

SAKKOS (*Gk.*, a sack). The principal eucharistic vestment proper to Byzantine bishops.

SCHEMA (*Gk.*). The monastic habit; a garment derived therefrom (*Syr., eskhimo*).

SKOUPHOS. The cap worn by monks under their veil and by minor clerics.

SOLEA. The step before the holy doors at which communion is given.

STAROSLAV. A name given, first by French writers, to Church Slavonic.

STAROVERY (*Russ.*). *See* Old Believers.

STASIDIA (*Gk.*, standing-places). The fixed seats behind the altar, in front of the *eikonostasis*, and around the walls of a Byzantine church: usually stood at rather than sat upon.

STIKHARION (*Gk.*). A vestment equivalent to an alb.

SYNAXARY (*Gk.*). A calendar or martyrology with brief notices of the saints; a passage from the same read in the office.

224

GLOSSARY

SYNAXIS (*Gk.*, assembly). 1. A feast on which are commemorated saints connected with the mystery of the previous day. 2. The council of seniors in a monastery.

SYNKELLOS. 1. A bishop's secretary or vicar general. 2. An auxiliary bishop.

SYNOD (*Gk.*, meeting). 1. Any ecclesiastical council. 2. A patriarch's permanent episcopal council. 3. The governing assembly of an Orthodox church.

SYNTHRONOS (*Gk.*). The bishop's seat and stalls for clergy behind the altar.

TEMPLON (*Gk.*). Another name for the *eikonostasis*.

THEOTOKOS (*Gk.*, *tokos*, childbirth). The Mother of God. *Theotokion*: a hymn in her honour.

THRONE. An expression used in the East equivalently with the Western "see" (episcopal).

TREBNIK (*Sl.*). A Slavonic book of the Byzantine rite, the Ritual of the Sacraments.

TRIKERION (*Gk.*). A three-branched candlestick.

TRISAGION, THE. The thrice-holy hymn: "Holy God, holy strong One, holy deathless One, have mercy on us."

TROPARION (*Gk.*). A generic name for the short hymns of the Byzantine rite.

TYPIKON (*Gk.*). 1. A book of the calendar and rubrics; each chief church of the Byzantine rite has one of its own. 2. A charter of monastic constitutions.

VARTAPET. A rank in the Armenian hierarchy, below the episcopate.

VICAR PATRIARCHAL. A local representative appointed by a patriarch.

VLADYKA (*Sl.*, ruler, master). The Slavonic form of address to a bishop.

XEROPHAGY (*Gk.*, dry food). The stricter form of Eastern fast.

ZEON (*Gk.*, boiling). Warm water poured into the chalice before communion.

ZONE (*Gk.*). Girdle.

GENERAL BIBLIOGRAPHY

REFERENCE BOOKS

Dictionnaire de théologie catholique.
Dictionnaire d'histoire et de géographie ecclésiastiques.
Dictionnaire d'archéologie chrétienne et de liturgie.
Dictionnaire de spiritualité ascétique et mystique.
The Catholic Encyclopaedia.
Échos d'Orient (Paris, 1898-1942).
Lexicon für Theologie und Kirche.
Enciclopedia cattolica.
Atlas of the Early Christian World (London, 1958).
List of Books in English about the Eastern Churches (Newport, R.I., 1960).

GENERAL

D. Attwater, *A Book of Eastern Saints* (Milwaukee, 1938).
N. H. Baynes, *The Byzantine Empire* (Oxford, 1943).
ed. N. H. Baynes and H. Moss, *Byzantium; an Introduction to East Roman Civilization* (Oxford, 1948).
L. Bréhier, *L'Église et l'Orient au moyen âge: les Croisades* (Paris, 1928).
L. E. Browne, *The Eclipse of Christianity in Asia* (Cambridge, 1933).
H. M. Chadwick, *The Nationalities of Europe* (Cambridge, 1945).
Le communisme et l'Église catholique (Paris, 1956). A documented report, 1939-55.
C. Dawson, *The Making of Europe* (London, 1946).
C. Diehl, *History of the Byzantine Empire* (Princeton, N.J., 1925).
F. Dvornik, *National Churches and the Church Universal* (London, 1944).
A. Fortescue, *The Lesser Eastern Churches* (London, 1913).
P. Hughes, *A History of the Church*, 3 vols. (London, 1934-46).
J. M. Hussey, *Church and Learning in the Byzantine Empire* (Oxford, 1937).
———— *The Byzantine World* (London, 1957).
W. Kolarz, *Myths and Realities in Eastern Europe* (London, 1946).
C. Lagier, *L'Orient chrétien des Apôtres jusqu'à Photius* (Paris, 1935).
F. J. McGarrigle et al., *The Eastern Branches of the Catholic Church* (New York, 1938).
H. Musset, *Histoire du christianisme spécialement en Orient*, 3 vols. (Harissa, 1948).
S. Runciman, *The Byzantine Civilization* (London, 1933).
———— *A History of the Crusades*, 3 vols. (Cambridge, 1951-54).

Sesostris Sidaruss, *Les patriarcats dans l'Empire ottoman* (Paris, 1907).

M. Spinka, *A History of Christianity in the Balkans* (Chicago, 1933).

A. A. Vasiliev, *History of the Byzantine Empire* 2 vols. (Madison, Wis., 1958).

W. A. Wigram, *The Separation of the Monophysites* (London, 1923).

LITURGY AND ART

D. Attwater, *Eastern Catholic Worship* (New York, 1945).

M. Beza, *Byzantine Art in Rumania* (London, 1940).

I. H. Dalmais, *The Eastern Liturgies* (London, 1960).

O. M. Dalton, *East Christian Art* (London, 1925).

I. Dirks, *Les saintes icones* (Amay, 1939).

H. Glück, *Die christliche Kunst des Ostens* (Berlin, 1923).

A. Grabar, *Byzantine Painting* (New York, 1953).

W. Hazzard, *Medieval Russian Churches* (Cambridge, Mass., 1949).

C. Korolevsky, *Living Languages in Catholic Worship* (London, 1957).

N. P. Kondakov, *The Russian Icon* (Oxford, 1927).

N. Liesel, *Eastern Catholic Liturgies* (Westminster, Md., 1960).

———— *Die Liturgien des Ostkirche* (Freiburg, 1960).

U. Monneret de Villard, *Le chiese della Mesopotamia* (Rome, 1940).

N. Nilles, *Kalendarium manuale utriusque ecclesiae orientalis et occidentalis*, 2 vols. (Innsbruck, 1896-97).

A. Raes, *Introductio in liturgiam orientalem* (Rome, 1947).

I. E. Rahmani, *Les liturgies orientales et occidentales* (Bairut, 1929).

D. T. Rice and S. Radojcić, *Yugoslavia: Mediaeval Frescoes* (New York, 1955).

S. Salaville, *An Introduction to . . . Eastern Liturgies* (London, 1938).

E. Tisserant, *Petit paroissien des liturgies orientales* (Rome, 1941).

PERIODICALS

The Eastern Churches Quarterly (Newman Bookshop, Oxford; C.N.E.W.A., 480 Lexington Ave., N.Y.).

Irénikon, quarterly (Prieuré bénédictin, Chevetogne, Belgium).

Istina, quarterly (25 bde d'Auteuil, Boulogne-sur-Seine).

Der christliche Osten, every two months (Catholica Unio, 153 Leopoldstrasse, Munich).

L'Orient Syrien, quarterly (93 ave Paul Doumer, Paris).

Proche-Orient Chrétien, quarterly (St. Anne's Seminary, Jerusalem, via Amman).

Unitas, quarterly (140 Strand, London, W.C.2; St Paul's Friary, Graymoor, N.Y.).

Vers l'unité chrétienne, monthly (25 bde d'Auteuil, Boulogne-sur-Seine).

Chrysostom, quarterly bulletin S.S.J.C. (Marian House, London, N.12).

INDEX

A

	PAGE
Abrikosova, Mother A.	122
Abyssinians, *see* Ethiopians	
Ad catholici sacerdotii, encyclical	25
Addai and Mari, SS.	195
Agathangelo of Vendôme, Bd.	129, 140
Aggami, Mother A.	160
Alba Julia, Union of	106–7
Albanians, Catholic	66, 126
Alexandria, Coptic patriarchate of	128ff., 138
Alexandrian rite, *see* Coptic and Ethiopic rites	
Allatae sunt, encyclical	17
Allatius, Leo	112
Altar vessels, vestments, etc.:	
Armemian	180–1
Byzantine	40ff.
Chaldean	194
Coptic	132
Ethiopic	144
Malabarese	205–6
Maronite	166
Syrian	152–3
Amay, *see* Chevetogne	
America, Eastern Catholics in	62
and *passim*; early examples	148, 179
Anaphoras	28
Chaldean	195–6
Coptic	133
Ethiopic	144–5
Maronite	167
Syrian	154
Anne's, St, seminary, Jerusalem	59–60
Antioch, patriarchate of:	
Maronite	158ff.
Melkite	55ff.
Syrian	147ff.
Antiochene rite, *see* Syrian (West) and Maronite rites	
Antonian monks	163–4, 193
nuns	164
Armenian monks	177–8
nuns	178
Armenian rite	180ff.

	PAGE
Armenians, Catholic	173ff.
Assemani, Joseph	160, 163n.
Assumptionists	109, 113, 118, 150, 213
sisters	109
Athanasius, Amba	129
Audo, Patr. J.	191, 198
Augustinians of the Assumption *see* Assumptionists	

B

Babylon, patriarchate of	192ff.
Bachynsky, Bp A.	94
Bait Marun monastery	158
Baradai, Jacob	147
Barbara's, St, Church, Vienna	89
Baptism by immersion	29, 48, 134, 155, 184, 196
Basilian monks and nuns	60–1, 83–4, 86, 87, 96, 97, 103, 109, 210
Bejan, Fr P.	191, 195
Belloc, H., quoted	34
Benedict XIV, Pope, quoted	17
Benedict XV, Pope, quoted	20, 34
Benedictines	97, 150–1, 213ff.
Bessarion, Cardinal	11, 68
Blessed Sacrament, cultus of	30, 63, 172
Bread, altar, leavened	29, 43, 132, 144, 153, 195
Bread, blessed	46, 172, 183
Brest Litovsk, Union of	73–4
Bulgars, Catholic	117ff.
Butler, Abbot Cuthbert, quoted	210
Byelorussians, Catholic	122ff.
Byron, Lord	178
Byzantine rite	38ff.

C

Cabrol, Abbot F., quoted	viii
Caesaeopapism	6
Calendar, Julian	51, 92, 135–6, 145
Calendars and penitential seasons:	
Armenian	185–6

PAGE

Byzantine, 9n., 51ff, 63, 70–1, 92
Chaldean . . 197–8
Coptic . . . 135–6
Ethiopic . . . 145–6
Malabarese . . . 207
Maronite . . . 168
Syrian . . . 156–7
Canon law, 20–1, and *passim*
Capuchin friars
123, 129, 140, 142, 213
Cardinals, eastern
11, 76, 150, 176, 177
Carmelites . . . 202, 204
nuns . . . 119
tertiary sisters . . 204
Cerularius, Patriarch . 8–9
Chalcedon, Council of
4, 128, 147, 173–4
Chaldean rite . . 194ff.
Chaldeans . . . 188ff.
Characteristics, religious xii, 28ff.
Chevetogne monastery 113, 213–14
Christian Brothers . 109
Christians of St Thomas 199ff.
Church books and music:
Armenian . . 181–2
Byzantine . 41, 43, 69
Chaldean . . . 195
Coptic . . 132–3
Ethiopic . . . 144
Malabarese . . . 206
Maronite . . . 166
Syrian . . . 153
Church buildings and furniture:
Armenian . . . 180
Byzantine . . 38ff.
Chaldean . . . 194
Coptic . . 131–2
Ethiopic . . . 143–4
Malabarese . . . 205
Maronite . . . 166
Syrian . . . 152
Cilicia, patriarchate of . 175ff.
Cistercians . . 142, 215
Colleges, pontifical:
Armenian . . . 177
Ethiopic . . . 142
Greek . . 112–13
Maronite . . . 163
Rumanian . . 109, 110
Russian . . . 124
Ruthenian . . . 82
Communion in both kinds
48–9, 63, 90, 134–5, 145, 156
Communism and religion . 35–6
Concelebration
45, 91, 133, 154–5, 167

PAGE

Confirmation by priest
29, 48, 134, 155, 184, 196
Constantinople, patriarchate of
5ff., 10ff.
Constaninople, rite of, *see*
Byzantine rite
Conventual Franciscans . 109
Coptic rite . . . 131ff.
Copts, Catholic . . 129ff.
Corsica, Greeks in . . 115
Crusades, the 10–11, 56, 159, 174
Cum data, decree . . 85, 97
Cyril VI Tanas, Patr. . . 56–7
Czarnecky, Bp N. . . . 123

D

Danbo, Abbot G. . . 193
Demandatum caelitus, decree . 17
Devotions . . 53 and *passim*
Diamper, Synod of . 201–2
Divine Office:
Armenian . . 183–4
Byzantine . . . 46
Chaldean . . . 196
Coptic . . . 133
Ethiopic . . . 145
Malabarese . . . 207
Maronite . . . 167
Syrian . . . 155
Dominicans
123, 138, 174–5, 189, 192, 213
tertiary sisters . . 122, 193
Douglas, Canon J. A., quoted 12, n.
Druzes . . . 160–1

E

Ea semper, letter . . . 85
East Syrian rite,
see Chaldean and Malabar rites
Eastern Congregation, Sacred. 20
Edward I, king of England 16, 189n.
Egyptian Christians, *see* Copts
Eikonostasis . . 39, 91
Eikons . . . 29
Emelyanov, Fr N. . . 122
Ephesus, Council of . . 4
Equidem verba, letter . . 213
Estonians, Catholic . . 127
Ethiopians, Catholic . . 141
Ethiopic rite . . 143ff.
Etsi pastoralis, bull . 17, 67

F

Fasilidas, Negus . . . 140
Feodorov, Fr L. . . . 36, 121

PAGE

Fermor, P. L., quoted . . 11
Filioque . . . 8, 46, 90
Finns, Catholic . . . 127
Florence, Council of
  11–12, 13, 56, 105, 120, 129, 138–9
"For thine is the kingdom . . ." 43
Fortescue, D. A., quoted
  8, 23, 33–4, 112, 201n., 175
Franciscan tertiary sisters 164, 204
Friars Minor
  86, 97, 103, 129–30, 161, 189, 213
Frumentius, St . . . 138

G

Gabra Michael, Bd . . 141
Galicia . . . . 76ff.
Gazeau, Dom R., quoted . 213
Genuflexion . . . 29
Georgians, Catholic . . 126
Ghika, Fr V. . . . 108
Goydich, Bp P. . . . 95
Great Britian, Eastern
  Catholics in . . 89, 124
Greek rite, *see* Byzantine rite
Greeks, Catholic . . 122ff.
Grégoire, H., quoted 6–7, 174n.
Gregory the Enlightener, St . 173
Grottaferrata monastery 42, 68–9

H

"Hail, gladdening Light" (hymn) 47
Hassun, Card. A. . 117–18, 176
Heresies . . . 3–4, 158–9
Hermits 164
Hierarchy and institutions:
  Armenians . . 176ff.
  Bulgars . . . 118–19
  Chaldeans. . . 192ff.
  Copts 130–1
  Ethiops . . . 141ff.
  Greeks . . . 114–15
  Hungarians . . . 100
  Italo-Greeks . . 67ff.
  Malabarese . . 203ff.
  Malankarese . . 171–2
  Maronites . . . 162
  Melkites . . . 58ff.
  Podcarpathian Ruthenians 96, 97
  Rumanians . . .108–9
  Russians . . . 123ff.
  Syrians 150–1
  Ukrainians . 82ff., 86, 87
  Yugoslavs . . 102–3
  other groups . . .126–7

Hinsley, Card. A., quoted . 140
Hybridization 26ff., 91 and *passim*

I

Iberians, *see* Georgians
Iconoclasm 29
Imitation of Christ, Order of 170–1
In suprema, encyclical . . 17
India, early Christians in 199–200
Innocent III, Pope, quoted .10–11
Inquisition, the . . . 201
Isidore of Kiev, Cardinal 11, 120
Italo-Greeks, -Albanians 10, 65ff.
Ivanios, Mar
  (George Panikkerveetil) .170–1
Ivanka, A. von, quoted . . 30–1

J

Jacobis, Bd J. de . . . 141
Jacobites:
  Indian . . . 169, 202
  Syrian . . . 147ff.
Jesuits 73, 106, 109, 122–3, 139–40,
  163, 165, 194, 213
John XXIII, Pope, quoted . 3
Josaphat of Polotsk, St . . 74

K

Kalavassy, Bp G. . . 113–14
Karolidis, Prof., quoted . 69
Karshuni 154
Katholikos (title) . 173, 176, 192
Kerala 199
Keumurgian, Bd Gomidas . 175
Khuzam, Patr. Mark . . 130
Kontaris, Patr. C. . . 112n.
Kostelnyk, Fr G. . . . 81
Krizanić, Fr Y. . . . 103

L

Lagier, Bp C., quoted . . 60
Languages, liturgical:
  Arabic . 44, 63, 133, 166
  Armenian . . . 182
  Coptic . . . 133
  English . . 44, 98
  Estonian . . . 127
  Finnish . . . 127
  Ge'ez . . 143, 144
  Georgian . . . 126
  Greek . . 44, 115
  Magyar . . 44, 101
  Malayalam . . 172, 206

PAGE

Rumanian . . 44, 110
Slavonic . 44, 92, 119, 125
Syriac . 154, 166, 195, 206
Latinization, *see* Hybridization
Latvians, Catholic. . . 127
Lazarists . 141, 192–3, 213
Lebanon massacres . . 161
Leclercq du Tremblay, Fr J. 129
Lesser Armenia . . . 173
Lesser Eastern Churches . 4
Lisle Abbey, U.S.A. . . 214
Liturgies, eastern, 28ff. and *passim*
Liturgy eucharistic:
  Armenian . . .182–3
  Byzantine . . . 44
  Chaldean . . .195–6
  Coptic . . . 133
  Ethiopic . . .144–5
  Malabarese . . .206
  Maronite . . .166
  Syrian 154
Liturgy of St Basil . . 44
Liturgy of St James . . 154
Liturgy of St John Chrysostom 44
Low Mass . . 28–9, 45, 182
Lyons, Missionaries of . 131
Lyons, Union of . 11, 56

M

Magna Graecia . . . 65
Makarios, Patr. C. . . 130
Malabar Catholics . 199ff.
Malabar rite. . . 205ff.
Malankara Catholics . 169ff.
Malta, Greeks in . . 115
Marian clerks regular . .123–4
Maro St 158
Maronite martyrs . . . 161
Maronite rite. . . 165ff.
Maronites . . . 158ff.
Married clergy . 23ff. and *passim*
  in North America . . 85
Maryamat sisters . . . 164
Mass, *see* Liturgy, eucharistic
Mass, names for the . . 27–8
Massacres, by Druzes . . 161
  by Turks . . . 176, 191–2
Mazlum, Patr. Maximos III . 57–8
Mekhitar of Sivas, Abbot . 177
Mekhitarist monks 177–8, 186, 210
Melkites, Catholic. . . 57ff.
Mellusians 203
Mendez, Fr A. . . . 140
Menezes, Abp A. de . . 201
Missions to the heathen
     163n., 171, 204

PAGE

Monasticism . . 209ff.
Monophysism 4, 128, 147, 173–4
Monothelism . . 158–9
Muakkad, Bp G. . . . 61
Music, *see* Church books
Muyser, Fr J. . . . 131

N

Neilos, St 68
Nestorianism . 3–4, 199ff.
Nestorians . . 188–9
Nineveh fast. . . .136
Nomenclature . . .10–11
Notaras, Luke, quoted . . 11

O

Old Believers . . 90, 121
Olivetan Benedictines 123, 214–15
Oriental Institute . . . 21
Orientalis ecclesiae, encyclical 17
Orientalium dignitas, constitution 18
Orthodox (the word) . 10n.
Orthodox Eastern church
     10 and *passim*
Ortynsky, Bp S. . . . 85

P

Paez, Fr P. . . . 139–40
Pallium 58
Panteleimon Zelov, monk 118n.
Patriarchal powers . . 58
Patriarchates, the Five . . 5
Paul, St, Missionaries of
  (Harissa) . . . 42, 61
Persecutions 35, 57, 75–6, 81–2,
  95–6, 119, 126–7, 140–1, 148, 178–9
Petrarch, quoted . . . 11
Photius, Patriarch . . 7–8
Pierling, Fr P., quoted . . 120
Pius XI, Pope, quoted viii, 25, 213
Pius XII, Pope, quoted 17–18, 34
Podkarpatska Rus. . . 94ff.
Political interference:
  French . . 148–9, 175
  Russian . . . 118
Popa, Bp A. A. . . .106
Portuguese missionaries
     139–40, 200ff.
pro Armenis, Instruction. . 175
Protestantism . . 105–6

R

Redemptorists 86, 88, 96, 123, 213
Reunions . 11ff., 56–7 and *passim*